EVANGELICALS AND AMERICAN
FOREIGN POLICY

EVANGELICALS
AND AMERICAN
FOREIGN POLICY

Mark R. Amstutz

OXFORD
UNIVERSITY PRESS

OXFORD
UNIVERSITY PRESS

Oxford University Press is a department of the University of Oxford.
It furthers the University's objective of excellence in research, scholarship,
and education by publishing worldwide.

Oxford   New York
Auckland   Cape Town   Dar es Salaam   Hong Kong   Karachi
Kuala Lumpur   Madrid   Melbourne   Mexico City   Nairobi
New Delhi   Shanghai   Taipei   Toronto

With offices in
Argentina   Austria   Brazil   Chile   Czech Republic   France   Greece
Guatemala   Hungary   Italy   Japan   Poland   Portugal   Singapore
South Korea   Switzerland   Thailand   Turkey   Ukraine   Vietnam

Oxford is a registered trademark of Oxford University Press
in the UK and certain other countries.

Published in the United States of America by
Oxford University Press
198 Madison Avenue, New York, NY 10016

© Oxford University Press 2014

Library of Congress Cataloging-in-Publication Data
Amstutz, Mark R.
Evangelicals and American foreign policy / Mark R. Amstutz.
pages cm
Includes bibliographical references and index.
ISBN 978–0–19–998763–4 (alk. paper)—ISBN 978–0–19–998764–1 (ebook)—
ISBN 978–0–19–998765–8 (ebook)   1. United States—Foreign relations—Religious
aspects.   2. Religion and international relations—United States.   3. Evangelicalism—
Political aspects—United States.   4. Christianity and politics—United States.   I. Title.
E183.7.A64 2013
261.7—dc23
2013006546

9 8 7 6 5 4 3 2 1
Printed in the United States of America
on acid-free paper

For Donna Ruth

CONTENTS

ACKNOWLEDGMENTS

In carrying out the research for this book, I have incurred numerous debts. First, I thank Wheaton College for granting me a sabbatical leave to commence work on this project. Second, I thank the Aldeen Fund, which provided funds that allowed me to carry out interviews with numerous religious and political leaders in Washington, D.C., and New York City. Third, I thank Josh Steddom, my teaching assistant, for research assistance and Stephanie Hagen, a former student of mine, for editorial assistance. Fourth, I am grateful to Theo Calderara, religion editor at Oxford University Press, for overseeing the transformation of a manuscript into a book. His editorial suggestions greatly improved the clarity and succinctness of the book's key themes and arguments. Finally, I thank Donna, my wife, for her continuing support of my work as a teacher and scholar of international affairs, and in particular for her encouragement on this project. It is to her that I dedicate this book.

EVANGELICALS AND AMERICAN FOREIGN POLICY

INTRODUCTION

In a seminal *Foreign Affairs* article in 2006, former Council on Foreign Relations senior fellow Walter Russell Mead argued that, since the end of the Cold War, American Evangelicals' political influence had increased significantly. Previously, mainline Protestants were the dominant religious voice in American politics. But the growth of conservative Protestant churches shifted power from the mainline to Evangelicals. Mead wrote: "The more conservative strains within American Protestantism have gained adherents, and the liberal Protestantism that dominated the country during the middle years of the twentieth century has weakened. This shift has already changed U.S. foreign policy in profound ways."[1]

This shift in influence mirrored a larger demographic shift. Between 1960 and 2003, mainline church membership fell from 29 million to 22 million, while its market share declined even more precipitously—from 25 percent of all religious groups to just 15 percent. During this same time period, Evangelical churches expanded dramatically. For example, in 1960, the Methodist Church had almost 2 million more members than the Southern Baptist Convention (SBC); but by 2003, the SBC had more members than the combined totals of the Methodist, Presbyterian, and Episcopalian Churches and the United Church of Christ.[2] A report by the Institute for the Study of American Evangelicals (ISAE) estimated that at the beginning of the new millennium, there were between 70 and 80 million Evangelicals in America, or about 25 to 30 percent of the population. Yet since this estimate does not include African-American Protestant churches, which generally share evangelical theology, the ISAE report concludes, "a general estimate of the nation's [E]vangelical population could safely be said to average somewhere between 30–35 percent of the population, or about 100 million Americans."[3]

The growing Evangelical engagement in politics, especially in international relations, is an important development in American religious and political life. Throughout much of the twentieth century, Evangelicals avoided public affairs, concentrating instead on religious work. This disregard of public affairs coincided with the emergence of fundamentalism. When mainline Protestant churches—under the influence of biblical criticism, scientism, and progressivism—began to drift away from the teachings of classical Protestantism, orthodox believers responded by forming a movement that emphasized the "fundamentals" of traditional Protestant Christianity. As this movement developed in the early twentieth century, it increasingly emphasized religious beliefs, biblical teachings, and the priority of spiritual matters over temporal concerns. To ensure authentic faith, Fundamentalists called for separation from liberal church denominations. Orthodox believers thus increasingly followed a separatist strategy where religion took precedence over political and social life.

Fundamentalists' disengagement from the social, cultural, and political concerns of society—a theological perspective that H. Richard Niebuhr calls "Christ Against Culture"—represented a radical departure from the more holistic Protestant faith that had dominated American culture throughout the eighteenth and nineteenth centuries. Challenging this separatist model, a group of orthodox Protestants began calling for a new (or neo) Evangelicalism based on a return to traditional Protestant belief and practice. Although the new movement shared fundamentalism's commitment to core doctrinal beliefs, it differed in its desire to be fully engaged in temporal affairs and to cooperate with other Christian groups in advancing common moral and social concerns. Some observers suggest that the real difference between Fundamentalists and Evangelicals is the latter's willingness to collaborate with mainline Protestants and Roman Catholics.

Evangelicals and Global Engagement

This book examines the impact of American Evangelicals on international affairs. While government officials regard foreign policy as a means to advance the national interests of states, Evangelicals view global affairs as a means of caring for the spiritual and temporal well-being of people in foreign lands. In pursuing this task, Evangelicals focus on preaching and teaching the gospel as well as on meeting human needs, especially those of people in impoverished societies. To promote evangelism, Evangelicals have built churches and seminaries, taught biblical and theological studies, and translated Scripture into indigenous languages. And to enhance human dignity, Evangelicals have established schools and promoted literacy, built clinics and dispensaries, promoted agricultural development and distributed food aid, created orphanages, and propagated values about the inherent worth of all persons. Thus, Evangelical global engagement has involved both spiritual and humanitarian dimensions, with spiritual concerns providing the primary motivation.

Evangelical global engagement first emerged in the early nineteenth century with the rise of the missionary movement. Although the primary missionary task was evangelism, this religious work spawned a variety of humanitarian services to meet people's social, educational, and medical needs. Thus missionaries served both as foreign emissaries of the gospel and as agents of international humanitarianism. In addition, missionaries served as agents of cultural transformation by teaching and modeling values and practices conducive to human dignity. Some of these values included the inherent worth of persons, freedom of conscience, the equality of persons, and the moral autonomy of individuals. Missionaries also were at the forefront of American internationalism, disseminating information about foreign societies and encouraging interest in international affairs. Finally, because American missionaries had the greatest expertise in foreign languages and cultures, they helped to educate government and business leaders traveling to foreign lands, especially in Asia, Africa, and Latin America.

Throughout the first half of the twentieth century, Evangelical missionary activity continued to expand. With the rise of the new Evangelicalism in the mid-1940s, the breadth and depth of Evangelicals' global reach increased still further with the development of humanitarian organizations and increased concern with public affairs. Although Evangelicals expressed few concerns about global politics, one issue animated them greatly—opposition to atheistic communism.[4] Throughout the Cold War, Evangelicals remained adamant critics of Soviet communism, not simply because of its totalitarianism but also because of its opposition to transcendent religion. Because Evangelicals regarded communism as a "counterfeit" religion,[5] they viewed the Cold War as a dispute between two conflicting religious worldviews. As a result, Evangelicals strongly supported the United States' containment policy.

Evangelical anticommunism spawned a secondary concern: support for victims of religious persecution. Because freedom of religion was curtailed in communist regimes, the National Association of Evangelicals (NAE), the informal association of some forty-five Evangelical denominations, adopted several resolutions expressing concern about rising religious persecution.[6] Yet the collapse of Soviet totalitarianism in 1990 did not end religious repression.

Indeed, the post–Cold War era has witnessed increased religious persecution from intolerant tribal, ethnic, and religious groups. As a result, the NAE has continued to champion the cause of religious freedom.

Beginning in the 1970s, Evangelicals became more overtly political. The issues that first animated them were domestic social issues like abortion and prayer in public schools. These and other related concerns were fueled by a perception of increasing secularism and materialism within American society. But as the Cold War wound down, Evangelical political concerns shifted toward global affairs and in particular toward issues such as religious persecution and related human rights concerns. As Mead noted, Evangelicals have played a more important role in influencing U.S. foreign policy since the early 1990s. At the same time, their advocacy has raised concerns about the efficacy of such initiatives and, more significantly, about the church's shift in priorities from spiritual concerns to temporal affairs. Some thoughtful observers have reminded religious activists that the church is not an interest group, and that it risks losing its spiritual and moral authority when it begins to function as one.

Evangelicals have thus participated in America's global engagement in two principal ways. First, missionaries have contributed directly to peaceful, humane international relations through their religious and humanitarian work. In particular, missionaries have provided expertise on foreign societies, nurtured the ideal of a morally integrated international community, and fostered awareness of global society. Evangelicals have been at the forefront of U.S. internationalism. More recently, however, Evangelicals have supplemented this direct global engagement with public policy advocacy on foreign policy concerns. Beginning in the post–Cold War era, Evangelicals have become more involved on a number of foreign policy concerns and have sought to influence foreign policy decision making. They have done so by emphasizing fundamental religious and moral values and by mobilizing grassroots support for specific public policy initiatives on issues like religious freedom and human rights.

Unlike the Roman Catholic Church, which has a well-established doctrine of social and political thought, Evangelicals have no social doctrine to guide political action. Nevertheless, Evangelicals have established a general theological framework that influences how believers approach public affairs. Fundamentally, the Evangelical strategy gives precedence to spiritual life over temporal concerns. This does not mean that the individual salvation of persons will inevitably resolve the world's social and material problems. Rather, it suggests that the moral reformation of individuals provides the foundation for a just and humane political society.

Given the diffuse, grassroots nature of American Evangelicalism, defining the movement's evolving impact on U.S. global engagement is difficult. Not surprisingly, some dubious claims have been advanced about the past and present role of Evangelicals in international relations. One of the goals of this book is to provide a more complete account of the extraordinary role of Evangelicals in global affairs by challenging prevalent misconceptions. Some of these are the following:

- *The rise of American Evangelicalism is a recent development,* following World War II. This claim is false since the emergence of Evangelicalism in the 1940s was not a new development but a return to the traditional Protestant faith—the religion that had prevailed in the United States before liberal religion emerged in the late nineteenth century.
- *Evangelical concern with social and political affairs is a modern development,* dating from the 1950s and 1960s. Neo-Evangelicalism emerged in the mid-1940s in response to fundamentalism's separatism and neglect of social and cultural life. Yet classical Protestantism—the American Evangelical religion of the eighteenth and nineteenth centuries—was fully engaged in the social, cultural, and political issues of the day. It is therefore untrue that Evangelical social and political engagement began in the aftermath of World War II.
- *Evangelicals' limited participation in public affairs is due to an underdeveloped and incomplete political theology.* This is a half-truth. To be sure, pietism—giving priority to personal religious beliefs and individual spirituality while deemphasizing formal church doctrines—undoubtedly inhibited Evangelical engagement in public life, especially in the first half of the twentieth century. But to the extent that Evangelicals deemphasized domestic and international public affairs, this was due less to an incomplete political theology and more to a deliberate strategy that gave precedence to spirituality over political action.
- *Evangelical global engagement is ineffective because of its weak institutions.* Unlike the Roman Catholic Church or mainline Protestant denominations, Evangelicals are an informal, grassroots movement. Evangelicals have no pope, and the associations that facilitate coordination among its member denominations have little authority. While the movement's informal institutions have impeded the capacity to influence public affairs, Evangelicalism's decentralized character has also ensured a vibrant, entrepreneurial faith that, when mobilized, can exert significant influence on social and political life.

- *American Evangelical engagement in international affairs began in the aftermath of the Cold War.* According to this view, Evangelicals first became politically and socially active in the 1970s and 1980s, in response to domestic social issues and subsequently over global concerns. In 2002, *New York Times* columnist Nicholas Kristof argued that Evangelicals were the "new internationalists" because of their important humanitarian contributions in developing nations.[7] But contrary to Kristof's claim, Evangelicals have been at the forefront of global humanitarianism for nearly two centuries. Indeed, Evangelical missionaries were involved in humanitarian projects long before the U.S. government began its foreign aid programs. It is not an exaggeration to suggest that Evangelical missionaries were the first American internationalists.

- *Evangelicals support Israel because of "end-times" theology.* Although this claim has some truth, it exaggerates the role of prophetic religion among Evangelicals. To begin with, only a small percentage of Evangelicals accept the prophetic teachings of dispensationalism—a theological perspective that emphasizes Israel's role in the events surrounding Christ's Second Coming. The far more convincing reasons for Evangelical support of Israel are based on God's covenants with the Jewish people and common democratic values. Evangelicals believe that, as God's chosen nation, Jews play an important role in salvation history. Supporting Israel is thus a way of affirming God's providential order. Equally important, however, Evangelicals sympathize with Israel because it shares with the United States common ideals and democratic institutions rooted in a Judeo-Christian worldview. The view that prophetic teachings explain Evangelical sympathies toward Israel is unconvincing.

- *Evangelicals are shifting their political identity from a conservative worldview to a more liberal worldview.* In an article in *The New Yorker*, Frances Fitzgerald claims that a new movement of moderate to left-center Evangelicals is gaining influence.[8] In recent decades, progressive Evangelical leaders like Jim Wallis, Tony Campolo, and Ron Sider have challenged the conservative politics of Evangelicals. Now, however, these leaders are being supported by a growing number of pastors, writers, and professors. This shift toward the political center is evidenced by the declining influence of the Christian Right and the advocacy of more progressive public policy concerns. The analysis in chapter 8 suggests that issues like climate change and immigration, however, do not reflect the concerns of rank-and-file Evangelicals. Notwithstanding the initiatives of progressive leaders, Evangelicalism remains a conservative theological and political movement.

- *Evangelicals do not support the political and economic development of nations.* This view derives in great part from the conventional wisdom that state-centered planning is necessary to foster economic development. But Evangelicals do care about development, but they do so by emphasizing decentralized, civil society initiatives and by giving precedence to the moral transformation of persons as a prerequisite to economic growth.

A major goal of this book is to provide a more compelling account of Evangelicals' influence on America's role in the world. The book describes how Evangelicals have influenced international affairs, both directly through missionary and humanitarian service and indirectly through reflection and action on global concerns like Third World poverty, Middle East politics, religious persecution, and the HIV/AIDS pandemic. The book also assesses and critiques the growing political advocacy of Evangelicals. As noted above, the declining membership and influence of mainline Protestant churches and the growth of Evangelicals has shifted political influence from the mainline to Evangelicals. This increasing role in American public life has provided Evangelicals with an opportunity to help advance important international concerns such as religious freedom and humanitarian relief. But rising political advocacy involves significant risks, since it can undermine the independence and moral authority of the church. Because religious groups make their most important contributions to the moral life of nations when they relate transcendent norms to domestic and international social, political, and economic concerns, public affairs advocacy can shift the church's focus from its mission of proclaiming the good news of the gospel. The challenge for Evangelicals is to engage public policy concerns without losing their focus on religious matters.

The Plan of the Book

This book is divided into two major sections. The first, chapters 1–4, explores the nature and rise of Evangelical global engagement. It examines the role of religion in foreign policy, the nature of Evangelicalism, the impact of the missionary movement, and the nature of Evangelical political ethics. Chapters 5–8 apply the Evangelical worldview to international relations, focusing on global poverty, America's ties to Israel, and several specific foreign policy issues, such as international religious freedom, human trafficking, climate change, and immigration. After identifying a number of shortcomings in Evangelicals' political advocacy, the concluding chapter 9 offers a number of suggestions for developing a more credible strategy of global engagement.

Since this book is about Evangelicals, it is important to say a word about the identity of this group of Christians. Although there is no consensus among theologians as to the definitional boundaries of Evangelicalism, I shall assume that Evangelicals are a distinct group of orthodox believers who share common beliefs and practices. Such Christians are to be found in mainline Protestant churches, nondenominational churches, independent congregations, and large associations like the Southern Baptist Convention and Pentecostal churches. Because of the distinctive nature of Evangelicalism, I capitalize *Evangelical* throughout this book. This decision is in keeping with the suggestion of "An Evangelical Manifesto," issued in May 2008, which correctly observes that the term needs to be uppercased like the names for other religious groups, including Roman Catholics, Orthodox, and Protestants.[9]

1 CHRISTIANITY AND FOREIGN POLICY

In order to illuminate the nature and impact of Evangelical global engagement, we'll begin by exploring the context in which such foreign policy initiatives are developed—in particular, by examining the nature and role of moral values and religious norms in the conduct of foreign relations. My aim is to describe the context in which Evangelical faith has influenced, and continues to influence, American global engagement. The chapter addresses four major issues: morality and foreign policy, religion and the development of the American nation, Christianity and foreign policy, and the integration of moral values with governmental decision making.

Morality and Foreign Policy

Before we examine the role of religion in international affairs, and more particularly the role of Evangelicals in American foreign policy, it is important to briefly address the question of whether and how moral values influence global politics.

Because of the evident cultural pluralism in the world, some theorists and government officials have gone so far as to conclude that international political morality does not exist.[1] But the view that the world has no common moral values is unpersuasive. This book is rooted in the assumption that norms, especially moral values, are an inescapable element of all human actions, whether individual or collective. As A. J. M. Milne notes, a complete diversity of values would be incapable of sustaining global social and political life. Some minimal morality is necessary. According to Milne, this global morality includes such norms as respect for human life, pursuit of justice, fellowship, social responsibility, freedom from arbitrary interference, and civility.[2]

Similarly, political theorist Michael Walzer argues that the international community is sustained by a thin global morality. He distinguishes between a developed or "maximal" morality and a less developed or "minimal" morality. Moral minimalism is "thin," he observes, not because it is unimportant or because it makes few claims on humans but, rather, because its claims are broad and diffuse.[3] Thus, while societies may differ in their beliefs about "maximal" values such as women's rights, distributive justice, criminal justice procedures, and the nature of marriage, they can agree on fundamental norms such as the peaceful settlement of disputes, the sanctity of human life, and protection of the environment. In his classic *Just and Unjust Wars*, Walzer offers a persuasive defense of moral minimalism. He argues that throughout history, leaders have validated the existence of moral values in wartime through their arguments and justifications. Walzer writes: "The clearest evidence for the stability of our values over times is the unchanging character of the lies soldiers and statesmen tell. They lie in order to justify themselves, and so they describe for us the lineaments of justice."[4] Thus, although international moral standards may be weak and at times difficult to discern, a thin body of moral norms exists.

In *The Moral Sense*, political scientist James Q. Wilson similarly claims that an underdeveloped political morality sustains all social and political life. This moral sense, writes Wilson, "is not a strong beacon light.... It is, rather, a small candle flame, casting vague and multiple shadows, flickering and sputtering in the strong winds of power and passion, greed and ideology. But brought close to the heart and cupped in one's hands, it dispels the darkness and warms the soul."[5]

Even if we accept the claim that a thin moral code exists in the world, we are still left with a question: How should political morality influence the international behavior of states? Fundamentally, moral principles can contribute to the development and implementation of foreign policy by (1) helping to define goals and purposes, (2) providing a standard for judging action, and (3) offering inspiration for action.

First, moral principles serve as a beacon, as a light guiding a ship through the stormy waters of international relations. They provide a constant reference point without which consistency in foreign policy would be impossible. Moral principles—justice, protection of the innocent, caring for those in absolute poverty—can play an important role in defining the fundamental aims of foreign policy. This does not mean that morality should be used to establish specific foreign policy goals. Rather, the purpose of political morality is to help structure the general contours and perspectives of foreign policy. According to international affairs scholar Alberto Coll, while transcendent norms cannot be applied directly to the actions of states, they can serve as "a guidepost, as illumination, and as a potential source of human action."[6] Historian Arthur Schlesinger, Jr., similarly emphasized the important but limited role of moral values in defining foreign policy objectives. Indeed, he argued that moral values should play a decisive role in foreign policy only in questions of last resort. In his view, the chief purpose of moral norms in foreign affairs is "to clarify and civilize conceptions of national interest."[7]

Moral norms also provide a basis for judgment. Without some notion of right and wrong, good and evil, it would be impossible to condemn horrific acts like genocide and ethnic cleansing or to support initiatives calling for greater human rights and increased religious freedom. In the aftermath of the 1994 Rwandan genocide, for example, President Bill Clinton expressed regret that the United States, along with other countries, had not done more to protect innocent Tutsi civilians from Hutu mass killings. Similarly, when it became clear that Serbs were carrying out ethnic cleansing and other human rights abuses against Muslims in the 1992–95 Bosnian civil war, there was widespread international condemnation of these atrocities. And when Libyan dictator Muammar Gaddafi threatened mass killings in 2011 against the citizens of Benghazi after rebel forces had taken control of that city, the UN Security Council authorized collective military action to protect civilians. In short, despite the "thin" nature of international political morality, moral norms were indispensable in providing a basis by which to judge governmental behavior. Without some idea of what constitutes a humane, just world order, identifying and critiquing political evil is impossible.

Finally, moral norms serve to persuade and motivate foreign policy action. In effect, morality provides the "fuel" for the governmental "engine." Since persons share a universal commitment to uphold human dignity and to demonstrate compassion for those in need, there is a widely shared presumption that governments should provide humanitarian assistance when calamities occur. For example, when Americans saw television footage of thousands of malnourished Somali children and learned that the bitter fighting among Somali warlords was preventing the distribution of food to those suffering from starvation, public opinion began to shift, calling for some type of humanitarian action in response to the crisis. Consequently, the U.S. government called on the United Nations to address it. In December 1992, soon after the UN Security Council had authorized military action, President George H. W. Bush ordered U.S. military forces to intervene to restore minimal order so that food could be distributed to some 300,000 persons facing death from starvation. Similarly, even though North Korea is a totalitarian communist nation that has misused scarce resources to maintain a formidable military, the U.S. government has provided food aid. It has done so despite the fact that such aid is contrary to the strategic goal of constraining the North Korean regime. In his important study of foreign aid, David Lumsdaine shows that morality was the principal motivation for the substantial aid given by Western developed nations to poor countries. He writes that donor countries' "sense of justice and compassion" was the chief inspiration for economic assistance.[8]

Integrating political morality with U.S. diplomacy has been difficult, in great part because "political realism" has been the dominant approach to international affairs among American scholars and government officials. According to this school of thought, since international politics is chiefly determined by the distribution of power among states, a prudent foreign policy needed to be guided by a country's interests, not by its moral aspirations. And since the world lacks a central authority, each country is ultimately responsible for its security and well-being. Not surprisingly, this realist perspective places a premium on economic and military power and deemphasizes moral values.

One of the most articulate exponents of realism during the Cold War was George Kennan, a distinguished U.S. diplomat and leading diplomatic thinker. In many of his writings, Kennan argued that moral values could contribute little to the making and implementation of foreign policy—first, because there were no widely accepted norms of international political morality, and second, because governmental decision making had to be based on political considerations, not moral values. Kennan expressed his skepticism about the role of morality in foreign affairs:

> Moral principles have their place in the heart of the individual and in the shaping of his own conduct, whether as a citizen or as a government official.... But when the individual's behavior passes through the machinery of political organization and merges with that of millions of other individuals to find its expression in the actions of a government, then it undergoes a general transmutation, and the same moral concepts are no longer relevant to it. A government is an agent, not a principle; and no more than any other agent may it attempt to be the conscience of its principle. In particular, it may not subject itself to those supreme laws of renunciation and self-sacrifice that represent the culmination of individual moral growth.[9]

Like other American realists, Kennan argued that the only way to pursue a prudent foreign policy was to ensure that the goals pursued in the international community were rooted in the country's vital interests, defined as national security, the integrity of political life, and the well-being of citizens. According to Kennan, these interests had no moral quality but were fundamental purposes that emerged from the decentralized character of international society—a society of distinct sovereign nation-states, each interested in its own security and welfare.[10]

Kennan underestimated the role of morality in foreign affairs for at least two reasons. First, he failed to distinguish between personal morality and political morality. Although the two are related, they are not identical. Individual morality consists of the moral principles and rules that apply primarily to individuals in their private relations. For example, the Sermon on the Mount, the admonition to "love your neighbor as yourself," and the obligation to tell the truth apply primarily to persons and cannot be used directly to devise public policies. Collective or political morality, by contrast, consists of moral norms that apply to the behavior of collectives like neighborhoods, colleges, corporations, cities, and states. Examples of such morality include norms like the right of sovereign independence of states and the corollary right of self-defense, the obligation to not intervene in other states' domestic affairs, the right to control borders, and the duty to settle interstate disputes peacefully. Since Kennan viewed morality through the prism of personal ethics, he failed to appreciate how values like promise-keeping, mercy, and generosity could be integrated into public life. Secretary of State Dean Acheson, an Episcopalian, similarly held to Kennan's narrow realist perspective. "What passes for ethical standards for governmental politics in foreign affairs," he observed, "is a collection of moralisms, maxims, and slogans, which neither help nor guide, but only confuse, decision making."[11]

A second reason why Kennan failed to grasp the importance of moral values in public affairs was his limited conception of government. Whereas many political theorists, including Christian thinkers, have regarded the promotion of justice as the fundamental task of the state, Kennan had a far more constrained view of government. In his view, governing was "a practical exercise" that called for the maintenance of social order, the promotion of economic prosperity, and the protection of society from foreign aggression. Although he, as a Presbyterian believer, undoubtedly believed that government was divinely ordained, he was reluctant to integrate his Christian beliefs with his work as a diplomat. In his view, pursuing moral goals like international justice, human rights, or poverty reduction may be noble, worthy ends, but they were not the fundamental tasks of government in a global society.

Despite Kennan's perceptive analysis of global and diplomatic affairs, his perspective on morality and foreign policy was ultimately unconvincing. Human life involves moral choices. To be human means to make choices every day regarding responsibilities to family, work, local community, and state. Of course, most decisions do not involve moral concerns—dimensions of right or wrong, good or bad, just or unjust hardly ever arise. Such perfunctory decisions are nonmoral. But when citizens address issues like climate change, arms control, protection of innocent civilians, the role of force in halting aggression and genocide, or environmental protection, such concerns necessarily will involve ethical concerns.

Foreign policy, like many aspects of human life, is inextricably a moral enterprise. When a government's goals are partly informed by moral values, the promotion of policy initiatives will necessarily entail ethical analysis—weighing competing moral goals and devising policies that advance the desired objectives in the most effective and least costly manner. Since moral values are often foundational for public policy decisions, the issue is not whether moral values will influence the conduct of foreign policy but, rather, which values and in what ways. As a result, foreign policy is not and cannot be a value-free enterprise. Arnold Wolfers, a noted Cold War international relations scholar, offers a sound perspective on this issue: "The 'necessities' in international politics, and for that matter in all spheres of life, do not push decision and action beyond the realm of moral judgment; they rest on moral choice themselves."[12]

After the Soviet Union introduced nuclear intermediate-range ballistic missiles into Cuba, the Kennedy administration was faced with the challenge of defining the nature of the threat and devising a response. In *Thirteen Days*, his account of this crisis, Robert Kennedy argued that moral considerations played a decisive role in how decision makers addressed policy alternatives. Kennedy claimed that, in the early stages of the crisis, officials spent more time weighing and assessing the moral consequences of military action than on any other matter. In his view, the principal reason why the United States did not carry out an all-out military attack against Cuba was that such action would have eroded, if not destroyed, "the moral position of the United States throughout the world."[13] To be sure, taking into account moral principles will not necessarily ensure an ethical response. But when decision makers take time to reflect on the justice and rightness of their actions, they introduce considerations that are likely to result in better foreign policies.

Despite the significant influence of the realist paradigm throughout the Cold War, international relations scholars and public officials now recognize that this perspective offers an incomplete account of what has motivated the American people's international concerns since the nation's founding. In his penetrating analysis of American foreign policy, *Special Providence*, Walter Russell Mead argues that one of the reasons why critics, especially those from Europe, have failed to understand American diplomacy is that they rely on a realist framework that fails to take into account distinctive features of American society. In particular, the tradition of European (continental) realism neglects the role of ideals, gives priority to politics over economics, and disregards the vibrant, participatory nature of American politics. Since the assumptions of European realism do not reflect American reality, using this approach will inhibit understanding of American global engagement. Mead writes: "It is like using a map of Oregon to plan a road trip in Georgia; there is no way to avoid getting lost."[14]

Not only has realism lost its singular appeal in the United States, but scholars have similarly lost faith in the prevailing secular assumptions that dominated the analysis of international relations. Throughout the Cold War, most of the Western intelligentsia believed that political development and economic modernization would inevitably result in a secularized global community where reason would displace faith. Because of the pervasive influence of the secularist perspective, scholars disregarded religion, viewing faith as irrelevant to the analysis of international affairs and even inimical to peace and global order. The secularization paradigm, however, has not been validated by historical experience. Indeed, since the second half of the twentieth century, religion has become more important in national and international affairs; only Europe has followed the predicted path of secularization.[15] As a result, scholars have begun to acknowledge the shortcomings of the secularization thesis and to analyze religion as an important phenomenon in global politics.

Religion and the Development of the American Nation

Although the impact of religion on public life varies from country to country, in the United States, religion has played a very important role from the start. Religion not only provides values and beliefs to define national identity but also sets forth goals and motivations for the country's policies and actions. As Walter Russell Mead observes:

> Religion has always been a major force in U.S. politics, policy, identity, and culture. Religion shapes the nation's character, helps form Americans'

ideas about the world, and influences the ways Americans respond to events beyond their borders. Religion explains both Americans' sense of themselves as a chosen people and their belief that they have a duty to spread their values throughout the world. Of course, not all Americans believe such things—and those who do often bitterly disagree over exactly what they mean. But enough believe them that the ideas exercise profound influence over the country's behavior abroad and at home.[16]

From the time that the first English migrants established settlements in New England in the early seventeenth century, the Christian religion has played an important role in public life, providing spiritual values, religious symbols, and moral inspiration for the emerging American nation. The most important early settlers in North America were the Puritans—Protestant Calvinists who fled "Christian" Europe to establish new communities based on alternative theological traditions and free from state control. These devout pioneers made two lasting contributions to the development of America's national identity. First, they helped to define and reinforce a belief in the exceptional character of the American nation; and second, they provided a foundation for the subsequent emergence of a national civil religion. The first development resulted in the emergence of a belief in American exceptionalism—the idea that the United States is qualitatively different from other nations. The second contributed to the rise of civil religion, which is not a system of religious beliefs but, rather, the use of sacred language and symbols to interpret national identity. As I note below, both ideas have played important roles in American public affairs. The early Puritan settlers believed that they had a responsibility to build and sustain political communities that embodied God's law. Following Augustinian thought, they believed that the "City of Man" would always be an imperfect, sinful society, but believers could, nevertheless, point to the "City of God" by the manner in which they lived their lives, individually and collectively. In carrying out this earthly project, Puritans drew much inspiration from God's promises to Israel, particularly those related to Israel's divine deliverance from Egyptian bondage. John Winthrop, leader of the Massachusetts Bay Colony, captured the covenantal nature of their worldview in a famous sermon delivered in 1630. In the sermon, Winthrop acknowledged God's blessings, called on the colonists to be a "city upon a hill," and reminded them that "the eyes of all people" were upon them.[17] He warned his listeners that if they did not follow God's commands, they would suffer harm and be cursed. Following the conditional promises given to Moses and the people of Israel in Deuteronomy 28, the Puritans' faith assumed that God would bless them and their new communities would prosper only if they followed His commands and lived virtuous, holy lives. Although some have interpreted the Puritan religion as a call to triumphalism and dominion, the primary concern of the Puritan pilgrims was godly living.

The idea of American exceptionalism emerged in the late eighteenth century. Although its primary ideas were political beliefs in liberty, equality, and constitutionalism, religious ideas and sacred symbols reinforced the belief in America's uniqueness. Indeed, the persistent influence of exceptionalism in American society is the result of its religious-political character. American exceptionalism was built on republican ideals of limited, participatory government, but it has been sustained by religious rhetoric. Political theorist James Skillen describes it thusly:

> The people who...organized themselves into...[a] republic believed that their project as a whole, including both its limited government and its free individuals, represented a unique, providential blessing and appointment of God in history. Consequently, the nation came to see itself as a chosen people called to serve as a light to the world. Thus, it would become possible in America's future for citizens to remain suspicious of government even while loving the nation.[18]

This integration of religious and political rhetoric has been evident throughout much of American history. During the colonial and post-independence eras, preachers, civic leaders, and government officials regularly attributed the rise and development of the American nation to God's providence. In a 1783 sermon celebrating independence, for example, Ezra Stiles, a Congregational minister and president of Yale College, suggested that God had blessed "his American Israel," and that still greater blessings were to come.[19] Similarly, George Washington often called attention to the providential character of the American nation. His Farewell Address emphasized that both religion and morality were indispensable to the well-being and prosperity of the nation. In modern times, President John F. Kennedy used religious rhetoric in his inaugural to remind citizens to "go forth to lead the land we love, asking His blessing and His help but knowing that here on earth God's work must truly be our own."[20] President Reagan, in a 1983 speech to religious broadcasters, similarly expressed his belief in the unique character of the United States:

> I have always believed that this blessed land was set apart in a special way, that some divine plan placed this great continent between the

two oceans to be found by people from every corner of the earth—people who had a special love for freedom and the courage to uproot themselves, leave their homeland and friends to come to a strange land. And, when coming here, they created something new in all the history of mankind—a country where man is not beholden to government, government is beholden to man.[21]

Civil religion is likewise a fusion of Christian and American ideas. According to sociologist Robert Bellah, who coined the term, *civil religion* refers to the "religious dimension, found … in the life of every people, through which it interprets its historical experience in the light of transcendent reality."[22] Civil religion is the foundation for exceptionalism. In effect, civil religion is the theology of the American political faith, whereas exceptionalism is the belief in America's uniqueness.

Since the Bible was the one book that was familiar to all literate Americans when the country was first emerging, biblical imagery provided the basic building blocks of the American civil religion. Biblical ideas like the Covenant, Promised Land, Chosen People, New Jerusalem, and the Exodus provided sacred concepts by which citizens could interpret the rise and evolution of the new nation. It is important to stress again, however, that civil religion involves the use of religion for nonreligious ends. As Bellah noted, civil religion was not a substitute for Christianity. Indeed, they performed radically distinct functions. Churches "were neither to control the state nor to be controlled by it."[23]

To be sure, many American Christians have failed to distinguish civil religion from the Christian faith. Indeed, many Americans have been tempted to regard America's prosperity and political power as expressions of God's providential partiality toward the United States. But Skillen correctly reminds us that American civil religion is not necessarily Christian. In his view, the tendency of some Evangelicals to identify with American exceptionalism is not grounded in theological or biblical analysis but in a desire to "recover the WASP moral consensus that informed the late 19th century Americanism."[24] Indeed, Skillen claims that civic faith—or what he terms "American new-Israelitism"—is contrary to the message of the Bible.[25]

We should not be surprised that most American Christians, and especially Evangelicals and Fundamentalists, support American civil religion. Public opinion surveys have repeatedly shown that a majority of Americans are strongly convinced of the exceptional nature of the United States. A Gallup poll in December 2010 found that 80 percent of respondents thought that the United States had a unique character "that sets it apart from other nations as the greatest in the world."[26] Additionally, a 2011 opinion poll by the Pew Research Center found that Americans are still far more convinced of their national superiority than are people of other countries. According to the twenty-three–nation poll, when asked if their culture was superior to others, 49 percent of Americans said yes. By contrast, only 32 and 27 percent of British and French people, respectively, supported this view.[27] Thus, while support for exceptionalism may be declining in the United States, Americans remain strongly committed to a belief in the unique and exceptional nature of their country. And because this idea is buttressed by sacred terms and religious ideas, Christians tend to provide even stronger support for the unique mission of the country.

Finally, some observers have suggested that American civil religion contributes to national self-worship. To be sure, the idea that God has blessed America can be misinterpreted and misused. No doubt some foreign policy initiatives, especially those during the era of Manifest Destiny, were direct by-products of this conviction. As Bellah emphasized in 1991, however, the tradition of American civil religion was to be conceived "not as a form of national self-worship but as the subordination of the nation to ethical principles that transcend it in terms of which it should be judged."[28] Viewed in this light, civil religion could both inspire moral action and provide an ethical framework by which to hold the American people morally accountable. Being a "city upon a hill" did not mean that America had to impose its values and institutions on others. Instead, it could demonstrate to the world the habits, traditions, and values that contributed to the prosperity, liberty, and human dignity of American society.

Historian Walter McDougall argues that America's founding fathers saw the nation's exceptionalism in its domestic identity, not in the ideals it sought to promote abroad. "Foreign policy," he writes, "existed to defend, not define, what America was."[29] Former Secretary of State Madeleine Albright captures this perspective in her book *The Mighty & The Almighty*. While acknowledging that the United States is "an exceptional country" with "a responsibility to lead," she argues that it should pursue foreign policy with care and discretion and with respect for international norms. She writes: "Our cause will not be helped if we are so sure of our rightness that we forget our propensity, as humans, to make mistakes. Though America may be exceptional, we cannot demand that exceptions be made for us. We are not above the law; nor do we have a divine calling to spread democracy."[30]

Christianity and Foreign Policy

Since Christianity is a religion, not an ideology, it is not primarily concerned with social and political issues. Rather, its focus is on personal spirituality—that is, on the meaning and purpose of life. As a result, the Christian faith does not provide ready-made prescriptions for social, political, or economic problems. This does not mean that membership in the "City of God" does not have implications for citizenship in the "City of Man." But discerning how Christians should fulfill their temporal obligations is a task requiring, at a minimum, biblical and theological knowledge, competence in international relations, and prudence in making judgments about public affairs. Even though the Bible is not a manual on political and economic life, it nevertheless provides general principles and broad perspectives that can help to guide thought and action in international affairs. In *Foreign Policy in Christian Perspective,* the mid-twentieth-century theologian John C. Bennett argued that although the Christian faith could not provide specific answers to the challenges of global politics, it could help structure and guide analysis and action. In particular, it could provide "ultimate perspectives, broad criteria, motives, inspirations, sensitivities, warnings, moral limits rather than directives for policies and decisions."[31]

Is there a biblical perspective on world politics? Do theological principles exist that can help structure the development and implementation of a just U.S. foreign policy? Is there a distinctive Christian worldview on international affairs, and if so, what are some of its elements? Although it is beyond the scope of this study to set forth a full account of a Christian worldview, below I sketch key principles that should ground a biblical framework on international affairs. I title this framework a Biblical Code of Peace and Justice, following the model developed by historian Dorothy Jones in her book *A Code of Peace.*[32]

The Biblical Code, a minimalist moral account of global politics, is based on eight principles rooted in Scripture that help to create and sustain peace and justice in global society: 1. the moral legitimacy of states; 2. God's sovereignty over nations; 3. the priority of persons; 4. the universality of sin; 5. the priority of love; 6. the demand of justice; 7. the presumption of peace; 8. the need for forgiveness.

1. *The Moral Legitimacy of States*: States—political communities ruled by government—are morally legitimate because they are a part of God's created order. In his letter to the Romans, Paul writes that persons should be "subject

to the governing authorities. For there is no authority except from God" (Rom. 13:1). And the writer of 1 Peter declares: "Be subject for the Lord's sake to every human institution, whether it be to the emperor as supreme, or to governors as sent by him to punish those who do wrong and to praise those who do right" (1 Pet. 2:13–14). Based on a careful analysis of Scripture, philosopher Nicholas Wolterstorff concludes that government is divinely instituted "as part of God's providential care for his human creatures."[33]

States are also morally significant because human beings are social creatures, created to live in association with others. However, the biblical code being advanced here does not specify which political arrangements are morally legitimate. Rather, it simply asserts that people's well-being is secured through divinely appointed political communities ruled by government. Such governmental institutions are not simply human conveniences that help to secure order. Rather, government is instituted by God to promote justice and to coordinate individual and collective activities that contribute to the common good. Additionally, this norm does not specify what type of regime is morally preferable. For example, it does not specify whether nationalism and patriotism are ethically valid, whether existing state boundaries are morally legitimate, whether nation-states have a right to sovereignty, or which of the world's more than 10,000 nations have a right to self-determination. Throughout history many different types of political communities have been institutionalized, including city-states, empires, and feudal kingdoms. Since the mid–seventeenth century, the nation-state has been the major political organization in the world. In short, states are not simply human constructs but also communities rooted in God's fundamental created order.

2. *God's Sovereignty over Nations:* Since God is sovereign, omnipotent, and omniscient, His authority extends to all peoples and all nations. All creation lives under the providence and judgment of God. This means that all human actions are finite and imperfect, always subject to God's sovereign will. The prophet Isaiah captures the greatness of God and the frailty of nations when he writes, "Behold the nations are like a drop from the bucket, and are accounted as the dust on the scales" (Isa. 40:15). And again: "He sits enthroned above the circle of the earth, and its people are like grasshoppers. He stretches out the heavens like a canopy, and spreads them out like a tent to live in. He brings princes to naught, and reduces the rulers of this world to nothing" (Isa. 40:22–23). Although God is sovereign, He uses humans to accomplish his purposes in the world. This is why Christians, as God's children, must obey Him by promoting righteousness

and justice within the international community. Finally, individuals and collectives are accountable to God and will be subject to His judgment.

Theologian John Bennett writes that since God is love, His love transcends all nations "in such a way that he keeps all their ideals and achievements and ideologies under judgment."[34] The truth about God's transcendence is important because it means that human initiatives are always an incomplete and partial fulfillment of divine will. Indeed, human actions will always be tainted because, as St. Paul asserted, they "fall short of the glory of God" (Rom. 3:23). However, recognizing God's sovereignty and transcendence over nations can free humans from national idolatry—from believing that they have a unique role in resolving the problems of global politics. The divine answer to human frailty is the acknowledgment of sin through repentance, both individual and collective.

3. *The Priority of Persons*: The third element of the Biblical Code is the special place of human beings in God's world. In contemporary political thought, the priority of persons is expressed in the notion of human rights—a concept that has become the most important basis for discourse on international relations. According to the doctrine of human rights, persons are entitled to basic claims by virtue of their fundamental worth as free, equal, and responsible moral agents. From a biblical perspective, human rights are rooted in the transcendent dignity of persons, who are created in the image of God and are the beneficiaries of divine salvation through Jesus's atonement. Theologically, human rights are important because, as Charles Villa-Vicencio eloquently explains: "In order to realize and fulfill their destiny as the bearers of God's image, the fundamental rights of all people are to be fully claimed and concretely appropriated, recognizing that without certain basic rights…people are not able to realize their full God-given potential. To deny these rights to people is to oppose the work and purpose of God in the world."[35]

Finally, since human rights are fundamental claims, the purpose of government is to secure and protect human rights. Vaclav Havel, the former president of the Czech Republic and a leading intellectual and civic leader, stressed the priority of individual rights over government when he noted that "the state is a human creation, human beings the creation of God."[36] Consequently, a biblical approach to global order is one that affirms the legitimacy of states but gives moral precedence to persons.

4. *The Universality of Sin*: According to Scripture, the corruption of human nature is universal and total. It affects all people and all of a

person's being—mind, body, and soul. Because of the pervasiveness of sin, humans can never act wholly justly and righteously, even when they do so in the name of God. Even the most noble and lofty expressions of justice cannot escape the grip of self-love. Since reason itself is tainted by sin, reliance on natural law and moral reflection can provide, at best, a proximate guide to ethical action. Reinhold Niebuhr argued that, given the limitations of moral ideals, the most effective way to advance the common good was not by seeking justice per se but by restraining self-interest.[37]

Because of the ubiquity and persistence of self-love, human action is always tainted by sin. Humans can never love God and their neighbor fully. The Bible teaches that oppression and injustice are caused by the misuse of human freedom. Although self-love is always lurking in the background, this does not mean that persons cannot promote justice and the common good. Indeed, since persons bear the image of their creator, they have the capacity to be co-creators—agents of the divine will, carrying out the work of human redemption. But they must always do so with the recognition that human thought and actions are conditioned by egoism and partiality.

The failure to recognize the limits of human action has often impeded progress. Niebuhr argued, in *The Irony of American History*, that progressive ideologies had a corrupting effect on American history because they disregarded sin. In Niebuhr's view, there could be no confidence in the improvement of society through idealistic ideologies.[38] Modesty and humility were necessary in all human initiatives, whether personal or collective. This view was strongly argued by H. Richard Niebuhr, Reinhold's brother, in his seminal study *Christ and Culture*, which examines different ways that Christians have historically related faith to social, political, and cultural life. Although Christians had developed a number of major approaches to the problem of how to relate Christianity to the temporal order, Richard Niebuhr concluded that no single approach could provide an authoritative way to advance the kingdom of God on earth. The reason was simple: the divine strategy was "in the mind of the Captain rather than of any lieutenants."[39] In short, since human actions are always finite, they can never fully embody the demands of justice. Consequently, there can be no confidence in human progress.

5. *The Priority of Love*: Jesus declared that the first commandment was to love God "with all your heart, and with all your soul, and with all your mind, and with all your strength" and that the second commandment was to "love your neighbor as yourself" (Mark 12:30–31). Love

involves unqualified giving, expressing human dignity through an all-encompassing, unselfish concern for others. Its purest expression is sacrificial love, while its most common manifestation in human communities is mutual love. Since human beings cannot fulfill the demands of love fully or consistently, however, mutual love cannot be a reliable foundation for political society. To be sure, love can contribute to harmonious voluntary cooperation, but only government has the capacity and legitimacy to ensure compliance from recalcitrant members. Thus, while love provides the moral foundation for communal solidarity, government provides the indispensable institutions to sustain communal order and foster social and political justice.

Since God's love is total and universal, Christians are called to follow His example by caring for others, whether they live in a crowded city or a remote village. It is a difficult commandment to fulfill because believers must reconcile the demands of love among different human communities, including family, friends, neighbors, professional colleagues, citizens, and persons from other nations. The real impediment to expressing love is not the challenge posed by the natural inclination to be partial toward family and friends but, rather, the failure to overcome self-love. Religious moralists, Niebuhr believed, were not very helpful in politics because they proclaimed the ideal of love as if it were self-enforcing. "The law of love" was not only an inadequate and incomplete political strategy; it was also a false religion. The gospel, he wrote, is not simply that we ought to love one another. Rather, it is the truth that people violate the law of love and need God's mercy and forgiveness.[40]

6. *The Demand of Justice*: A sixth key element of a Christian worldview is justice—one of the most difficult concepts in public affairs. The biblical idea of justice is associated with, among other things, the fair and impartial administration of the law, the proper treatment of the poor, protection of the weak and the oppressed, and support and care for strangers. It is also associated with righteousness (Ps. 33:5; Ps. 112:4; Prov. 29:7). From an Old Testament perspective, the pursuit of justice is rooted in law, which provides standards by which to judge the behavior of individuals and collectives. For Nicholas Wolterstorff, the Old Testament conception of justice is best captured in the vision of *shalom*, or right relationships—an ideal that is fulfilled when people are at peace in all their relationships: "with God, with self, with fellows, with nature."[41]

In the New Testament, there is little concern with law and justice; instead, the emphasis is on the fulfillment of justice and righteousness through love.

Love, of course, is not justice, since the former involves unqualified giving, while the latter involves calculation and judgment.[42] Divine love, as expressed in the redemptive work of Christ, provides the foundation for justice since it is the only way of partially overcoming human sinfulness. Rightly understood, the love of God provides an authentic and complete foundation for pursuing temporal justice in domestic and global affairs. But the most that humans can achieve is a partial or relative justice based on the weighing and balancing of conflicting and competing interests. The communal harmony that is achieved through government and legal institutions is at best an approximation of brotherhood, or mutual love, because humans are never free from the power of egoism. Emil Brunner captures the interrelationship of love and justice well: "Justice is nothing but the form of love which has currency in the world of institutions."[43]

7. *The Presumption of Peace:* According to the Scriptures, our Heavenly Father is a source of peace within human beings but also a source of peace within and among political communities. The Bible repeatedly admonishes humans to live justly and harmoniously with others. Indeed, the work of peacemaking and peacekeeping is so important that God takes special note of those who pursue and implement peace. In the Sermon on the Mount, Jesus observes that peacemakers will be "blessed" and "will be called the sons of God" (Matt. 5:9).

As noted earlier, the biblical ideal of peace is *shalom*—a vision of communal harmony and justice set forth in the Old Testament prophetic literature. This conception differs from the notion of peace as conceived by most contemporary journalists and statesmen in a number of ways. First, the biblical peace of shalom is all-encompassing, describing not only interpersonal and intercommunity relationships but also inward harmony based on being rightly related to God. Second, whereas shalom seeks peace through righteousness and justice, political peace is based on the application of rules and laws, backed by the coercive power of the state. Third, whereas political peace is essentially a negative conception, rooted in the absence of war and conflict, shalom is a positive conception, involving rightly ordered community life in the pursuit of the common good. Finally, whereas political peace is often viewed as an instrumental condition that helps to realize other important social, economic, and political goods, shalom views peace as an intrinsic moral end.

The vision of shalom is important for Christians because it provides an ideal that they should seek to fulfill. But as Saint Augustine noted long ago, this ideal can never be fully realized in the Earthly City. Shalom thus will be established in God's time by his action at the completion of human history. This does not mean that humans should be resigned to achieving peace only through power and force. Rather, it means, as Wolterstorff has written, that shalom "is both God's cause in the world and our human calling."[44]

8. *The Need for Forgiveness:* Forgiveness—the lifting of a deserved debt—is an important dimension of Christian ethics. It is significant because people are called to forgive others even as God, through Christ's redemption, has forgiven human sins. But practicing forgiveness is an especially difficult and challenging ethic, in part because it is contrary to the natural human desire to retaliate. Yet retaliation does not heal the wounds of wrongdoing. The ethic of *lex talionis* may provide some limited form of retributive justice, but it does not restore trust and repair broken relationships. Indeed, forgiveness is needed precisely because the communal ties ruptured by wrongdoing cannot be fully healed through strict, compensatory justice. In his account of the work of South Africa's Truth and Reconciliation Commission (TRC), Archbishop Desmond Tutu, the commission's chairman, argues that healing the wounds of apartheid would have been difficult if the state had relied on the existing criminal justice system. What was needed was an alternative approach that emphasized healing and reparation rather than punishment. Tutu's central argument is captured by the book's title: *No Future Without Forgiveness.*[45]

Historically, forgiveness has been regarded as an interpersonal ethic, not a norm applicable to political life. The Jewish philosopher Hannah Arendt was one of the first political theorists to recognize the potential role of forgiveness in politics. In *The Human Condition,* she argued that the viability of human communities depended upon two practices—promise-keeping and forgiveness. The first principle was important in sustaining communal solidarity; forgiveness, by contrast, was necessary to help overcome the evils and injustices of social and political life.[46] In his book *An Ethic for Enemies,* theologian Donald Shriver argues that the ethic of forgiveness needs to be incorporated into public life, since it would help to more effectively reconcile the demands of justice and restoration of broken relationships.[47] As with interpersonal relationships, acknowledging culpability and expressing contrition increases the potential of forgiveness. Since past offenses cannot be undone, truth-telling and forgiveness are desirable because they can facilitate the restoration of communal ties and promote national reconciliation.[48]

Although the application of forgiveness poses major challenges in politics, forgiveness is important because it may help overcome the legacy of past injustices that feeds the cycle of revenge and thus help create the preconditions for reconciliation among former enemies. If retributive justice—that is, the punishment and compensation for past wrongs—is a necessary condition for overcoming past evils, then creating a more stable, humane world may be impossible in many human communities. Political ethicist Jean Bethke Elshtain has written: "not every wrong can be righted. Not every injustice can be reversed."[49] If groups are trapped by memory and are unable to forgive, then the desire for revenge will continue to impede the development of humane, forward-looking communities. The ferocity of the mid-1990s Balkan wars illustrates the dangers of backward-looking political ideologies rooted in historical myths and memories of past injustices. This does not mean that nations should adopt a policy of historical amnesia. But at some point some forgetting will be necessary if people are to shift their collective concerns from revenge to hope, from retribution to reconciliation.

Integrating Moral Values with Foreign Policy Decisions

Since moral values are essential to governmental decision making, how can Evangelicals contribute to development and implementation of foreign policy? How can the Christian faith, and more particularly the Biblical Code, help to structure American global engagement?

First, religious beliefs and moral values of elected leaders and appointed government officials can influence foreign policy decisions. Since the conscience of leaders is an important determinant in decision making, advancing moral goals necessitates leaders who identify with fundamental moral norms. Clearly, leaders' beliefs and values are a major factor in policy making. This is illustrated, for example, in the different ways that presidents have approached foreign assistance on family planning. In 1984, President Ronald Reagan initiated a policy prohibiting the use of federal funds for organizations that perform or actively promote abortion. The so-called Mexico City policy prohibited the funding of clinics and family-planning centers that performed or encouraged abortions, even if the funding for such services came from nongovernment sources. This meant that American foreign aid could not go to medical and humanitarian organizations that actively promoted abortion. The policy was continued until 1993, when President Bill Clinton issued an executive order overturning that policy soon after taking office. And when George W. Bush became president, one of his first executive decisions called for the restoration of the Mexico City policy. President Barack Obama reversed this policy in 2009, three days after he took office, demonstrating again that the moral beliefs of leaders can result in different public policies.

Another example of how religious values influence foreign policy is President Harry Truman's decision to support the creation of the state of Israel. Truman, a Baptist who had a simple yet deep personal faith, believed that the Jewish people had a special place in God's plan of redemption. Moreover, since Jews had suffered continued persecution and discrimination during their two-thousand-year exile, and had experienced the most extensive genocide in the history of humankind during World War II, Truman believed that they were entitled to humanitarian support. Although it is impossible to prove that Truman's religious beliefs were responsible for his support of Israel, it seems inconceivable that his core religious and moral convictions did not play an important part in his thinking, especially since he had to overcome the staunch opposition of Secretary of State George C. Marshall and senior personnel at the Department of State.[50]

More recently, some of President George W. Bush's foreign policy initiatives demonstrate even more explicitly how leaders' religious dispositions and moral values influence decision making. On December 13, 2000, in a Republican presidential primary debate, Bush stated that his favorite political philosopher was Jesus. And after winning office, he explained the religious foundation of his decision making, declaring: "I base a lot of my foreign policy decision on some things that I think are true. One, I believe there's an Almighty. And, secondly, I believe one of the great gifts of the Almighty is the desire in everybody's soul, regardless of what you look like or where you live, to be free. I believe liberty is universal."[51]

Unlike most of his predecessors, Bush did not shy away from offering moral judgments on international issues. Indeed, unlike realists, who regard global politics as a struggle for power, Bush viewed many of the problems of the world as conflicts between justice and injustice, good and evil, right and wrong. This tendency to reduce issues to fundamental moral verdicts was illustrated in his 2002 West Point Commencement Address: "Some worry that it is somehow undiplomatic or impolite to speak the language of right and wrong. I disagree. Different circumstances require different methods, not different moralities. Moral truth is the same in every culture, in every time, and in every place.... We are in a conflict between good and evil, and America will call evil by its name."[52] Philosopher Peter Singer found that in the first two and a half years of his presidency, Bush spoke of evil in 319 speeches, using the word as a noun far more than as an adjective.[53]

To be sure, it is impossible to demonstrate that the religious beliefs and moral values of President Bush, or any other leader, have resulted in particular actions or decisions. Too many factors are typically involved in the choices and decisions that humans make. Still, it is important to emphasize that religion and morality are important determinants of human behavior. As historian Paul Merkley notes, if people's beliefs do not influence human action, then "history is an utterly meaningless field of study."[54] In short, leaders will necessarily act in ways that are consistent with their beliefs and values, unless some compelling factor impedes them from doing so.

A second way that religious beliefs can influence foreign policy is through the expressed views and sentiments of citizens. Since the United States is a democratic state where governmental legitimacy is based on consent, the beliefs and ideas of its citizens matter. Not only do citizens elect government officials at the local, state, and national levels, but they also influence leaders' actions directly through lobbying and indirectly through media campaigns.

Although U.S. foreign policy is typically initiated by government leaders, mass public opinion can support and constrain leaders' actions. Public opinion studies have shown that the public's sustained preferences matter in foreign policy decision making.[55] Indeed, while foreign policy initiatives need not have the public's support at first, sustaining a policy will necessitate public support or at least the absence of opposition. Of course, organizations mobilize mass public opinion and help to initiate, modify, or reform government policies.

As with all nongovernmental organizations, religious groups and church associations can play important roles in mobilizing public opinion. For example, church governmental offices can monitor legislative initiatives, help keep church leaders informed on specific issues, and pursue lobbying on issues they regard as morally significant. Additionally, they can seek to keep their members informed and to influence their views and sentiments. Ironically, while mainline Protestant churches have reduced significantly their political advocacy in the post–Cold War era, Evangelicals—who historically deemphasized social and political concerns—have greatly expanded their foreign policy advocacy. This, as we shall see later, does not come without risks.

In the following chapters, I examine the role of Evangelicals in promoting global political engagement based not on their religious rhetoric but on their religious beliefs and commitments. The aim is to illuminate the nature and evolution of such engagement and to assess its overall impact.

2 THE NATURE AND RISE OF EVANGELICALS

Evangelicalism can be difficult to define. It is not a church association with an established ecclesiology, nor is it a cohesive, coherent movement with an established creed. Rather, Evangelicalism is a transdenominational Protestant movement rooted in shared beliefs and commitments. Moreover, since Evangelicals share a natural affinity with fellow believers, Evangelicalism can be viewed as an ecumenical movement of different traditions and national groups in which shared biblical beliefs are more important than ecclesiastical differences.[1] In the pages that follow, I will trace the origins and development of Evangelicalism in America.

The Development of Evangelicalism

The word *evangelical* derives from the Greek noun *euangelion*, which the writers of the New Testament used to refer to the "good news" or "gospel" that Jesus, the Son of God, has atoned for human sin and offers salvation. The seeds of Evangelicalism were first sown during the Protestant Reformation, when a small group of church leaders, including Martin Luther, John Calvin, and John Knox, began to call for a renewal of the Christian faith that emphasized Bible reading, personal faith in Christ, and the role of Jesus as the sole mediator of human salvation. Since this movement challenged the traditions, practices, and authority of the Roman Catholic Church, it came to be called Protestantism. For Luther and Calvin, salvation was not something to be dispensed by the clergy but, rather, was a gift from God to any person who believed in Jesus as Savior and Lord. Thus, when Protestant churches emerged in the seventeenth century, some of them began using the word *evangelical* to emphasize the denomination's commitment to historic Christian beliefs. To this day, the descendants of many of these churches retain the name Evangelical.

The word *evangelical* as it is now commonly used has its origins in the eighteenth-century revivals in England, Wales, Scotland, and especially in Britain's North American colonies. The renewal of the Protestant faith in the colonies began early in the eighteenth century with the so-called Great Awakening, when preachers like Jonathan Edwards, George Whitefield, and John Wesley began calling for a revival of personal faith and piety. At the same time, this renewal movement challenged the prevailing Reformed creed—the so-called Puritan canopy—that America's founding was rooted in a divine covenant in which God bestowed blessings on his people but also held them to account for the fulfillment of his will. Puritans had been quite confident that through their faithful service to Christ they could fulfill the demands of authentic religion. Yet it became clear that Puritanism could not eliminate the temptations of power and wealth. While Reformed theology proclaimed the universality and totality of human sin, it underestimated the power of sin in the lives of believers, especially those holding positions of political and social responsibility. The Great Awakening called believers to authentic personal piety.[2]

During the second half of the eighteenth century, church growth declined, failing to keep pace with the significant population growth in the colonies. This all changed with a second Protestant renewal movement. Indeed, from the 1780s through the mid–nineteenth century, historic Protestant Christianity (Evangelicalism) experienced dramatic growth in both the number of believers and their level of commitment to a church. As historian Mark Noll observed, "No other period of American history ever witnessed such a dramatic rise in religious adherence and corresponding religious influence on the broader national culture."[3]

Throughout the nineteenth century, American Protestantism remained committed to the classical doctrines of orthodox Christianity. Mainline denominations were thus Evangelical. As Robert Putnam and David Campbell note in *American Grace*, their magisterial study of religion in the United States, "Evangelicalism was the dominant strain within American Protestantism through most of the nineteenth century."[4] Along with numerical growth came a significant expansion of foreign missionary activity. While the sending of missionaries to foreign lands began rather slowly in the early part of the nineteenth century, by the end of the century American Protestant churches had more than 5,000 missionaries working throughout the world, with the bulk of them serving in Hawaii, China, India, and the Middle East. And between 1906 and 1915, the number of U.S. missionaries doubled from 7,500 to 15,000.[5] The missionary enterprise would eventually have an extraordinary impact on American global engagement.

But all was not well in the major Protestant denominations. By the end of the nineteenth century, Protestant church leaders, influenced by secularism, modern science, rationalism, and biblical (higher) criticism, began to question the authority of Scripture, the core beliefs of Christianity, and traditional approaches to biblical interpretation. Whereas Evangelical Protestantism assumed the universality and totality of human sin, this new liberal faith took on a progressive view of human nature. As Alister McGrath observes, the liberal creed "was inspired by the vision of a humanity which was ascending upwards into new realms of progress and prosperity."[6]

As liberal theological beliefs and assumptions became more pervasive among Protestant churches in the early twentieth century, tensions grew between believers committed to the classical Evangelical faith and believers committed to a progressive, liberal faith. Whereas traditionalists assumed that final authority rested with biblical revelation, the liberal faith was more concerned with reconciling modernity with religious beliefs. As this conflict intensified in the 1920s, the traditionalists began calling for a return to the fundamentals of Christianity and for separation from mainline denominations. Beginning in 1910, a series of books was published to highlight the core beliefs of the Christian faith. Titled *The Fundamentals*, the twelve volumes consisted of some ninety essays that described and defended key elements of the classical Protestant faith and critiqued ideas and practices that threatened orthodoxy. Because of the pivotal role that these books played in the liberal–orthodox conflict, the term *fundamentalist* came to be associated with the defenders of biblical Christianity.

At first, the Fundamentalist movement was primarily concerned with a return to biblical orthodoxy. But with the growth of religious polarization between liberal and Fundamentalist believers, Fundamentalist leaders adopted an increasingly oppositional character, calling for disengagement from society. Indeed, the dominant perception of Fundamentalists became that they were more concerned with attacking modern science and the prevailing culture than with spreading the gospel. Even more injurious to the orthodox faith was fundamentalism's focus on eschatology. Rather than exploring how the Christian faith can equip believers to be faithful servants of Christ in the temporal world, Fundamentalists focused on preparation for eternal life and the final judgment. This focus was rooted in premillennial dispensationalism—a theological approach that interpreted biblical revelation as unfolding in distinct epochs, or dispensations. (Since this theological method has had significant influence on believers' views on Israel, I examine it more fully in chapter 6.) Since dispensationalism emphasized holy living through piety and separation, it encouraged, in the words of Mark Noll, a "Gnostic supernaturalism" that pushed analysis from the visible present world to the invisible future.[7] In effect, this religious perspective shifted concern from stewardship of God's creation to the contemplation of salvation and redemption of the world, reinforcing the separatist and otherworldly tendencies of fundamentalism.

Although some aspects of fundamentalism were inconsistent with classical Evangelicalism, the two movements shared many core beliefs. In particular, Fundamentalists emphasized the authority of Scripture, the sinfulness of humans, Christ's atonement as the sole basis of personal salvation, the need for personal acceptance of Christ's sacrifice, and the priority of sharing the gospel. But fundamentalism's emphasis on personal piety, separation from the temporal demands of the world, and view of salvation as deliverance from society's social, political, and economic problems were contrary to classical Evangelical thinking. Not surprisingly, a group of orthodox Protestant leaders began calling for a renewal of the traditional Evangelical faith—one that called believers into cultural and social engagement. Dr. Harold Ockenga, one of the leaders of this movement, defined the "new" or "neo" Evangelicals as follows:

> The new evangelicalism embraces the full orthodoxy of fundamentalism, but manifests a social consciousness and responsibility which was strangely absent from fundamentalism. The new evangelicalism concerns itself not only with personal salvation, doctrinal truth and an eternal point of reference, but also with the problems of race, of war, of class struggle, of liquor control, of juvenile delinquency, of immorality, and of national imperialism.... The new evangelicalism believes that orthodox Christians cannot abdicate their responsibility in the social scene.[8]

The "new" Evangelicalism got its official start when Ockenga, Stephen Paine, William Ayer, Charles Fuller, and other church leaders established the National Association of Evangelicals (NAE) in 1943. Evangelical leaders had concluded that fundamentalism no longer represented them. Additionally, they believed that just as mainline Protestant churches had established the Federal Council of Churches to facilitate collective action, so too Evangelicals needed an organization to foster greater cooperation on shared concerns. Thus, some one thousand church leaders gathered in Chicago and adopted a constitution and doctrinal statement. Although the NAE has grown significantly in the past half-century, especially with the addition of Pentecostal denominations, the movement remains a loose association of more than fifty denominations representing some 45,000 congregations with roughly 30 million members. Ironically, the Southern Baptist Convention (SBC), the largest Evangelical denomination with more than 16 million members, never joined the NAE, not because of doctrinal disagreements but because of its desire for autonomy.

The rise of Evangelicalism is thus tied to the liberal–fundamentalist controversy of the early twentieth century. Because fundamentalism and Evangelicalism share a common commitment to orthodox beliefs, the media often treats these two groups as synonymous. But important differences exist, not so much in theology as in strategy and missiology. Gerald McDermott has identified seven areas in which members of these two constituencies differ:

1. *Interpretation of Scripture*: Fundamentalists tend to emphasize a literalist interpretation of Scripture more than Evangelicals.
2. *Culture*: Fundamentalists tend to question the value of secular culture, whereas Evangelicals regard "common grace" working in and through all society and cultural institutions.
3. *Social Action*: While Fundamentalists have tended to view social and economic action as peripheral, Evangelicals have viewed them as central to the gospel.
4. *Separatism*: As noted above, Fundamentalists believe that authentic faith requires separation from the world in order to fulfill the mandates of biblical religion. As a result, they give priority to personal pietism and minimize engagement with secular society. Evangelicals, by contrast, believe that participation in cultural, social, and political life is imperative in reforming and transforming society.
5. *Dialogue with Liberals*: Fundamentalists have avoided discussions with liberal Christians, believing that little could be learned from such engagement. Evangelicals, by contrast, have been far more eager to learn from and perhaps to influence them.
6. *The Nature of Faith*: Although both Fundamentalists and Evangelicals emphasize salvation by grace, the former have tended to emphasize rules and prohibitions far more than Evangelicals.
7. *Divisiveness*: While division and fractures are common to both Fundamentalist and Evangelical churches, this pattern has been more pronounced among the former group than the latter. Because Evangelicals emphasize the difference between essentials and nonessentials more than do Fundamentalists, they tend to be more willing to accommodate to

challenging circumstances, such as remaining in a mainline Protestant denomination.[9]

Who Is an Evangelical?

Three common ways of identifying Evangelicals are through denominational affiliation, adherence to distinctive religious beliefs, and self-identification.[10] Although these approaches are interrelated, each approach captures a slightly different group of Christians. Moreover, each is potentially problematic since they do not necessarily correspond to authentic Evangelical belief and practice. For example, denominational affiliation assumes that people who attend conservative Protestant churches and denominations are Evangelicals and that those who attend progressive mainline Protestant churches are not. But Evangelicals form a significant segment of mainline denominations. Similarly, self-identification does not guarantee authentic religious belief and practice. Finally, if religious beliefs are used to identify Evangelicals, the character and number of the Evangelical population will vary greatly, depending on measurement criteria. The Barna Research Group, for example, uses a demanding set of standards that tends to limit the size of the Evangelical population. According to Corwin Smidt, a scholar of American religious politics, the number of Evangelicals is roughly one-fourth the U.S. population when measured in terms of church affiliation, but only one-seventh when using the belief system developed by Barna.[11]

Since our investigation is chiefly concerned with the nature of Evangelicalism and its role in international affairs, we are primarily interested in the religious character of the Evangelical movement. Of the three ways of identifying Evangelicals, the most relevant is people's religious beliefs. According to theologian Alister McGrath, the Evangelical faith is based on four central beliefs: (1) Scripture is the ultimate authority in matters of spirituality, doctrine, and ethics; (2) the death of Jesus Christ on the cross is the only source of salvation; (3) conversion or "new birth" is a life-changing experience; and (4) sharing the Christian faith, especially through evangelism, is an indispensable element of authentic faith.[12] Historian David Bebbington has similarly identified four convictions and attitudes that are central to the Evangelical Christian faith: (1) conversion—the priority of salvation; (2) biblicism—the belief that all necessary spiritual truth is found in the Bible; (3) activism—the belief that faith needs to be expressed through service to God, including sharing the gospel with others; and (4) crucicentrism—the belief that Christ's death on the cross provides the means by which people can be reconciled to God.[13]

Using McGrath's and Bebbington's conceptualizations, I conceive of Evangelicalism as a movement within Protestantism that emphasizes three beliefs: (1) the primacy of the Scriptures as the final authority for religious faith, (2) the need for conversion through the personal acceptance of Jesus's atonement on the cross, and (3) the imperative of sharing the "good news" of the gospel through evangelism.[14]

Missiologist Andrew Walls has written that Evangelicalism is "a religion of protest against a Christian society that is not Christian enough."[15] Evangelicalism emerged, he writes, when Protestant churches failed to inspire individual spiritual transformation and personal holiness. Formal religion and creeds were important but not sufficient to ensure authentic religion. "Evangelical faith," Walls writes, "is about inward religion as distinct from formal, real Christianity as distinct from nominal."[16] William Wilberforce, the great English parliamentarian who led the campaign against the slave trade, observed that what distinguished "real" Christians from "professing" Christians was a commitment to three doctrines—original sin and consequent human depravity, the atonement of Christ, and the sanctifying power of the Holy Spirit. Since the established Christian churches did not understand the radical nature of sin, they failed to understand the nature of Christ's atonement and had little place for holiness. For Wilberforce, Evangelicalism began with an acknowledgment of sin, a personal trust in Christ's redemption from sin, and a call to holy living.

One of the distinctive traits of Evangelicalism is that, unlike formal church denominations, it is a decentralized, entrepreneurial movement. This entrepreneurial spirit was especially evident in the Christian revivals of the nineteenth century—the Second Great Awakening, which lasted from the late eighteenth century through the mid–nineteenth century, and the Third Great Awakening, which stretched from 1880 to 1910. These renewal movements not only increased religious devotion among believers but also contributed to the numerical increase and societal impact of Evangelicalism, including the growth of the missionary movement.

Reverend Rufus Anderson, a pioneer of the missionary movement, claimed that this voluntary, informal ethos was rooted in the nature of Protestantism itself, which he described as "free, open, responsible, embracing all classes, both sexes, all ages, the masses of the people."[17] This ethos provided the organizational flexibility and empowered the faithful to focus on the task of evangelism. In time, voluntarism not only dominated missionary societies but influenced the nature of church life itself. According to Walls, the influences of voluntarism and decentralization were so profound that by the twentieth century, "the line between church and association had in America become so fine that the church itself often came to be seen almost in terms of a voluntary society."[18]

Because Evangelicalism is a tendency or movement within Protestantism, it is less cohesive and coherent than well-established theological traditions like Calvinism or Anabaptism. As a result, some observers question the validity of Evangelical identity. Historian Nathan Hatch, for example, claims that "there is no such thing as Evangelicalism,"[19] while religion professor Jon R. Stone has argued, based on his analysis of the postwar Evangelical coalition, that "evangelicalism is a fiction."[20] Similarly, while David Gushee and Dennis Hollinger question the coherence of the Evangelical identity, they suggest nonetheless that it is a valid identity rooted in the supremacy of biblical revelation. They observe that when Protestant orthodoxy has been challenged, Evangelical renewal movements have responded based on their allegiance to Scripture. Thus, they view Evangelicalism "as a renewal movement within Christianity that continually calls the churches back to deeply committed biblical faith and practice."[21]

Since identifying who is an Evangelical is a challenging task, estimating the size of the American Evangelical population is especially difficult. Using survey data from a variety of sources, the Institute for the Study of American Evangelicals (ISAE) suggests that the number of Evangelicals in the United States is roughly 25 to 30 percent of the population, or about 70 to 80 million people. This estimate, however, underestimates the total number of Evangelicals, since it does not include the African American Protestant population (estimated at 8 to 9 percent of the U.S. population), which is overwhelmingly Evangelical in theology. Thus, the ISAE claims that a more accurate estimate of all American Evangelicals is 30 to 35 percent of the U.S. population, or about 100 million Americans.[22] According to their exhaustive study of American religion titled *American Grace*, Robert Putnam and David Campbell argue that Evangelicals are the largest religious tradition in the United States, accounting for roughly 30 percent of the U.S. population.[23] Christian Smith, a leading sociologist, offers a similar estimate. Using multiple data sources, he concludes that the number of Evangelicals is about 29 percent of the American population—or roughly 82 million persons.[24]

The Rise of Evangelicals—And the Fall of the Mainline

In recent decades, American Evangelicalism has grown in both size and influence. What might explain this? One factor that has undoubtedly contributed to Evangelicalism's growth is its strong commitment to spiritual formation. While mainline Protestant churches have diluted the spiritual teachings of the church, Evangelicals have continued to give priority to the spiritual task of proclaiming the gospel and the preaching and teaching of the Bible as the foundation of faith. For Evangelicals, the purpose of the church is to worship God, proclaim the good news of the gospel, and serve the temporal and spiritual needs of the world. Fundamentally, the church seeks to equip its members to be faithful in serving Christ's kingdom.

A second source of Evangelicalism's dynamism is its grassroots, populist nature. Whereas most mainline denominations have well-developed institutions, Evangelicalism is a decentralized movement where local congregations are responsible for their own affairs. As a result of strong congregational ownership, Evangelical churches tend to have a comparatively high level of member involvement and financial support. And because of the lack of institutional hierarchy, Evangelical churches are free to experiment and adapt to changing cultural and social norms, but doing so without compromising their spiritual mission. Indeed, the growth of Evangelicals has undoubtedly been fueled by the continued innovation and adaptation to modern commercial society and popular culture.

A third factor contributing to the rising influence of Evangelicals is the belief that domestic and international issues are part of the redemptive mission of the church. The 1974 Lausanne Congress on Evangelism declared that while evangelism remained the church's primary task, its redemptive task also included caring for the social, economic, and political issues of society. A renewed concern with these issues began in the late 1940s, when theologian Carl F. H. Henry called attention to the "uneasy conscience" believers possessed because they had neglected social and political concerns.[25] Although the Evangelical political agenda in the 1950s and 1960s was limited to a few issues—such as opposition to communism, support for chaplains in the armed forces, and prayer in public schools—in time the agenda expanded both domestically and internationally to address such issues as pornography, homosexuality, immigration, refugees, foreign aid, and religious freedom. Indeed, owing to increased resources and a more strategic approach to international affairs, Evangelical influence on global issues increased notably in the post–Cold War era, resulting in important public policy decisions and the enactment of legislation such as the International Religious Freedom Act of 1998 and the Sudan Peace Act of 2002.

A fourth factor that has contributed to the rising influence of Evangelicals is the increased, often sympathetic coverage by the media. Press reporting on Evangelicals began to expand during the presidential campaign of Jimmy Carter in 1976, with *Newsweek* calling 1976 "the year of the evangelical" shortly after Carter's election. Subsequently, media coverage expanded both in breadth and depth with the increased political mobilization of conservative Christians—first through the Moral Majority spawned by Reverend Jerry Falwell and later by the Christian Coalition initiated by Pat Robertson. Although the growing identification of Republicanism with both Evangelicals and Fundamentalists resulted in increased influence and media coverage, the coverage was not always well informed, with reporters typically failing to distinguish Evangelicals from Fundamentalists. Nevertheless, even though the American media has remained largely secular and politically liberal, coverage of Evangelicals has become not only more nuanced but also more sympathetic.

Fifth, the political influence of Evangelicals has risen as their leaders have learned to collaborate with other political groups pursuing similar political and legislative goals. At the same time Evangelicals, building on their flexibility and grassroots organizations, have learned the importance of mobilizing public opinion. The priority of collaboration and mobilization was evident in the successful passage of the International Religious Freedom Act of 1998 and the Sudan Peace Act of 2002.

Evangelical influence is also growing because, as Evangelicals have become better educated and more sophisticated, they have joined the leadership ranks in business, education, the professions, and government and politics. As Michael Lindsay has shown in his book *Faith in the Halls of Power*, Evangelicals have greater influence in politics because a growing number of political leaders and government officials publicly identify as Evangelicals.[26]

Finally, and most significantly, the decline of mainline Protestantism has created a vacuum that is being filled by other religious groups, including Evangelicals. As the mainline adopted more progressive social and political causes, neglecting its primary task of proclaiming the gospel, its membership declined significantly. Whereas mainline Protestant denominations accounted for 25 percent of all church members in 1960, by 2003 this figure had fallen to 15 percent.[27] In the past four decades (1965 to 2005), membership has declined for all mainline churches—with the most precipitous declines experienced by the United Methodist Church (UMC; 11 million members to 8.2 million), the Episcopal Church (3.6 million members to 1.9 million), and the Presbyterian Church USA (3.2 million members to 2.4).[28] As Kenneth Woodward wrote in a feature article in *Newsweek* in 1993, mainline churches were "running out of money, members, and meaning."[29]

While the numerical decline of the mainline is noteworthy, the most important religious development has been these churches' loss of credibility and influence. Historically, mainline churches played an important role in defining and structuring the dominant values and political morality of the

American people. In spite of their theological diversity, leading Protestant denominations contributed to the American moral order, providing a vocabulary and political morality that helped to structure the conceptualization of important domestic and international public affairs. Through their public witness the mainline helped to advance Christian ideals and to provide moral guideposts on public policy concerns. According to Joseph Bottum, "Protestantism helped define the nation, operating as simultaneously the happy enabler and the unhappy conscience of the American republic—a single source for both national comfort and national unease."[30] In the 1950s and 1960s, at the height of their influence in American public life, mainline Protestant churches were major cultural institutions.

To a significant degree, this influence was the result of interdenominational cooperation—facilitated by the Federal Council of Churches, established in 1908, and its successor organization, the National Council of Churches (NCC), created in 1950. The fall in membership in mainline Protestant denominations has led to dramatic changes in the NCC. Indeed, since the mid-1980s, the NCC has all but vanished from public life. Whereas the organization boasted more than 600 staff in their New York City headquarters at the height of their influence in the 1960s, by the beginning of the new millennium the NCC, with fewer than 35 staff, was on the brink of bankruptcy.

Ironically, as Protestant churches pursued religious ecumenism and increased their social and political engagement, they adopted progressive social positions and made accommodations with modern cultural life. This shift from spirituality to social engagement, from inwardness to outwardness, led to a loss of the transcendent resources that had served as the foundation of these churches' credibility and influence. Thus, as they became more involved in social and political affairs, the churches—at least as represented by the NCC and their respective Washington, D.C., governmental affairs offices—began to look more like progressive interest groups than religious teachers with a unique spiritual message. The result of this shift in priorities was predictable: the mainline churches began to decline in membership and lose influence.[31]

Thus, while Protestant thinkers like Reinhold Niebuhr profoundly influenced political analysis in the mid–twentieth century, in contemporary America the mainline leaders are offering few noteworthy contributions to public life. Moreover, since Protestant political ethics played a critical role in structuring debate on public affairs throughout much of American history, the decline of mainline Protestantism in the late twentieth century is a development of singular significance for the American people. Mainline Protestant institutions no longer influence America's moral-cultural ethos. In Bottum's words, "the Mainline has lost the capacity to set, or even significantly influence, the national vocabulary or the national self-understanding."[32]

Had mainline churches remained faithful to their sacred mission, they would have undoubtedly continued to play an important, even dominant, role in American cultural and political life. This is especially the case since mainline denominations, unlike Evangelical churches, have well-developed institutions that facilitate efficient individual and collective decision making. By contrast, Evangelicals have weak organizational structures and pursue public affairs concerns through decentralized, local-level activity. Since Evangelicalism is a grassroots movement with few established institutions to promote shared beliefs and actions, the fact that Evangelical groups have been able to influence national and global affairs is itself quite remarkable.

The Institutionalization of Evangelicalism

Historian Mark Noll has observed that the Evangelical movement is diverse, flexible, adaptable, and multiform.[33] Indeed, the strength of Evangelicalism is its decentralized character that allows it to adapt to the shifts in dominant social and cultural patterns and seek to communicate faith in market-friendly ways. The institutional flexibility and adaptability of Evangelicalism has been especially visible with the emergence in the 1980s and 1990s of what theologian David Wells has termed the "marketing church."[34] The distinctive feature of this new expression of Evangelicalism is that it seeks to adapt faith to the shifting contours of modern culture in order to attract nonbelievers. This market-friendly faith contrasts with traditional Evangelicalism, which is rooted in discerning and applying biblical truth to everyday life. Moreover, whereas traditional churches meet in conventional church structures and use hymns, choirs, Scripture reading, and communal confession in worship, contemporary market-oriented churches use buildings resembling sports arenas and rely on informal worship patterns that include contemporary music, drama, and teaching (rather than preaching).

Another distinguishing feature of Evangelicalism is its lack of a central governing authority. The movement has no leader equivalent to the Roman Catholic pope. Its leaders are drawn from the ranks of preachers and theologians whose authority derives simply from their ability to attract followers. Because of his international impact as an evangelist, Billy Graham is commonly regarded as the most influential American Evangelical of the second half of the twentieth century.

Evangelicalism is flexible, continually adapting to changes in the world. Indeed, the growth and dynamism of the movement is the result of creative, entrepreneurial initiatives of pastors and lay leaders. One of the strengths of Evangelicalism is its entrepreneurial, grassroots initiatives and the spread of informal networks of communication and voluntary associations. But because of its weak institutions, Evangelicals have historically tended to limit their level of engagement in civic life, especially when contrasted to the far better organized religious institutions of mainline Protestantism and Roman Catholicism.

The development and growth of Evangelicals, however, would have been impossible without the creation of institutions—principally the National Association of Evangelicals (NAE). One of the NAE's first actions was the establishment of a governmental affairs office in Washington, D.C., to promote causes such as including Evangelical chaplains in the armed forces, assisting mission agencies in dealing with the Department of State, expanding religious broadcasting, and opposing communism. The director of the governmental affairs office, Reverend Clyde Taylor, not only played a crucial role in promoting such shared concerns among public officials but also contributed significantly to the organization's development during his three decades of service.

The NAE is an umbrella organization, and the loose, fragile ties joining its different denominations have limited its social and political engagement. Given the institutional weakness of Evangelicalism, the NAE has been most effective when its leaders have affirmed positions widely supported by members. During the Cold War, for example, the NAE regularly condemned communism as an ideology antithetical to Christianity, knowing that the vast majority of American Evangelicals supported this view. Similarly, while the NAE has affirmed the legitimacy of the state of Israel and called for peace in the Middle East, it has wisely refused to take a position on specific policy issues in this conflict because of members' different views on the matter. When leaders advance positions that don't have the widespread support of their members, their initiatives have limited impact. Such advocacy not only is ineffective but, more significantly, also tends to undermine the credibility of the organization itself.

At the beginning of the new millennium, the total membership of the NAE was about 30 million, representing more than 45,000 churches from forty-eight denominations. This number, however, represents only a part of the American Evangelical community. To begin with, a large segment of believers within mainline denominations are Evangelical. Indeed, the largest, most dynamic churches within mainline Protestant denominations are theologically conservative. Thus, while the mainline denominations are themselves led by a liberal, progressive staff, a large percentage of members remain attached to their denominations and local churches in the hope that religious orthodoxy will be renewed and restored. In addition, there are other denominations that, while theologically conservative, have remained independent of the NAE. The largest and most important of these is the Southern Baptist Convention (SBC), with more than 16 million members. Additionally, a significant portion of Evangelicals are associated with independent churches and parachurches unaffiliated with any established church.

Beginning in the 1980s, one of the most important institutional developments in contemporary Evangelicalism has been the rise of independent mega-churches such as Bill Hybels's Willow Creek Church, in Barrington, Illinois; Joel Osteen's Lakewood Church, in Houston; and Rick Warren's Saddleback Church, in Lake Forest, California. Unlike the more structured, formal worship services common in traditional churches, these new institutions meet in large auditoriums and provide biblical teaching through a consumer-sensitive approach to faith. Although these mega-churches are large—some with ten to twenty thousand members—they also seek to increase the level of members' participation through a host of small-group experiences that allow greater opportunity for learning, fellowship, and service. Not surprisingly, these "seeker sensitive" churches account for a significant part of the Evangelical movement's growth.

The Future of Evangelicalism

American Evangelicalism remains a loose coalition held together by slender bonds. These weak ties are being challenged by growing theological and ecclesiastical pluralism, evident not only in the varied approaches to worship but also in the growing social and political pluralism of the movement. Some observers think that Evangelical influence is likely to decline because of these divisions. Indeed, one journalist goes so far as to predict the breakup of the Evangelical movement.[35]

Although American Evangelicalism remains a predominantly conservative religious movement, some observers have suggested that a moderate political center is gaining strength. For example, ethicist David Gushee argues that an Evangelical "center" is emerging, one that lies between the dominant religious right and the minority Evangelical "left," represented by writer Jim Wallis and others.[36] Gushee supports his contention by claiming that a growing number of influential Evangelicals have adopted a more moderate and comprehensive approach to public life, taking up previously peripheral issues such as the environment and global poverty. He notes that the NAE, by adopting the framework statement "For the Health of the Nation," has moved toward the political middle, while ethicist Ronald Sider and his Evangelicals for Social Action have shifted from the left toward the center. Gushee also highlights NAE's adoption of "An Evangelical Declaration Against Torture" and the growing support among some Evangelicals for initiatives to curb human-initiated global warming as evidence of growing political moderation. The NAE failed to endorse "Climate Change: An Evangelical Call to Action," but many Evangelical leaders signed the statement nonetheless.

Progressive Evangelicals like Jim Wallis have been especially critical of the narrow social and economic agenda of traditional Evangelicals. For them, if Evangelicals are to overcome the widespread perception that they are the Republican Party at prayer, they have to broaden their political program. This means that concerns such as foreign aid, climate change, torture, and immigration must supplement the typical social issues like abortion, prayer in public schools, and same-sex marriage. Additionally, progressives are much more critical of American exceptionalism and the nationalistic sentiments that characterize Evangelical conservatives. As noted above, some church leaders have called for a retrenchment from political engagement. For them, politics has distorted the priorities of the church. In 2008, a group of Evangelicals issued a public declaration entitled "An Evangelical Manifesto" that emphasized the distinctive features of the Evangelical faith. According to its authors, the manifesto was developed in order to address misunderstandings about Evangelical identity and to clarify where Evangelicals stand on public affairs. The manifesto, which says that Evangelicals are believers defined by the "Good News of Jesus of Nazareth," reminds readers that Christians hold dual citizenship: they are "Citizens of the City of God" but also "resident aliens in the Earthly City." Since authentic faith calls believers to be "in" but "not of" the world, the manifesto affirms that Evangelicals "are fully engaged in public affairs, but never completely equated with any party, partisan ideology, economic system, class, tribe, or national identity."[37]

The manifesto declares that Christians have often committed two major errors. Their first mistake has been to privatize faith, interpreting religion as applicable solely to the personal and spiritual realm. The second error has been to politicize faith—viewing religious life chiefly as a way of improving society. Authentic Evangelical faith must engage public life but never compromise its higher commitment to Christ. The manifesto states: "we Evangelicals see it our duty to engage with politics, but our equal duty never to be completely equated with any party, partisan ideology, economic system, or nationality."[38]

As noted earlier, the emergence of the New Evangelicalism in the early 1940s was in great part a response to Fundamentalism's excessive pietism, isolation, and lack of cultural and social engagement. But by the 1980s, Evangelicals were so involved in political action that they risked compromising the transcendent message that authentic religion can bring to political society. The rise of the so-called Religious Right—a broad movement of conservative Christians—encouraged significant political action by Fundamentalist and Evangelical churches, especially on domestic social concerns. Thus, by the end of the Cold War in 1990, Evangelicals had greater political influence than mainline denominations.[39]

But for many Evangelicals, the rise of politicized religion was deeply troubling, not only because it compromised the fundamental spiritual role of churches but also because the American public had deep reservations about such activity. According to Putnam and Campbell, survey data have shown that the American public disapproves of preachers trying to influence political action. "Overwhelmingly," they write, "Americans do not think clergy should be in the business of political persuasion." They go on: "Most people come to church to hear about God, not Caesar. Too much talk of Caesar risks driving them away."[40]

In view of the dangers involved in public policy analysis and action, how should organizations like the SBC or the NAE carry out political initiatives? How should they address global social, political, and economic concerns without neglecting the fundamental task of preaching and teaching the gospel? If Evangelicals are to avoid the mistakes of mainline churches—mistakes of excessive involvement in politics and a neglect of the transcendent mission of teaching and propagating religion—they need to carefully balance spiritual and temporal responsibilities. Additionally, when undertaking political initiatives they need to do their teaching and advocacy work with great skill, lest political advocacy call into question the church's competence and spiritual authority.

Clearly, the winds of American Evangelicalism are blowing in different directions. But if Evangelicals become excessively concerned with public affairs and neglect their primary spiritual mission, they may soon find themselves following the path of decline traced by mainline Protestant churches.

Finally, it is important to address the declining influence of American Evangelicalism in the world—a decline tied to the demographic shifts in the world's Christian population. Historian Philip Jenkins argues in *The Next Christendom* that the center of Christendom is shifting from the global North to the global South because of the significant growth of Christianity in Africa,

Asia, and Latin America and the dwindling role of Christianity in rich, modern societies in Europe and North America. According to one estimate, the number of Christians in North America and Europe in 1900 was 428 million, or 82 percent of the world's Christians, while the rest of the world's Christians, roughly 94 million, accounted for 18 percent. By 2005, however, European and North American Christians were estimated at 758 million, while the rest of the world accounted for 1.4 billion believers. Thus, only 35 percent of Christians lived in Europe and North America in 2005, while 65 percent lived in the global South.[41] More significantly, if current trends continue, by 2025 the number of Christians in the global South is projected to increase to 1.85 billion, or 71 percent of the world's total Christian population, while the number of Christians in North America and Europe is expected to fall to 29 percent of the world's total.[42]

To a significant degree, the dramatic growth of Christianity in the global South has been led by the increasing influence of Pentecostalism.[43] And Pentecostal and Charismatic Christianity has also spread among Protestant denominations as well as the Roman Catholic Church, both in Europe and North America but especially in the global South. According to one estimate, in 1970 there were about 72 million Pentecostals and Charismatic Christians in the world, but because of the significant growth of such believers in Africa and Latin America, the total Pentecostals/Charismatics had increased to almost 590 million by 2005. And if current trends continue, the total number of Pentecostals and Charismatics in the world is expected to be close to 800 million in 2025.[44]

In sum, although Evangelicals continue to account for about one-fourth of the American electorate, the growing theological and political diversity among American Evangelical groups is threatening the religious movement's religious and social influence in the United States. Whether Evangelicals can restore the movement's earlier coherence and cohesiveness is unclear. But if they are unable to constrain the religious and theological pluralism currently under way, Evangelicalism is likely to become even less influential in religious and social life in the United States. Additionally, if Evangelicalism becomes more diverse, it will undoubtedly impede the movement's ability to influence public affairs, domestically as well as internationally.

3 THE GENESIS OF EVANGELICAL GLOBAL ENGAGEMENT

THE MISSIONARY MOVEMENT

Official international relations are determined largely by intergovernmental relationships—the bilateral and multilateral cooperation among officials from different countries. Since foreign policy is concerned chiefly with advancing the national interests of states, the work of missionaries, strictly speaking, is not a part of American foreign policy as it is commonly understood.

Yet foreign relations are not the exclusive domain of government. Indeed, global society is profoundly influenced by the beliefs and actions of nonstate actors, including organizations, associations, movements, and groups representing an array of transnational concerns. Additionally, U.S. nongovernmental organizations (NGOs) influence not only events abroad but also American foreign policy. Religious organizations are no exception—for example, Christian missionaries have traditionally had a strong influence on the communities in which they serve. Therefore, while missionaries have not been directly involved in the conduct of American foreign relations, they have nonetheless played, and continue to play, an important indirect role in America's engagement in the world.

The Rise of the American Missionary Enterprise

In the early nineteenth century, Congregational, Methodist, Episcopalian, and Presbyterian churches began sending missionaries overseas—first to Hawaii and then to the Middle East and the Far East. Although some American Protestants had undertaken sporadic missionary initiatives in the late eighteenth century, the modern missionary movement dates to 1806. In that year, Samuel Mills and a group of friends at Williams College gathered under a haystack, seeking refuge from a sudden thunderstorm. There they

vowed to dedicate their lives to foreign missions, and so the modern missionary movement began at the "haystack prayer meeting." Mills subsequently
organized another group—the Society of Brethren—to encourage foreign
evangelistic activity at other educational institutions, including Yale College
and Andover Theological Seminary. And though he himself traveled only
briefly to Africa to help identify a territory (Liberia) to which freed slaves
could return, Mills played a crucial role in promoting the cause of missions
and in recruiting church leaders to serve as missionaries.

Despite his youth, Mills was permitted to address the 1810 Assembly
of the Congregational Churches of Massachusetts in order to promote the
cause of foreign missions. In his passionate presentation, he called on church
leaders to develop an organization to encourage foreign missions. Partly in
response to his promotional work, New England church leaders established
a centralized, interdenominational organization—the American Board of
Commissioners for Foreign Missions—to manage and direct the missionary
enterprise.

Since most Protestant missionaries were sent under the auspices of the
American Board, the organization had a profound impact on overseas missionary activity. From the outset, the Board emphasized evangelism and
encouraged missionaries to address social and cultural matters only as they
impacted human dignity. As an 1823 Board directive noted, the missionary
was to "abstain from all interference with local and political views of the people. The Kingdom of Christ is not of this world; and it especially behooves
a missionary to stand aloof from the private and transient interests of chiefs
and rulers."[1] Rufus Anderson, who served as head of the Board from 1832
to 1866, was especially influential. He believed that it was important to distinguish between the work of indigenous church leaders and that of foreign
missionaries, and emphasized that missionaries should carry out their work as
itinerant teachers and preachers rather than as settled pastors.

Perhaps the most influential early missionary couple was Adoniram
and Ann Judson, who went to Burma (now Myanmar). After learning the
Burmese language, they devoted themselves to evangelism and teaching—
she promoting literacy among women and he teaching Western technologies
to men. But early in their missionary service war broke out between Britain
and Burma, leading to Adoniram's imprisonment and torture. Despite the
tragic deaths of his wife and two infant daughters—owing in great part to
the physical hardships and persecution they endured—Adoniram continued
his evangelistic and educational work until his death in 1850. The quality and
scope of his scholarly work was truly remarkable. Among other things, he

translated the entire Bible into Burmese, prepared a scholarly grammar, and nearly completed a comprehensive Burmese-English dictionary. Evangelism was difficult; he made no converts in his first four years of service. Yet by the time of his death, Adoniram was supervising 163 Burmese church leaders who ministered to some seven thousand church members.[2]

The growth of American foreign missions was slow at first, but the number of missionaries continued to increase rapidly in response to the Second Great Awakening—the religious renewal movement of the mid–nineteenth century that encouraged revivalism and social reform, or what some observers have called "practical Christianity." The expansion of missionary activity was even more dramatic in the latter part of the century as another revival movement swept the American heartland. This decentralized renewal movement, known as the Third Great Awakening, encouraged believers toward a deeper commitment to the Christian faith. It thus led to more evangelistic initiatives, increased pietism, and greater social engagement, especially in addressing such social ills as slavery, alcoholism, and poverty. D. L. Moody, one of the movement's leaders, established an educational training center—Moody Bible Institute, in Chicago—that helped to equip countless students for foreign missionary service. It is estimated that the number of Protestant missionaries increased from 5,000 at the end of the nineteenth century to roughly 10,000 in 1915.[3]

After World War I, Protestant missionary activity changed as mainline churches became less concerned with evangelism and more concerned with social justice. As a result, the number of mainline Protestant missionaries remained rather stable for several decades, while the number of nondenominational and interdenominational Evangelical groups expanded rapidly, eclipsing the number of mainline missionaries by the 1940s. William Hutchison claims that the "heyday" of Protestant foreign missions was from 1880 to 1930.[4] This judgment is unwarranted, however, in view of the even greater expansion of missionary activity in the aftermath of World War II. Indeed, the heyday of foreign missions did not come until the 1950s and 1960s, with the expansion of interdenominational and nondenominational Evangelical missions associations.

In 1958, mainline Protestants had 7,901 missionaries, while Evangelical missions groups had nearly twice that many (13,468).[5] In subsequent decades these trends became even more pronounced as the number of Evangelical missionaries continued to expand relative to those from mainline churches. Between the 1950s and the 1990s, the number of nondenominational missions agencies increased threefold—rising from 178 agencies to 575—whereas the number of denominational and interdenominational organizations increased by fewer than 30 (from 87 to 115).[6] Not surprisingly, the number of Evangelical missionaries affiliated with these agencies also continued to expand rapidly. The Southern Baptist Convention continued its spectacular expansion, more than doubling the size of its missionary force between 1969 (2,564) and 2001 (5,437).[7] By 2001, the total number of full-time U.S. missionaries was more than 44,000, with the vast majority of these serving under Evangelical organizations.[8]

Significant change in the nature and scope of missionary enterprise, however, is under way. This change is the result not only of globalization and the growing ease and decreasing cost of international travel but also of the growth of what might be termed "populist Evangelicalism." As the Evangelical movement has become further decentralized and more informal, the traditional structures of foreign missions have similarly become less institutionalized, resulting in a dramatic rise in smaller, less structured missions organizations. The proliferation of small missions associations has also influenced another noteworthy development: the rise of short-term missions trips by church groups and a decline in the number of long-term missionaries. Later in this chapter, I briefly explore some of the implications of the shift toward informal, shorter-term missions.

The Missionary Movement and Foreign Cultural Engagement

Scholars have offered widely differing interpretations of the nature and influence of missionary activity, especially for the first phase of the missionary enterprise in the nineteenth century. For some observers, missionary work was chiefly spiritual, designed to share the gospel with people in foreign lands who were unfamiliar with Christianity. According to this perspective, missionaries traveled to foreign lands to proclaim the good news of salvation in Christ and were chiefly interested in religion, not social and cultural life. Missionary activity, however, was never solely religious. Indeed, from the outset missionaries were inevitably involved in educational, medical, social, and cultural activities, if for no other reason than to facilitate the teaching of religion. And this work often challenged prevailing customs and social practices. As a result, some scholars have argued that the missionary movement was also deeply engaged in cultural, economic, and social transformation. The noted historian Daniel Boorstin, for example, has argued that:

> Missions became a way of hallowing American democracy and the American Standard of Living and in the course of the nineteenth

century, the foreign-missionary effort actually helped give a religious authenticity to the ways of Americans at home. Education, which was becoming a secular religion within the Untied States, became an agency of missions abroad. American missionaries carried this gospel of education to the farthest corners of the world. They established schools of every kind with American money, which they collected in millions of dollars and in millions of pennies.[9]

Some critics have claimed that the American missionary movement was an expression of imperialism, with missionaries serving as agents of social and cultural domination. For example, Stephen Neill writes: "whatever may have been the beneficent intentions of missionaries, they were in fact the tools of governments, and that missions can be classed as one of the instruments of western infiltration and control."[10] Jean and John Comaroff similarly claim that when missionaries set out to save Africa, their goal was "to make her peoples the subjects of a world-wide Christian commonwealth." They were not simply bearers of the Christian religion but also "the human vehicles of a hegemonic worldview."[11] A more convincing interpretation is that the missionary movement was fueled by mixed motives. To be sure, missionaries not only benefited from their association with great powers but also, at times, reinforced foreign political and business interests. But just as often, missionaries defended indigenous cultures and protected the interests and welfare of natives. As Lamin Sanneh writes:

> The evidence paints a complicated picture of the diverse and unpredictable indigenous responses to Christianity because the premise of missionary hegemony is faulty. There were equally as many examples of Christianity coalescing with anti-colonial activities and movements as there were of imperial collusion and acquiescence. A chain is only as good as its weakest link, and the weakest link in the argument of hegemony is evidence of Christian-inspired protest and resistance, both in the church and in politics. Colonized societies produced a class of national champions as well as imperial supporters.[12]

Similarly, historian Andrew Preston claims that missionary enterprise was a mixture of imperialism and service. He writes: "Often the expansion of Americanism and Christianity was an explicitly imperial project. But just as often, missionaries displayed a unique sensitivity to the concerns of native peoples that superseded their national prejudices."[13] According to Stephen

Neill, most missionaries held mixed views about Western colonialism and the dominant role of Western values. While some missionaries regarded Western hegemony as "something undesirable in itself," others, he writes, "were prepared to accept it for the sake of the good, but sometimes to turn all too blind an eye to the evil."[14] While acknowledging that missionaries' primary concern was with "the well-being of the people whom they had come to serve," Neill notes that this did not mean that missionaries carried out their work in an impartial and dispassionate manner. "All too often the missionary held that he could judge better of the real interests of his people than they could themselves," he writes; "his objectivity was blurred by a certain patronizing, and sometimes even contemptuous, attitude towards men whom he could never quite persuade himself to regard as grown up."[15] There can be little doubt that missionaries, when confronted with cultural and social practices that they regarded as oppressive and unjust, sought to uplift indigenous peoples by liberating them through education. But for the most part, such initiatives were not motivated by a quest for imperial domination or political control but, rather, by a fundamental commitment to the dignity of human beings, regardless of their status, gender, wealth, or social class. In writing about the American missionary enterprise in China, historian John Fairbank argues that missionaries, besides carrying out religious work, were agents of American social and cultural values. In effect, missionaries were "apostles of liberty under law, of one-class egalitarianism (except for the anomaly of black slavery), and of self-determination of peoples."[16] According to Arthur Schlesinger, Jr., since native societies were not "gardens of innocence and tranquility," missionaries frequently challenged customs that they considered evil and condemned discriminatory practices. And from time to time they sought to reform oppressive institutions and transform unjust cultural traditions.[17] In short, while the missionary enterprise emphasized evangelism, missionaries did not hesitate to confront values and traditions that they considered inimical to human dignity.[18]

It is easy to regard missionary activity solely as religious work and to dismiss its potential impact on the social and cultural life of foreign societies. But as Mead has aptly noted, it is a mistake to view missionaries as "nothing more than psalm-singing fishers of souls."[19] From the outset missionaries were involved in promoting human welfare through educational, social, and cultural initiatives, including the building of clinics, hospitals, and schools. And as they carried out their religious and humanitarian work, they modeled values and practices that reinforced the inherent dignity of all persons. In particular, missionaries contributed to human dignity by challenging gender discrimination, child labor, and other human rights abuses. In light of the important humanitarian work of missionaries, there can be little doubt missionary activity, in the words of Arthur Schlesinger, Jr., provided "a means to advance social progress."[20] Their contribution came in four primary areas.

Advancing Human Dignity

Protestant missionaries were pioneers in promoting the notion of the inherent worth of human life. For missionaries, people mattered because they were God's creation. What was important was that human beings accept the gift of salvation in Christ; conversion, missionaries believed, was the "*sine qua non* for improved morality," without which creating and maintaining a decent human society was impossible.[21] Human liberty was important because human responsibility was possible only where people had some fundamental choices over their conscience and aspects of their physical existence.

Many Evangelical missionaries taught and modeled values that affirmed the inherent worth of all persons, regardless of gender, social class, or ethnicity. For them, human dignity was not a legal doctrine or a political ideology. Rather, it was the basis of their evangelistic mission, which was to share the good news of salvation in Christ. Because Christianity assumes that all persons are created in God's image and that salvation is available to all who accept the divine gift of Jesus as Savior, the message of God's universal love represented a potential threat to societies that were unequal, oppressive, and discriminatory. From the outset, however, missionaries were reluctant to get involved in politics. The leaders of the American Board of Commissioners for Foreign Missions expected that missionaries would avoid interfering in native political affairs unless rulers threatened basic religious or moral beliefs and practices. For missionaries, the most effective way of advancing human welfare was through conversion and the nurturing of humane values and traditions.

Missionaries regarded advancing human dignity as part of their religious work, not a political project. In proclaiming the message of salvation in Christ, however, missionaries inevitably also advanced social, political, and cultural values that had nurtured economic enterprise and democratic practices in the United States. According to historian John Fairbank, missionaries were "apostles" of common values of American life. In his view, these included

a strong sense of personal responsibility for one's own character and conduct; an optimistic belief in progress toward general betterment, especially through the use of education, invention, and technology; and a conviction of moral and cultural worth..., justified both by the religious teachings of the Holy Bible and by the political principles of the Founding Fathers.[22]

Although the most important and influential method of advancing human dignity was through the proclamation of the Christian faith, missionaries did not hesitate to promote human welfare by challenging repressive social and political practices and by condemning human rights abuses, such as slavery, torture, and degradation of women and children. The important role of missionaries in challenging inhumane practices is best illustrated by William Carey, a British Baptist who carried out missionary work in India from 1793 until his death in 1834. Carey publicly condemned Sati—the Hindu practice of immolating widows on the funeral pyres of their husbands.[23] As a result, Sati was eventually declared illegal by the Indian government.

Education

From the outset, missionaries played a key role in fostering literacy and technical skills through the establishment of schools and colleges. Education was deemed important not simply as a means of learning to read the Scriptures but also as a way of enhancing people's skills and knowledge. Since education had improved human dignity and standards of living in Western societies, missionaries assumed that natives would benefit similarly. Moreover, missionaries believed that schools could contribute to the development of values and practices that would be conducive to greater social equality. Since the few educational opportunities in foreign societies were limited to the boys of rich, powerful families, the development of missionary schools provided a means by which poor children could develop skills that might free them from abject poverty. Finally, schools were important as a means of modeling gender equality in traditional cultures in which women were considered unequal. Not surprisingly, Protestant missionaries established countless schools and colleges for women throughout the Ottoman Empire as well as India and China.

Although education was an important element of all missionary enterprise, it was especially significant in areas where the evangelistic task was slow and difficult, such as the Near East and the Far East. The educational legacy of missionaries in the Middle East is especially noteworthy. In Syria (including present-day Lebanon), for example, missionaries had established thirty-three schools by 1860; by 1900 the number had increased to ninety-five, serving more than 5,300 students.[24] According to one estimate, by World War I, missionaries in the northern area of the Ottoman Empire (modern Turkey) had established ten colleges with 2,500 students, fifty high schools with 4,500 students and more than four hundred elementary schools with 20,000 students. And in Syria there were another 6,000 students in schools and colleges.[25]

Education was also a major element of missionary work in the Far East. John Fairbank estimates that by 1935 American missionaries in China had established thirteen Christian colleges that enrolled 5,800 students and 255 middle schools with nearly 44,000 students.[26] Thus, when American educational missionary work is combined with the educational service of British missionaries, the impact of Protestant missionaries on global education is truly remarkable. By one estimate, at the beginning of the twentieth century, American and British missionaries had established ninety-four colleges and universities and 29,458 schools.[27]

The long-term impact of missionaries' educational work was especially significant in the Middle East. In 1866, Daniel Bliss, a Congregationalist missionary in Beirut, began a small college (the Syrian Protestant College, later called American University of Beirut). This institution was remarkable for a number of reasons. First, although missionaries established the college to introduce students to the Christian faith, the approach to evangelism was nuanced and indirect. Bliss expressed his vision for the college as follows:

> This College is for all conditions and classes of men without regard to colour, nationality, race or religion. A man white, black or yellow, Christian, Jew, Mohammedan or heathen, may enter and enjoy all the advantages of this institution for three, four, or eight years; and go out believing in one God, or in many Gods, or in no God. But it will be impossible for any one to continue with us long without knowing what we believe to be the truth and our reasons for that belief.[28]

Second, the college carried out instruction in the native language (Arabic), rather than in English or French—the common pattern with British and French religious schools. Robert Kaplan writes that the decision to use Arabic reflected the American missionaries' desire "to convert Syrian society from within, as partners, rather than as self-declared outsiders like the French or British."[29] The missionary effort to establish institutions of higher learning that encouraged free inquiry and were accessible to indigenous people in their own language had a profound impact on Syrian (later Lebanese) society. Kaplan argues that the establishment of the Syrian Protestant College was probably "the most inspired idea in the history of foreign aid." He goes on: "Not only was it a quintessential cottage industry project for filtering Western values into the Arab world over time, but it also provided a permanent aesthetic monument to America in the region, a monument that posed no threat to anyone else's sovereignty."[30]

The educational effort of American missionaries in Turkey and Iran was even larger than that in Syria. Beginning in the mid–nineteenth century, missionaries began developing schools and colleges. Robert College, a men's high school north of Constantinople, was the first missionary institution of higher learning in the Near East. The Constantinople Women's College (later American College for Girls) was a similar institution for girls.[31] Euphrates College, located in Harput, in eastern Turkey, was established as a seminary and a coeducational high school for Armenian students. In 1895, the Kurds destroyed much of the campus, and in 1915, Turkish military authorities took it over, permanently closing the institution soon after.

Missionaries developed close relationships with indigenous people through their educational work. In Egypt, Syria, Turkey, and elsewhere, missionaries became fluent in indigenous languages and learned the social and cultural norms of the people. The decision to use Arabic at the Syrian Protestant College undoubtedly contributed to the close relationship between Arabs and Americans at this institution and had profound symbolic impact on the region. Because the college provided a safe environment for free inquiry and open debate, it played an important role in facilitating the emergence of an Arab collective identity that has been the foundation of the Pan-Arab Movement and a major political force in modern Middle East politics. Thus, while the college was established to promote Christian education, it had its most significant impact in social and political life. This pattern was also repeated at the American University of Cairo.

Humanitarianism

A third important dimension of missionary work was the provision of relief and development services. From the outset, missionaries built clinics and orphanages to care for those in need. American missionaries established the Protestant Medical College in Syria in 1867 and four years later created the School of Pharmacy. Within a few years American missionaries were treating 40,000 patients annually in hospitals and clinics located throughout the Ottoman Empire. Besides establishing clinics to offer basic medical care, missionaries developed model farms to teach effective agricultural practices and encouraged more effective enterprise by modeling values and practices necessary to increase economic efficiency. In Chile, for example, Anglican missionaries provided relief and development assistance to Araucanian Indians, a small, impoverished group of indigenous people in the central region of the country. Similarly, Methodist missionaries established a large model farm (known as "el Vergel") in the central agricultural region to offer education and training to local peasants. The school still provides technical training to young people.

One of the most significant initiatives in missionary humanitarianism was the relief provided to impoverished, persecuted Armenians and other minorities at the outset of World War I. In response to the massacres and displacement of tens of thousands of Armenians in the northern part of the Ottoman Empire (now Turkey), American missionaries in the Near East collaborated with U.S. government officials and American philanthropists to respond to the humanitarian crisis. In 1915, missionaries, supported by the U.S. government, established the American Committee for Armenian and Syrian Relief (ACASR) to spearhead humanitarian assistance to the Near East. ACASR—its name was later shortened to Near East Relief—was overseen by a large group of influential civic, business, and religious leaders. James Barton, the general secretary of the American Board of Commissioners for Foreign Missions, served as chair. It is estimated that in its first fifteen years, Near East Relief provided aid to more than 1 million refugees and housed, clothed, and educated more than 100,000 orphans.[32]

Evangelical humanitarianism greatly increased after World War II. One of the early pioneers of postwar Evangelical humanitarianism was Bob Pierce, founder of World Vision. Dr. Pierce first traveled to China as a war correspondent and saw the devastation and human misery firsthand. He subsequently traveled to Korea, where he initiated a sponsorship program to provide long-term care to children orphaned by war. The sponsorship program was later expanded to include orphans and children from other poor lands. By the beginning of the new millennium, World Vision was the world's largest Evangelical humanitarian organization. But it was hardly the only one. Faith-based nongovernmental organizations (NGOs) like Bread for the Hungry, Compassion Alliance, MAP (Medical Assistance Programs) International, Opportunity International, Samaritan's Purse, and World Relief all help people in need. To foster greater cooperation among Evangelical relief and development agencies, leaders established an association AERDO (Association of Evangelical Relief and Development Organizations). The association has been renamed Accord and currently has more than seventy member organizations.

It is important to stress that humanitarianism is not the chief work of missionaries. Of course, concern with meeting basic human needs—as with advancing the inherent dignity of all persons—is an important missionary task. But it is ancillary to the fundamental evangelistic ministry of proclaiming the good news of salvation in Christ. Still, because of their close relationships with indigenous peoples, missionaries are especially well equipped to undertake the humanitarian task in a knowledgeable and competent manner. Whereas American government officials and business leaders typically interact with a relatively small sector of society, missionaries maintain close ties with the masses and are therefore far more knowledgeable about the needs, problems, and challenges facing native peoples. Additionally, because of the close interpersonal ties between missionaries and natives, the former can model and teach values that foster better health, improve productivity and increase confidence, and uphold the inherent dignity of all persons.

Civil Society

American missionaries also promoted civil society by creating and strengthening nongovernmental institutions, such as religious denominations, medical associations, publishing groups, and educational associations. These mediating institutions—whether focusing on business, religion, education, or vocational associations—are essential in the development of humane, participatory social and political systems. According to democratic theorists, civil society is important because it fosters social cohesion and trust—what social scientists refer to as social capital. Indeed, since participation and trust are indispensable to democracy, it is impossible for a democratic government to function without a vigorous civil society.

According to Robert D. Woodberry and Timothy S. Shah, Protestantism played an important role in the rise and expansion of civil society because, unlike the centralized Roman Catholic Church, Protestants had no established authority to resolve theological disputes.[33] As a result, Protestant churches encouraged pluralism, which, in turn, nurtured what Alfred Stepan has termed the "twin tolerations"—the independence of the state from religion and the independence of religion from government.[34] The first "toleration" made it more difficult for religious bodies to control the state, thereby encouraging political activity free from interference by church authorities. In time, this development permitted the rise of mediating institutions of civil society and eventually the establishment of democratic institutions. The second "toleration" was equally significant since it led to the development of freedom of religion and freedom of conscience. It would have been difficult to develop democratic institutions without a deep and sustained religious pluralism. Thus, to the extent that the Protestant faith nurtured pluralism and civil society, it facilitated the development of democratic governance.[35]

When American missionaries traveled to foreign lands, they brought Protestant ideas with them: a belief in human sin, the inherent dignity of all persons, the priority of personal responsibility, the importance of individual accountability, human freedom, and a distrust of authority, including government. The dissemination of such notions played an important role in developing special-interest groups, associations, and voluntary organizations. While different religions had competed for centuries in India, the Middle East, China, and Japan, Woodberry and Shah claim that "no widespread budding of voluntary organizations happened in these lands until Protestant missionaries from nonestablished churches appeared on the scene."[36]

Missionaries did not travel to foreign lands to build civil society. Rather, the nongovernmental institutions they helped build were a by-product of their multifaceted missionary work. The broad scope of missionary activity is evident in the contributions that American and European missionaries could claim by the beginning of the twentieth century: 558 missionary societies, 7,319 mission stations, 14,364 churches, 94 colleges and universities, 29,458 schools, 379 hospitals, 7,682 dispensaries, and 152 publishing houses. The movement employed some 18,682 missionaries and 79,396 national workers.[37] In view of accomplishments such as these, Woodberry and Shah do not exaggerate when they claim that missionaries played a crucial role in the development of "organized civil society" across the non-Western world.[38]

The Missionary Movement and U.S. Foreign Policy

Although missionaries are not agents of the U.S. government, they nevertheless have made noteworthy contributions to the conduct of American foreign policy. While their most significant contributions have come through the indirect dissemination of knowledge and values, missionaries have, on rare occasions, also influenced decision making directly, chiefly by championing core moral values, advocating specific public policies, and disseminating knowledge about foreign societies.

Direct Engagement

Perhaps the best illustration of direct missionary engagement in American diplomacy occurred around the time of World War I. Missionaries had established close relationships with Armenians, Syrians, and other peoples in the

Ottoman Empire. Their years of work gave them knowledge about the Near East that no other Americans had, and they helped define American foreign policy interests in the region.[39] When the Turks committed genocide against Armenians in 1915–17, missionaries played a pivotal role in publicizing the atrocities, pleading for help, and mobilizing humanitarian aid.

Later, when the Ottoman Empire collapsed, and the territory was partitioned, missionaries provided invaluable perspectives on the needs and wants of indigenous peoples. And when Turkey prevailed militarily against Britain and France in its war of independence, James Barton, the head of the American Board of Commissioners for Foreign Missions, was present at the negotiations that led to the Lausanne Treaty of 1923. Like most American Protestants, he opposed the accord because it reduced freedom of religion in Turkey, curtailed missionary enterprise, and reduced Armenia's territory. However, Greece, Turkey, Britain, Italy, and Japan subsequently ratified the treaty, thereby establishing the borders of modern-day Turkey. In Joseph Grabill's view, the ratification of the Lausanne accord signaled "that both the ascendancy of Protestant diplomacy and the heroic age of Protestantism in the Near East had ended."[40]

Although missionaries were primarily concerned with evangelism and humanitarian work, they nonetheless also contributed directly to policymaking in geographic regions in which they worked. In the early Cold War years, missionaries were active in U.S. policy toward China. Throughout the late 1940s, as the Chinese civil war raged between the Nationalists, led by Chiang Kai-shek, and the Communists, led by Mao Zedong, missionaries and religious leaders not only helped shape the policy debate but also advanced specific goals. Although some missionaries and Protestant leaders identified with Mao's communist ideals, most were strongly supportive of Chiang Kai-shek, not only because he himself was a Christian but also because of deep misgivings about the anti-religious character of communism.

Missionaries with extensive cross-cultural experience could bring unique perspectives to complex, challenging foreign policy problems. When President Truman was seeking a diplomat to advance American interests in China, he chose a lifelong missionary, J. Leighton Stuart. Stuart, who had been born and reared in China as the son of missionary parents, and had served for more than forty years as a Presbyterian missionary educator, knew the history, language, and culture of China as well as anyone. He proved to be an effective ambassador, serving from 1946 to 1953, when Chinese communists defeated the nationalists. The new regime soon imposed severe restrictions on Christian worship and, more specifically, on the work of foreign missionaries. In time, the deep distrust and political conflicts between Communist China and the United States led to a rupture of diplomatic relations between the two states.

In his important book on religion and U.S. foreign policy during the early Cold War years, William Inboden tells the story of how former missionaries participated in the debate about "saving China."[41] Besides highlighting Ambassador Stuart's contribution to the evolution of U.S.–China policy, Inboden also examines the important political advocacy of two other former missionaries—Walter Judd and William Richard Johnson. Judd, who was elected to Congress in 1943, had served in China for ten years as a medical missionary of the Congregational Church. He became deeply concerned about the rising influence of revolutionary communist forces led by Mao in the late 1940s. As the guerrilla war began to make significant inroads against the Nationalist government, Judd became a leading spokesman for the anti-communist movement in American society, especially among religious elites.

Johnson, who had served for forty years as a Methodist missionary educator in China, similarly took up the cause of Chinese anti-communism upon his retirement. But whereas Judd carried out his advocacy as a U.S. congressman, Johnson took up the cause as a political activist, seeking to influence White House officials, diplomats at the Department of State, and members of Congress. It is important to stress, however, that while Judd and Johnson strongly supported the Nationalist cause and opposed Mao's Communist Party, there was no unified perspective on U.S–China relations among former missionaries. Inboden observes that while many American missionaries sought to influence the evolution of U.S.–Chinese ties, they did so not as a missionary lobby but as a group of independent religious activists, each with his own perspective. He writes: "there was not a unanimous 'missionary position'; while all agreed that spiritual imperatives should guide American policy, they disagreed in which direction it should go."[42]

Moreover, to the extent that former missionaries sought to influence U.S. foreign policy on China, they did so not on religious or theological grounds but, rather, based on their knowledge of Chinese society, love of the people, and desire to foster a free, tolerant culture. Thus, when former missionaries participated in public debates on the evolving political conditions in China or the actions that the U.S. government should take toward the communist regime, they did so chiefly as persons with competence in Chinese affairs.[43]

Missionaries also played an important role in providing information about foreign societies threatened by revolutionary communism. Because missionaries had firsthand knowledge of foreign lands and a strong anti-communist orientation, many were eager to assist the U.S. government's anti-communist campaign. Thus, in the 1950s, the Central Intelligence Agency (CIA) began to interview missionaries periodically as a way to gather intelligence. Under the CIA initiative, missionaries serving in regions where communist influence was rising, such as Latin America and Southeast Asia, were debriefed when they returned to the United States for home leave. According to one estimate, at the height of the Cold War, between 10 and 25 percent of all U.S. missionaries provided some information to American intelligence authorities.[44]

After this practice became public knowledge in the mid-1970s, the NAE and other missionary organizations condemned it, arguing that it compromised their religious missions and their perceived independence from governmental authority. Partly in response to strong criticism of the project, the intelligence community announced in 1977 that it was prohibiting the use of missionaries and journalists for intelligence collection. In 1996, however, CIA Director John Deutch raised new concerns about the ban when he announced that the earlier prohibition could be waived when confronting special threats to national security. Once again, the NAE and other religious organizations protested vigorously.

Indirect Engagement

Missionaries' most significant contribution to the conduct of American foreign policy has been their indirect influence on beliefs, values, and practices about the world in general, and about foreign societies in particular. By developing knowledge of the world, understanding the values and perspectives of other cultures, and heightening concern about foreign peoples, missionaries have been leaders in promoting concern for the welfare of other nations. In particular, missionaries have developed and disseminated knowledge of foreign cultures, promoted transnational interests and concerns, encouraged global humanitarianism, fostered the idea of the world as a coherent moral community, nurtured democratic ideals and practices, and promoted transnational, nongovernmental ties that have contributed to the development of transnational institutions—what scholars now define as global civil society.

1. *Promoting Knowledge of Foreign Societies*: Because missionaries were often the first Americans to live abroad for extended periods, they became the most knowledgeable persons about foreign cultures. This knowledge proved highly beneficial to government officials and businessmen traveling abroad and especially to U.S. diplomats. For example, when the Allies

were remaking the Middle East after the collapse of the Ottoman Empire, President Woodrow Wilson's administration relied heavily on missionary leaders for perspectives on the peoples of the Near East. Similarly, at the end of World War II, General Douglas MacArthur relied on the cultural and historical expertise of missionaries who had served in the Far East, especially in Burma, China, and Japan. Walter Russell Mead writes that MacArthur's reconstruction of Japan was "essentially an implementation of the missionary program at the point of bayonets." He goes on: "Without the long missionary experience America would have had neither the chutzpah or the know-how that characterized the occupation of Japan, a foreign policy venture that despite all the attendant controversy is generally considered one of the most important successful initiatives in American history."[45]

Mead argues that the work of missionaries helped prepare the United States for world leadership following World War II.[46] The United States was equipped to lead in the creation of global institutions and the cause of freedom and economic prosperity largely because of the significant international experience that missionaries had given American society in general and the U.S. government in particular. Although many missionary children followed their parents into full-time Christian service, a significant number pursued international careers in business, diplomacy, or related foreign vocations. As the United States assumed a global leadership role, the government's need for foreign experts increased significantly. Not surprisingly, a growing number of diplomats had missionary backgrounds, especially in the non-Western regions of the Near East, Far East, and Asia. According to one estimate, about one half of "foreign-culture experts" at the time of World War II were missionary children.[47]

2. *Promoting Global Interests*: Missionaries played important roles in promoting a greater national commitment to the interests and well-being of foreign peoples. In the early period of the American republic, the U.S. government was chiefly concerned with the development and consolidation of its political and economic institutions. The dominant foreign policy doctrine was isolationism. Although the United States faced periodic foreign challenges, its major goal was to avoid foreign entanglements. The rise and expansion of the missionary movement in the latter nineteenth century, however, helped fuel public concern for global issues. According to Preston, missionaries were in the vanguard of American internationalism, viewing themselves as "citizens of the world." In effect, they were "significantly ahead of their fellow Americans' thinking on

foreign affairs," perceiving "the world as fundamentally interconnected much earlier than most others did."[48]

To be sure, political and military officials and business leaders, independent of the concerns of missionaries, sought to expand American power internationally. In his important study of the rise of American international power, Warren Zimmerman shows how thinkers like Alfred T. Mahan and political leaders like Theodore Roosevelt encouraged and celebrated the rise of American global influence.[49] But missionaries also played a crucial role in America's shift from isolationism to internationalism. Schlesinger, for example, argues that missionaries contributed significantly to the rise of American expansionism in the late nineteenth century. Indeed, he suggests that the missionary movement may have influenced America more than it influenced foreign cultures. In Schlesinger's view, the self-confidence and self-righteousness of the missionary cause reinforced an expansionist ethos:

> Cultural aggression not only threatened the self-image of the violated nation but fed the self-righteousness of the intruders. Americans had long seen themselves as in some sense, first religiously and then politically, a chosen people. The Founding Fathers supposed that America would spread its influence by example rather than by intervention. But missionaries saw their responsibilities more urgently.... Their evangelical spirit helped to infuse the American role in the world with the impulses of a crusade.[50]

In short, although the rise of American globalism was chiefly political and economic, the missionary impulse to proclaim the gospel and to meet human needs in impoverished societies also helped to shape American public opinion about the world.

3. *Advancing Global Humanitarianism*: Missionaries contributed to American foreign policy by highlighting the needs and concerns of foreign peoples and by developing institutions to care for them. As noted earlier, missionaries pioneered in promoting education, developing healthcare facilities, and providing humanitarian relief. Noted historian Daniel Boorstin has observed: "the roots of foreign aid, of the Peace Corps, and of numerous other American institutions of diplomacy and foreign relations lay deep in the American missionary tradition which thrived in the nineteenth century."[51]

Missionary humanitarianism has influenced the ideas and practices of American foreign policy in a number of ways. First, missionaries reinforced the belief that all persons were entitled to dignity. Missionaries cared for the material and spiritual needs of others because they viewed people as children of God. To a significant degree, missionary humanitarianism was, therefore, rooted in moral assumptions about the international system. A second important influence of the missionary model was its focus on meeting local human needs. Since missionaries provided medical, educational, and economic aid through clinics, schools, and charity centers, missionary humanitarianism has offered an important model of decentralized service. This example has been especially influential in the post–Cold War era, as the United States has shifted its foreign aid strategy from direct government-to-government transfers to indirect aid through nongovernmental institutions. Under this new model, the U.S. government seeks to advance human dignity and meet basic human needs by supporting economic, educational, and social initiatives through institutions with strong ties to indigenous peoples.

4. *Nurturing the Idea of an International Community*: Another, related way that missionaries have influenced the foreign relations of the United States is by promoting the notion of the world as a universal community. Although missionaries tended to identify strongly with the United States and its ideals and interests, the overseas experience also contributed to the emergence of strong transnational ties and to the idea that all persons had matchless value, regardless of their nationality, ethnicity, or social class. And since all people were part of God's creation, the world was not simply a collection of tribes, cultures, and nations, but a coherent moral community. According to Dana Robert, "[t]he global vision intrinsic to Christianity—that of one world, one kingdom of God under Jesus Christ—has been both the motive and purpose behind much missionary fervor."[52] While missionaries continued to acknowledge national boundaries, they played an important role in celebrating the intrinsic unity and moral coherence of the world.

The claim that the world was a coherent moral community was not based on political ideology but on the fundamental truth that all persons were members of God's created world. Since people mattered in God's sovereign order, ethnic, religious, cultural, social, and political divisions were less significant than the overriding unity among all persons. To be sure, missionaries did not invent this notion. What was new, however, was the fresh impetus given to the concept of global society. The claim of transnational and transcultural unity was especially relevant for Christian believers who assumed that they were, collectively, part of the universal church, "the body of Christ."

To a significant degree, missionaries were the first American internationalists. Even before entrepreneurs began to establish overseas business interests, missionaries were deeply involved in the task of world evangelization, believing that all peoples should have the opportunity to hear the gospel message of salvation in Christ. Charles Denby, an American diplomat in China, noted that missionaries anticipated foreign businessmen. "The missionary," he observed, "inspired by holy zeal, goes everywhere, and by degrees foreign commerce and trade follow."[53]

Evangelical missionaries contributed significantly to the rise of internationalist dispositions among the public. These dispositions encouraged concern with global issues, such as human rights, care for women and children, and poverty reduction. Such global concerns, however, did not translate into support for the development of formal international governmental institutions. From the outset, Fundamentalists and many Evangelicals expressed deep skepticism about the rise in international governmental institutions, such as the League of Nations and its successor, the United Nations. When President Woodrow Wilson sought to establish the League of Nations at the end of World War I, conservative Christians strongly opposed him. According to Markku Ruotsila, Christian anti-internationalism emerged as a by-product of the controversy between modernists and conservative Christians.[54] Ruotsila argues that conservative believers, especially Fundamentalists, believed that the effort to create global governmental institutions was misconceived because it presumed that world peace could be achieved without a fundamental spiritual transformation. During the interwar period, and even throughout the Cold War, Fundamentalists and many Evangelicals continued to express grave misgivings about international organizations like the United Nations. In short, while Evangelicals have been strong advocates of global concerns, and have been strongly committed to the idea of the world as a coherent moral community, they have nonetheless been skeptical of the role of international governmental organizations.

5. *Fostering Democratic Ideals and Practices*: Although missionaries were not directly involved in creating and reforming governmental institutions, they nonetheless played a pivotal role in fostering the preconditions under which democracy could thrive. From the outset, American missionaries placed great emphasis on the role of Scripture in propagating the faith and in developing self-sustaining churches. As a result, they emphasized mass education, literacy, and Bible translation so that converts could read and study the Bible on their own.

In a pioneering study on the role of missionaries and the spread of democracy, Robert Woodberry shows that missionaries (what he terms "conversionary Protestants") contributed significantly to the rise and spread of stable democracy around the world. He writes that missionaries "were a crucial catalyst initiating the development and spread of religious liberty, mass education, mass printing, newspapers, voluntary organizations, and colonial reforms, thereby creating the conditions that made stable democracy more likely."[55] To support his claim, Woodberry uses both historical and statistical evidence. His historical analysis shows that missionaries had a unique role in spreading mass education, literacy, printing, and civil society, while his statistical analyses show that the role of missionaries explains about half the variations in democracy in Africa, Asia, Latin America, and Oceania.

Although Woodberry studied all Protestant missionaries from Europe and America, his conclusions about the pivotal role of missionaries in propagating democratic values and practices applies in particular to the U.S. missionary enterprise. Whereas many European missionaries served under state-supported Protestant churches, the American missionary movement was a private religious movement from the outset. As a result, U.S. missionaries were not only able to carry out their spiritual tasks with fewer constraints than missionaries from established European denominations, but they were also freer to encourage social reforms, religious freedom, and civil society.[56] While missionaries were not in the business of political development, their religious beliefs motivated and inspired them to carry out educational, social, and humanitarian initiatives that helped to create preconditions for the subsequent emergence of democracy.

6. *Promoting Global Civil Society*: Finally, missionaries contributed to the development of the notion of global civil society. Building on the idea of international community, the missionary movement played a key role in fostering transnational ties and in building nongovernmental institutions to sustain such cross-cultural relationships. Based upon his analysis of the missionary movement in the Far East, Fairbank concludes that overseas missions were America's "first large-scale transnational corporations."[57] And for Mead, the idea of international civil society emerges from the missionary movement itself. He writes:

> Apart from a handful of isolated intellectuals, no one before the missionaries ever thought that the world's cultures and societies had or could have enough in common to make a common global society

feasible or desirable. Certainly before the missionaries no large group of people set out to build just such a world. The concept that "backward" countries could and should develop into Western-style industrial democracies grew up among missionaries, and missionary relief and development organizations like World Vision and Catholic Relief Services remain at the forefront of development efforts. The idea that governments in the Western world had a positive duty to support the development of poor countries through financial aid and other forms of assistance similarly comes out of the missionary world. Most contemporary international organizations that provide relief from natural disasters, shelter refugees, train medical practitioners for poor countries, or perform other important services on an international basis can trace their origin either to missionary organizations or to the missionary milieu.[58]

The missionary enterprise, through its international humanitarian and religious work, not only helped nurture a global consciousness but also advanced transnational relationships buttressed by international institutions, including missionary societies, Bible societies, humanitarian organizations, and church denominations. Building on their extensive global networks, missionaries have continued to structure and influence American global engagement, fostering cooperation among groups and nongovernmental organizations, promoting global civil society, and providing relief and development aid.

The Future of Missions

The challenges of proclaiming the gospel message in foreign lands have changed dramatically in recent decades. Throughout the nineteenth century and much of the twentieth, missionaries were full-time church emissaries. Traditionally, they were expected to carry out their religious work by becoming fully embedded in indigenous societies, which presupposed significant religious and linguistic training beforehand. In time, missionaries were expected to know the language, customs, and traditions of the host society and be able to effectively communicate their religious message to the indigenous community. Increasingly, however, traditional missionary service is being superseded by a more flexible, less formal approach. This new, postmodern paradigm is characterized by less institutionalization, broader participation, shorter terms of service, and more specialized forms of ministry. In most cases, the initiative and financial support for these projects come from the volunteers themselves, their own churches, or from gifts. The new model emphasizes shorter-term missions focused on strengthening the religious work of local churches and providing support services in such areas as medical assistance, construction, education, and professional training.

To be sure, organizations like the Southern Baptist Convention (SBC) have continued to follow the traditional model. As of mid-2011, the SBC supported close to 5,000 overseas missionaries with a budget of more than $300 million.[59] But most Protestant denominations have reduced the number of foreign missionaries, while faith-based organizations and small-scale associations have expanded their operations. The missionary enterprises that have expanded dramatically in recent years are loosely organized, placing most responsibility on volunteers to garner their own financial support and to determine the type and location of service. One example is Youth with a Mission (YWAM), an informal association begun in the 1960s. By 1985, it had over 1,700 full-time volunteers, and by 2010, the number exceeded 18,000. Unlike traditional missionary organizations, however, YWAM is a loose association; each group ministry is a relatively autonomous body. Indeed, YWAM, which views itself as a "family of ministries," does not have a central headquarters. Staff members must raise their own funds and serve for shorter terms than traditional missionaries. In 2010, YWAM did mission work in some 180 countries.

Perhaps the most visible manifestation of the new, postmodern approach is the proliferation of short-term mission (STM) trips sponsored by churches, denominations, and specialized religious agencies. These STM trips—which typically last two weeks or less—give young people and adults the opportunity to provide humanitarian, medical, educational, and related services while also fostering closer relationships with believers from other regions of America or foreign countries, who often represent different standards of living. The growing importance of STMs is evident in most Evangelical churches, which send groups overseas to provide a wide variety of humanitarian and religious services. For example, Saddleback Community Church—a large mega-church in Mission Viejo, California—has sent more than 1,000 of its members on STM teams to Rwanda. The Rwandan outreach was considered so important that Rick Warren, Saddleback's pastor, has made numerous trips to the country, while Paul Kagame, Rwanda's president, has visited Saddleback and spoken to the congregation. According to Robert Wuthnow, approximately 1.6 million adults participate every year in overseas STMs.[60] Most STM trips, however, involve high-school-age youth. Although many of these trips occur within the United States, a significant portion involve overseas travel. In the college where I teach, most incoming freshmen have participated in at least one STM trip, with some having made three or four. Although it is impossible to determine how many young people are involved in STM trips, some religious observers claim the number may be as high as 2 million annually.[61]

Earlier generations of missionaries strongly influenced U.S. foreign policy. Is the new model of missionary work contributing similarly to America's role in the world? Are the new types of missionary activity, including STM trips and specialized missions projects, reinforcing U.S. global engagement? Although it is premature to draw any firm conclusions about the impact of the newer form of missionary service, some preliminary judgments are possible.

To begin with, since the new style of missionary service is more transient, workers are much less concerned with learning foreign languages and developing knowledge of foreign cultures and societies. And because they serve for shorter terms and often fail to acquire significant cross-cultural knowledge, they do not develop expertise about foreign societies. Consequently, contemporary missions personnel, unlike their traditional counterparts, will be less able to share knowledge about foreign countries. Additionally, given the decentralized, informal nature of contemporary missions organizations, such religious activity is also unlikely to strengthen global civil society. Global civil society presupposes the institutionalization of nongovernmental activities across national boundaries. Thus, while the highly institutionalized Roman Catholic Church can foster the development of global civil society, the fragile institutions binding American Evangelicals are unlikely to do so. They simply do not have the organizational foundations to contribute to the development of transnational nongovernmental organizations. To be sure, American Evangelicals have periodically hosted international conferences to promote increased religious cooperation, but such gatherings—such as the Third Lausanne Conference, held in Cape Town in 2010—are unlikely to establish institutions that are the bedrock of civil society.

On the other hand, the postmodern U.S. missionary movement can contribute to American global engagement by continuing three positive influences begun in earlier decades—namely, promoting global interests, providing relief and development assistance to poor societies, and strengthening the notion of the world as a moral community. To a significant degree, the continuation of these influences is a consequence of increased globalization, which has contributed to the shift from traditional, long-term missionary service to the informal, shorter-term missions projects. As the cost of and barriers to international travel have declined, the number and scope of missionary projects have dramatically increased, further nurturing transnational interests and concerns. The American missionary enterprise continues to be an important antidote to the isolationist sentiment that emerges from time to time, especially when the United States confronts an intractable foreign problem or costly war. Similarly, the contemporary missionary movement highlights the need for Americans to provide humanitarian assistance. Missionaries continue to influence U.S. decision making, not by political action or lobbying, but by modeling humanitarian action. They have done so by proclaiming the infinite worth of every human being and, more concretely, by providing food, development aid, medical care, and education. As I will argue later, Evangelicals have been so successful in dispensing humanitarian aid and in nurturing preconditions to economic development in poor societies that the U.S. government has increasingly relied on religious groups to meet overseas humanitarian needs.

Finally, contemporary missions have also unwittingly helped to disseminate belief in the world as a moral community. As with traditional missionary enterprise, contemporary missions groups have not intentionally sought to propagate the idea that the world is a global society where territorial boundaries are of dubious moral significance. Rather, the notion of a coherent moral world is a by-product of the Christian belief that God created the world and loves all persons, regardless of their ethnicity, nationality, or social class. The notion of the inherent value and unity of the world is thus rooted in religion. Political idealists also celebrate the moral unity of the world. But whereas the Christian appeal for world unity is based on religious claims, political idealists call for increased centralization of authority in order to advance global peace and prosperity among nation-states.

American missionaries have not only proclaimed the good news of Christ's redemption but have also influenced American global engagement. Although the missionary enterprise has been primarily concerned with religion, missionaries have influenced the nature and scope of America's relations with the world both directly and indirectly. They have done so directly by meeting human needs, emphasizing education, and teaching and modeling values and practices that nurture human dignity. Additionally, missionaries have contributed indirectly to America's role in the world by advancing ideas and values that have helped build a more peaceful, stable, and democratic world. Missionaries have fostered the idea of the world as a coherent moral society and have affirmed the inherent worth and equality of all persons. To be sure, the temporal initiatives of missionary groups are not a formal part of U.S. foreign policy. Still, the contributions of the United States to foreign societies would have been impossible without the pioneering contribution of its missionaries.

4 THE POLITICAL ETHICS OF EVANGELICALS

Do Evangelicals possess core principles and doctrines that help them navigate the political world? To what sources can Evangelicals turn to structure their reasoning and guide their actions in public affairs? As I have noted, Evangelicalism is a religious tendency based on core beliefs but characterized by a broad range of religious, social, and political preferences. Because Evangelicalism is held together by slender religious bonds and fragile institutions, it has no formal political theology to guide thought and action. Unlike the Roman Catholic Church, which has a well-developed body of social and political teachings and a robust institutional structure that makes public policy pronouncements, Evangelicals must usually fend for themselves. As a result, Evangelical political analysis and action have historically been more limited and less compelling than that of Roman Catholics or even mainline Protestants.

To the extent that a political ethic exists, its dominant feature is the priority of inward spiritual development over political action, of personal morality over public policy. Moreover, Evangelicals tend to prioritize the moral responsibility of persons over the development and enactment of public policies. Not surprisingly, the rise of Evangelical influence in domestic politics in the 1970s was a direct response to the growth of public policies that Evangelicals considered inimical to fundamental Christian norms. Indeed, the rise of the Moral Majority in the late 1970s and the Christian Coalition in the 1980s was inspired by the conviction that government had become excessively intrusive and that public policies were undermining traditional values.

This chapter maps the landscape of Evangelical social and political ethics.

Some Building Blocks of Evangelical Political and Social Thought

As noted earlier, neo-Evangelicalism emerged when orthodox Protestant leaders concluded that Fundamentalists had gone too far in their disengagement from society. These new leaders believed that Fundamentalists were right to challenge liberalism's progressive humanism by stressing theological orthodoxy. Nevertheless, they regarded the movement's isolation from cultural and social life as inconsistent with the demands of the gospel. The first significant call for a broader social engagement by Evangelicals came in 1947 with the publication of Carl F. H. Henry's *The Uneasy Conscience of Modern Fundamentalism*. Henry argued that the Evangelical mind was "uneasy" because it had not fully worked out the implications of the gospel for social, cultural, and political life: "no voice is speaking as Paul would, either at the United Nations sessions, or at labor-management disputes, or in strategic university classrooms whether in Japan or Germany or America."[1] Rather than engaging culture, Fundamentalists had dissipated their energies on doctrinal disputes. Especially troubling to Henry was the failure of Fundamentalists to work out the implications of their divergent eschatological perspectives. Instead, they focused on internal religious concerns, thereby neglecting the spiritual and tangible needs of the present world. "Nothing is so essential," he observed, "as the relevance of the gospel to the entire world. Whatever in our kingdom views undercuts that relevance destroys the essential character of Christianity as such."[2]

The impact of Henry's *Uneasy Conscience* on the Evangelical mind can hardly be overstated. J. Budzieszewski claims that while Henry's argument has become the "epitome of the [E]vangelical social ethos," the project of devising a full-bodied social and political theology is yet to be completed.[3] But important developments and initiatives have been undertaken in the intervening years.

The Chicago Declaration

The Chicago Declaration is a short statement on the need for Evangelicals to be more concerned with social and economic justice. Signed by a small group of moderate and progressive Evangelicals in November 1973, the statement was a major public call for Evangelical civic engagement at a time of significant social unrest.[4]

Although the convening group included established Evangelical leaders like Carl F. H. Henry and Vernon Grounds, the statement was influenced significantly by the concerns and beliefs of young, progressive Evangelical thinkers and activists. Since these assertions did not reflect the conservative orientation of the majority of Evangelicals, the declaration had little immediate impact and went largely unnoticed. Billy Graham did not sign the statement, and the NAE failed to endorse it.

The declaration begins with the affirmation that "God lays total claim upon the lives of his people," and acknowledges that believers have failed to care for those suffering injustice. It calls on Evangelicals to repent of their sin and to fulfill the demands of the gospel by defending "the social and economic rights of the poor and oppressed." Although the declaration emphasizes domestic injustices, it also addresses global poverty and international economic inequalities. The declaration states: "Before God and a billion hungry neighbors, we must rethink our values regarding our present standard of living and promote a more just acquisition and distribution of the world's resources." The statement also calls attention to the excessive nationalism and reliance on economic and military might that contribute to "a national pathology of war and violence which victimizes our neighbors at home and abroad."

Given the small number of signers, the declaration had little discernible impact on Evangelical social and political ethics at the times. The statement, however, is noteworthy because it highlights the growing Evangelical concern with public affairs.

The Lausanne Covenant

A document endorsed at a world congress on evangelization in Lausanne, Switzerland, in 1974, this is a declaration that illuminates the core beliefs and commitments of Evangelicalism. The covenant, like the Chicago Declaration, is important because it describes how Evangelicals approached the relationship between church and state, evangelism, and socioeconomic justice at that time. Although drafted by a group of Western Evangelical leaders, it was an international declaration adopted by some 2,300 church leaders from 150 countries.

Most of the Lausanne Covenant is concerned with spiritual issues and highlights the church's task of evangelism. At the same time, the covenant calls on believers to carry out the redemptive work of Christ in social and economic affairs, including the need for religious freedom in all societies. The covenant expresses "penitence" for neglecting human welfare and for regarding evangelism and social concern as mutually exclusive, calling on believers to engage in both. The covenant explains the interrelationship of the spiritual and the temporal as follows: "When people receive Christ they are born again into his kingdom and must seek not only to exhibit but also to spread its righteousness in the midst of an unrighteous world. The salvation we claim should be transforming us in the totality of our personal and social responsibilities. Faith without works is dead." Finally, the covenant reminds believers that since persons are made in the image of God, every individual has "an intrinsic dignity." Christians have a duty to protect and defend the fundamental worth of all persons.

One of the forward-looking dimensions of the covenant is its emphasis on the priority of religious freedom. Paragraph 13 calls on government leaders "to guarantee freedom of thought and conscience, and the freedom to practice and propagate religion in accordance with the will of God and as set forth in the Universal Declaration of Human Rights." This topic eventually captured the Evangelical imagination in the late 1990s, resulting in the U.S. Congress adopting the International Religious Freedom Act of 1998. Yet at the time, Evangelicals rarely addressed the topic of religious freedom except to repeatedly condemn the atheistic nature of Soviet communism and the persecution of believers under such a regime. The covenant's call for international religious freedom was ahead of its time.

The Peace, Freedom and Security Studies Program

In 1986, the National Association of Evangelicals, with the assistance of external advisers, established an educational initiative—known as the Peace, Freedom and Security Studies (PFSS) Program—that sought to develop a more informed approach to national security affairs. The initiative sought to broaden the public policy debate from military affairs alone to the challenge of advancing the multiple goals of national security, international human rights, and global peace.[5] At the time that the PFSS Program was launched, religious elites in America were deeply involved in the national debate over how to promote peace and, more specifically, how to reduce the threat of nuclear conflict with the Soviet Union. Mainline Protestant churches issued numerous declarations and framework statements on how to think about nuclear arms and the global order, while the U.S. Conference of Catholic Bishops issued an influential pastoral letter in 1983 titled "The Challenge of Peace."[6] Unlike Roman Catholics and mainline Protestants, Evangelicals remained largely silent on nuclear arms control. The creation of the PFSS Program was an effort to provide a framework to facilitate moral analysis of peace, freedom, and security concerns.

The aim of the PFSS initiative was educational: to offer a set of guidelines that could contribute to the moral analysis of foreign policy goals, humanitarian concerns, and global order.[7] In the words of Billy Melvin, the NAE's executive director, the aim of the program was to "improve the skills of Evangelical leadership in supporting religious liberty, promoting the security of free societies and encouraging progress toward the nonviolent resolution of international conflict."[8] Contrary to the one-dimensional peacekeeping initiatives of mainline Protestant churches, which focused almost exclusively on arms control, the NAE program sought to confront two threats simultaneously: "the twin threats of nuclear destruction and totalitarianism."[9]

The NAE's program was generally seen as informed and credible. The New York City–based Carnegie Council on Ethics and International Affairs sponsored a one-day symposium on the PFSS Program that drew leading representatives from the U.S. government, universities, foreign policy think tanks, advocacy groups, and religious nongovernmental organizations. While some Christian thinkers critiqued the framework for failing to emphasize justice, leading international relations scholar Joseph Nye, Jr., called the guidelines "impressive."[10] And unlike other church documents on peacekeeping and arms control issued at that time, the PFSS did not seek to provide public policy recommendations on such issues as nuclear strategy, military tactics, or the promotion of human rights. Rather, it sought to illuminate the interconnected nature of human rights, global order, and national security.

For the Health of the Nation

Perhaps the most significant and comprehensive Evangelical initiative on political and social ethics was the development of a framework document titled "For the Health of the Nation: An Evangelical Call to Civic Responsibility" (FHN).[11] Commissioned in 2001 by the NAE and prepared by a group of Evangelical scholars, FHN was formally adopted by the NAE in 2004 and signed by more than ninety Evangelical leaders. The document was inspired by the realization that, owing to their increasing numbers, American Evangelicals have a "historic opportunity" to influence public affairs. The FHN declares: "We make up fully one quarter of all voters in the most powerful nation in history. Never before has God given American [E]vangelicals such an awesome opportunity to shape public policy in ways that could contribute to the well-being of the entire world."[12]

A major aim of the FHN was to increase awareness of and concern over domestic and international affairs. But the goal was not simply to increase Evangelical political engagement; it was also to develop a more informed and sophisticated understanding of the complex issues facing America, domestically and abroad. Accordingly, the document sets forth two elements to guide believers' thought and action in social and political affairs: (1) the basis, method, and goals of political engagement; and (2) biblical principles that can contribute to a Christ-centered politics.

In the first section, the FHN reminds readers that, notwithstanding the growing awareness that political and social action are a central part of the church's redemptive ministry, American Evangelicals continue to be "ambivalent about civic engagement." At the same time, the FHN declares that political engagement is necessary because redemption, as theologian Richard Mouw rightly observes, involves all of creation, including the political domain.[13] The NAE statement captures this truth by declaring, "just governance is part of our calling in creation."[14] The FHN also importantly emphasizes the role of both individuals and institutions in pursuing Christian civic action. While assuming spiritual transformation to be an essential precondition for Christian political engagement, the document asserts that saving souls alone is not sufficient to ensure justice. Thus, the FHN declares that "[l]asting social change requires both personal conversion and institutional renewal and reform."[15] Finally, the FHN reminds readers that Christians' primary allegiance is to Christ and his kingdom, not to temporal authorities. This means that believers must give priority to the global church rather than to any political community. It also means, as the FHN asserts, that believers must balance their affection for their own country with an active love for foreign peoples.

In its second section, the FHN sets forth seven core principles that should guide political action. They are: religious freedom, the priority of family life and the protection of children, the sanctity of life, compassion for the poor, protection of human rights, the pursuit of peaceful conflict resolution and the restraint of violence, and environmental protection.[16] While each of these norms is potentially relevant to the pursuit of peace and justice in the international community, some—such as religious freedom, compassion for the poor, pursuit of peaceful conflict resolution, and environmental protection— are especially applicable to global politics and foreign policy. But because of its brevity, the FHN offers little analysis of how such norms should influence international relations.

The FHN is an important document, representing the first significant effort by American Evangelicals to develop a comprehensive framework for engaging in social and political life. Throughout the Cold War years, the NAE issued many public policy pronouncements on a wide variety of domestic and international political concerns. But because there was no accepted body of Evangelical political ethics on which the NAE could base its actions, the policy declarations reflected preferences rather than a deeply rooted Christian vision of public life. The 2004 document does not provide a framework in political ethics to address specific global challenges such as climate change, genocide, humanitarian intervention, or nuclear proliferation. But the FHN does offer an important resource for structuring social and political thought from a biblical perspective.

The Cape Town Commitment

The Third Lausanne Congress on World Evangelization was held in Cape Town, South Africa, in October 2010. The congress's core document—called "The Cape Town Commitment" (CTC)—was structured around the theme of love. The statement begins by declaring that the task of the church derives from the primacy of God's love. The CTC declares: "The mission of God's people flows from our love for God and for all that God loves. World evangelization is the outflow of God's love to us and through us." Whereas religious belief can be easily expressed through mental assent, an authentic religion demands the passionate expression of values. For the Christian, a faithful commitment to Christ requires adherence to properly ordered loves—for God, for neighbor, and for the world for which Christ died. Biblical scholar Christopher Wright, who led the drafting of the CTC, observed that the greatest challenge to God's mission in the world was not persecution or other religions but the disobedience of God's people.[17] Accordingly, the leaders of the congress challenged delegates to acknowledge that they had not been fully obedient in loving what God loves. The renewal of the church first required repentance.

The conference captured important ongoing international developments in global Evangelicalism. Two of the most significant of these are the rapid growth of Christianity in the global South and the increased acknowledgment that authentic faith demands both belief and behavior, or faithfulness both in spiritual life and in temporal life. Accordingly, a major goal of the congress was to ensure that the diversity of the global Evangelicalism was represented.[18]

In his pathbreaking book *The Next Christendom*, historian Philip Jenkins argues that the significant rise in believers in the global South is transforming the demography of Christianity.[19] The rising influence of church leaders from the global South was dramatically evident at the 1998 Lambeth Conference of the global Anglican Communion, where church leaders from the global South successfully blocked the effort of liberal bishops from the global North to allow ordination of practicing homosexuals. After intense and bitter debate, a majority of the bishops adopted a policy, over objections from liberal church leaders from Europe and North America, declaring that homosexual behavior was inconsistent with Christian ministry.

More recently, a 2010 survey of global Evangelicals by the Pew Research Center documents this shift in influence from the global North to the global South. According to the survey, which was based on the views of participants at the Cape Town Congress, 44 percent of global Evangelical leaders believe that the United States and Europe have too much influence on global Christianity, while 68 percent of the respondents believe that Evangelical leaders in Africa, Asia, and Latin America have too little influence. The survey also found that Evangelical leaders were more optimistic about Christianity in the global South than in the global North. According to the survey, 58 percent of global South leaders thought their own influence was increasing in their countries, while only 31 percent of global North leaders thought so. Indeed, 66 percent of Evangelical leaders in the global North thought their own influence in society was declining.[20]

The second noteworthy development was the acknowledgment of the centrality of social and economic witness to the church's mission of sharing the gospel. As one congress observer noted, "[E]vangelicalism's past debates over evangelism taking priority over service seemed finished. Speaker after speaker emphasized how integrally the two are related in witness."[21] Not surprisingly, the 2010 Pew Survey confirms widespread support for a Christian faith that integrates both religious belief and social practice. According to the survey, while virtually all respondents indicated that following the teaching of Christ in one's own life (97 percent) and working to lead others to Christ (94 percent) were essential to Evangelical Christianity, nearly three-fourths (73 percent) of the respondents said that helping the poor and the needy was also important to authentic Christianity.

After the congress concluded, conference leaders developed a second part of the CTC based on the discussions and deliberations at Cape Town. The second section, titled "Call to Action," sets forth concrete goals based on the ideas developed in the first part of the report. The call to action focuses on such themes as evangelism in a pluralistic world, the promotion of peace, and the development of a more faithful witness of the Christian faith—one characterized by humility, integrity, and simplicity. Some of the noteworthy recommendations include:

- Opposing the false dichotomy between the sacred and secular realms
- Viewing the workplace as a legitimate realm of ministry
- Supporting public policy initiatives that help care for the poor (e.g., the UN Millennium Development Goals)
- Demanding that governments respect religious freedom of all people
- Opposing slavery and human trafficking
- Affirming ethnic identity, provided it is subordinated to "our redeemed identity as the new humanity in Christ through the cross"
- Rejecting consumerism and materialism, which impair faithful discipleship[22]

Although this overview of declarations and initiatives illuminates some of the changing religious orientations and values among Evangelicals, it also highlights a number of core values that have remained constant: God's gift of salvation through Christ's atonement, the need to personally accept salvation, the authority of Scripture as a guide to faith, and the priority of evangelism.

Our brief overview of Evangelical declarations suggests a number of preliminary generalizations about Evangelical political theology. First, notwithstanding the increasing awareness that the gospel has implications for both spiritual and temporal life, Evangelicals continue to give priority to evangelism. Second, Evangelicals increasingly acknowledge that social and political affairs are a legitimate concern for the church. Third, even though the Bible is not viewed as a direct guide to political action, Evangelicals nevertheless believe that Scripture provides the framework for structuring political reflection and action. Fourth, Evangelicals emphasize the role of individual belief and action over the logic of collective action. Finally, Evangelicals are globalists, viewing the world as a coherent human society that calls for international responsibilities and transnational perspectives.

Distinctive Features of Evangelical Political Ethics

One reason why Evangelicals may not have been as politically influential in the past as other religious groups is their limited concern with public affairs. According to the pietist tradition, the Christian faith is chiefly about personal salvation, not the moral transformation of the world. According to Richard

Mouw, president of Fuller Theological Seminary, "the problem with a lot of Evangelicalism...is that it often focuses exclusively on personal religion."[23] To be sure, the Evangelical priority on the atoning work of Christ is central to New Testament faith. But the truth that Jesus is a savior needs to be supplemented with the truth that Jesus is king, he writes. Mouw quotes Abraham Kuyper, the Dutch theologian and politician (prime minister), who insisted "there is not a square inch in the whole domain of our human existence over which Christ, who is sovereign over all, does not cry 'Mine!' "[24] Evangelicals do differentiate between their responsibilities as citizens of a temporal kingdom and their responsibilities to the kingdom of God. This does not mean, however, that they believe the worlds of faith and politics should be kept totally separate. Authentic faith should, as Kuyper implied, inform all aspects of life.

Another reason why some scholars think that Evangelicals have not been very effective in public affairs is that they have failed to develop a political theology. Os Guiness, for example, notes that there has been no serious Evangelical public philosophy in the twentieth century,[25] while historian Mark Noll writes that diverse theological approaches among Evangelicals "leave [E]vangelical political thought scattered all over the map."[26]

Why have Evangelicals failed to develop a coherent political doctrine? One reason is the belief that Scripture is an adequate guide not only for religion but also for public life. Political theorist Jay Budzieszewski writes: "Although all traditional Christians believe in the truth and authority of Scripture, [E]vangelicals surpass all others in their determination to study and follow it. Their first thought on almost every subject is, 'What does the Bible say?' "[27] However, the challenge for Evangelical political thinkers, he notes, is not that the Bible fails to address government and politics but, rather, that "the Bible does not provide enough by itself for an adequate political theory."[28] Thus, when Christians seek to ground political action solely on the Bible, they inevitably pursue what Budzieszewski terms "inflationary policies"—that is, drawing conclusions from Scripture that are unwarranted.[29] While the Bible will remain the foundation of Christian political ethics, Scripture alone is insufficient to develop a comprehensive Christian approach to domestic and international political ethics.

Budzieszewski argues that the missing link to the development of Evangelical political ethics is God's revelation in the natural order of creation—what is usually called "general revelation." Whereas "special" revelation communicates God's guidance through Scripture, "general" revelation communicates God's will in the moral order of the world itself. Such revelation, which is evident to all humankind, is manifest in the created moral order and is expressed through the idea of natural law and more particularly through such notions as the right to life and the right to freedom. For Budzieszewski, therefore, the task of building a more comprehensive and developed Evangelical political worldview will necessarily require the integration of both Scripture and natural law.[30]

Ethicist Ronald Sider similarly attributes the limited impact of Evangelical political action to the weak and undeveloped nature of Evangelical political ethics. In his book *The Scandal of Evangelical Politics*, he argues that Evangelical political action in domestic and international affairs has been a "disaster." This failure, he observes, is evident in the pursuit of contradictory policies, the use of dishonest tactics, and the resort to foolish strategies in promoting legitimate goals. "At the heart of the problem," Sider writes, "is the fact that many Christians, especially [E]vangelical Christians, have not thought very carefully about how to do politics in a wise, biblically grounded way."[31] According to Sider, if political engagement is to be more effective, then Evangelicals must develop a more "biblically grounded, systematic approach to the complicated task of politics."

Although Evangelicals have not developed a comprehensive political theology, they nevertheless have established an approach to social and public life that guides their political analysis and action. It is important to stress that this underdeveloped framework is based on the writings, theological ideas, and perspectives of Evangelical thinkers, not on the prevailing beliefs of parishioners themselves. Given the pluralistic nature of the Evangelical movement, opinion polls of Evangelicals' political ethics would undoubtedly uncover different levels of commitment to the core principles described below. Still, we can discern an Evangelical approach to public affairs, characterized by five principles.

1. *The Primacy of the Spiritual Realm*: The primacy of spiritual development is a direct consequence of Evangelicals' belief that salvation—that is, redemption from sin—is the basis of the moral life. Accordingly, Evangelicals tend to assume that the development of stable, humane societies is possible only where individuals are rightly related—first to God and then to each other. Spiritual regeneration is thus a precondition for sound politics. Although human rights and individual responsibility are important elements of Evangelical personal agency, Evangelicals give priority to the inward spiritual condition of persons over the outward manifestations of behavior. Carl F. H. Henry captures the centrality of the gospel to social change: "The [E]vangelical task primarily is the preaching

of the Gospel, in the interest of individual regeneration by the grace of God, in such a way that divine redemption can be recognized as the best solution of our problems, individual and social."[32]

Whereas secular politics focuses on the temporal necessities of life, a Christian perspective regards spiritual renewal as the foundation for a good society. According to political scientist Timothy Shah, this represents a repudiation of the Western tendency to give primacy to the state in the moral formation of persons. According to classic Western thought, an important task of the state is to improve the human condition by assisting persons in acquiring virtues conducive to the good life. Thus, rather than advancing "statecraft as soulcraft," to use George Will's felicitous formula, Evangelicals have propounded the opposite doctrine—namely, "soulcraft as statecraft."[33] According to this perspective, moral human beings make justice possible. And what nurtures personal morality is individual conversion—the personal, inward acceptance of Christ's atonement for sin. Although state structures and sound public policies are important in fostering a just society, Evangelicals believe that spiritual redemption is the foundation for a humane and just politics. Indeed, the moral transformation of persons is the precondition for authentic political development and social reform.

Because spiritual transformation can result in dramatic changes in the beliefs, attitudes, and behaviors of individuals, we should not underestimate the importance of personal conversion. Indeed, while personal moral transformation can lead to important changes in individual life, it can also result in society-wide reforms that contribute to the development of more prosperous and humane political communities. Such improvements in social and economic life are possible because faith can nurture such virtues as integrity, truth-telling, diligence, and honesty—habits and values that are essential to a humane, just society. In her study of development in Guatemala, Amy Sherman corroborates this claim. She shows that individual conversion, by fostering desirable personal habits and values, can contribute to greater economic enterprise and social stability.[34] In a related study of Latin American Pentecostals, Douglas Peterson shows that while Pentecostals have rarely developed a sophisticated social ethic, they nonetheless have implemented effective humanitarian practices.[35] Thus, even though Evangelicals have not developed political and social doctrines to guide action, they nevertheless have contributed, indirectly if not directly, to more humane and economically prosperous political communities.

One of the dangers of this norm is that it has been used to over-spiritualize issues and thereby offer simplistic religious slogans as solutions to complex political and social problems. For example, some Evangelical preachers have proclaimed that international peace is best advanced through the spiritual salvation of individuals. However, the primacy of the spiritual realm does not mean that temporal issues should be ignored. To the extent that Evangelicals approach problems with simple biblical slogans, they will contribute little to the development of policies that are consistent with Evangelical political theology. Indeed, the effort to over-spiritualize issues will lead to the perpetuation of the Gnostic heresy that confronted the early Church—a heresy that viewed Christ as spirit rather than a person, and that regarded the material world as evil (or illusory). The challenge for Evangelical churches, therefore, is to confront temporal concerns directly while giving precedence to the proclamation and teaching of the gospel.

2. *The Dual Nature of Christian Citizenship*: Evangelical political ethics is characterized by dual citizenship. Christians are members of two societies: the physical location in which they reside, and the heavenly kingdom comprising a worldwide community of believers, Christ's Church. The classic statement on dual citizenship was set forth by Saint Augustine in the fifth century, in his masterpiece *The City of God*. According to Augustine, two worldviews or ways of life have resulted in the establishment of two distinct societies or "cities." The earthly realm, or "City of Man," is guided by love of self and relies on power and authority to maintain order; the spiritual realm, or "City of God," is guided by love of God. In the earthly city, governmental power is used to restrain sin and human greed. By contrast, in the heavenly city, comprising the voluntary community of Christian believers, there is no need for coercive authority since justice and peace are natural by-products of divinely inspired love.

All persons are subject to the influence of human and divine imperatives. The conflict between good and evil does not exist only between the two cities but also within every person. And since all human beings are subject to sin, the best that can be realized in this world is an imperfect, tentative peace through the coercive power of government. For Augustine, therefore, the purpose of the state is chiefly negative: to limit wrongdoing and maintain order.

Christians are called to fulfill their temporal responsibilities to the state and their spiritual responsibilities to the kingdom of God. When government rulers issue commands that are contrary to Scripture, believers must follow their moral conscience and disregard temporal commands. From a biblical perspective, governmental power must always be subservient to God's authority. Although the Bible encourages obedience to legitimate government authority, the Scripture is also clear that believers should disobey rulers when their demands contradict divine commands. When Peter and other apostles are brought before the Jewish Council (Sanhedrin) for teaching allegedly false doctrines, they declare that their first responsibility is to God, not the state. Peter boldly declares: "we ought to obey God rather than men" (Acts 5:29). Jesus himself says that his disciples should first pursue the "kingdom of God" and then fulfill other desires and obligations (Matt. 6:33).

Ever since the Pharisees asked Jesus whether it was lawful to pay taxes to Caesar, Christians have struggled to define the appropriate boundaries between the altar and the throne, between faith and politics. Jesus's answer—that we should "render to Caesar the things that are Caesar's and to God the things that are God's" (Matt. 22:21)—did not provide a conclusive answer. As a result, Christians continue to struggle to define the boundaries between church and state.

Living in the "City of Man" while fulfilling the spiritual admonitions and moral obligations of the "City of God" presents a never-ending challenge. One way of resolving the tension between temporal commitments to the state and the responsibilities toward spiritual authority is to pursue a strategy of detachment and withdrawal, with monasticism serving as the ultimate expression of such an option. Historically, Fundamentalists and some Evangelicals have been tempted by pietistic disengagement from temporal concerns. But Jesus commands his followers to be in the world but not of it (John 17:15,16). Believers are to work and serve Christ in the temporal city while maintaining their ultimate allegiance to God.

3. *The Imperative of Human Dignity*: A third key feature of Evangelical political ethics is the supreme importance of persons. Because human beings are created in God's image (*imago dei*), they are entitled to dignity and respect. Although human beings may differ in their social, economic, political, and intellectual capabilities, as bearers of God's image they are fundamentally equal. From a Christian perspective, the dignity and glory of persons are based not on the rational or moral nature of humans but on God's unlimited and all-embracing love (*agape*). And because God's love is unconditional and all-inclusive, human dignity is universal, extending to every person regardless of age, race, gender, or nationality. The Apostle Paul expresses this powerfully: "there is neither Jew nor Greek, there is

neither slave nor free, there is neither male nor female; for you are all one in Christ Jesus" (Gal. 3:28).

Glen Tinder argues that the most fundamental premise of Western social and political theory is the notion of human dignity, which he defines as "the idea of the exalted individual."[36] According to Tinder, this idea is not only "the spiritual center of Western politics" but also provides the foundation for Christian political reflection and action. Catholic social thought similarly emphasizes the priority of persons. According to a group of leading American Catholic thinkers, the most basic principle of Catholic social teaching is "the inalienable dignity of every single human person."[37] This dignity, they stress, is not given by the state but is inherent in all persons.

The idea of exalted individuals is important because it provides the basis for claims of human rationality, sociability, creativity, and moral autonomy. More particularly, the notion of the uniqueness of persons is the foundation for the claim of inalienable human rights, which includes the necessity of human freedom. Freedom is essential to authentic personhood because moral agency—that is, the assumption of responsible action—is only possible when people are responsible for their own thoughts and actions. Indeed, without freedom there can be no responsible action—no authentic expressions of love, no pursuit of the common good, no creative labor, and no justice.

4. *The Priority of Individual Responsibility*: A fourth feature of Evangelical political ethics is the important role of the individual. Since sin is personal, Evangelicals believe that redemption from sin is possible only by personally accepting Christ as Savior and Lord. Unlike the Roman Catholic faith, which emphasizes the role of the church in mediating salvation, Protestants regard salvation as God's gift to each person, available solely by individual acceptance of this divine gift through faith, not through any human initiative. Consequently, Evangelicals view spiritual development as a largely individual enterprise, where each person acquires the habits and disciplines that nurture a deeper reliance on God and a more faithful fulfillment of his Word. In *The Cost of Discipleship*, theologian Dietrich Bonhoeffer reflects on the radical individualism of the Protestant faith:

> Through the call of Jesus men become individuals. Willy-nilly, they are compelled to decide, and that decision can only be made by themselves. It is no choice of their own that makes them individuals: it is Christ who makes them individuals by calling them. Every man is called separately, and must follow alone.[38]

Given Evangelicalism's emphasis on personal spirituality, it is not surprising that this movement also places a high priority on personal morality and individual virtues in building just, humane political communities. This does not mean that social and political institutions are not important but, rather, that the development of just policies and institutions is possible only through the moral actions of persons. It is important to stress that the emphasis on individual agency is not to be associated with the radical notion of individualism rooted in political liberalism. To the extent that modern liberalism fosters a view of persons as solitary, atomistic individuals, this view is inconsistent with a Christian worldview. A Christian perspective on human nature begins by acknowledging that persons are made in the image of God and have infinite worth—not because they are autonomous but because they are God's children. For the Christian, the highest good is realized when persons individually acknowledge their sin and need of Christ, and they commence a process of spiritual reformation that in time makes possible a new type of politics.

Evangelical ethics thus places a premium on individual responsibility. And since responsibility is maximized when individuals are fully accountable, Evangelicals tend to prefer decentralized organization and to be skeptical of centralized, top-down government initiatives. In effect, Evangelicals strongly identify with the Catholic idea of subsidiarity, one of the core elements of Catholic social teaching. According to this norm, decision-making responsibility should be entrusted at the lowest possible level within an organization or political community in order to allow initiative, freedom of action, and maximum responsibility. Evangelicals support decentralization not because it is more effective or efficient but, rather, because it is consistent with their view of the human person—an individual morally accountable to God, to other persons, and to self.

The importance of the dual dimensions of spiritual transformation and individual responsibility has been repeatedly demonstrated. For example, spiritual reformation provided much of the impetus to the anti-slave-trade campaign of William Wilberforce, a member of the British Parliament. His deep faith in Christ led him to battle major British institutions, including the Church of England, to bring an end to the slave trade in the early nineteenth century. Similarly, after accepting Christ as personal savior, and upon his release from prison for his involvement in the Watergate scandal, former White House official Charles Colson established Prison Fellowship, a global organization that has contributed more to the reformation of the penal systems in the United States and many foreign countries than any other organization in modern times.[39]

5. *The Need for a Limited State*: A final feature of Evangelical political ethics is the desire for a limited state. The need to limit political authority is derived from two fundamental biblical principles. First, since human beings are created in the image of God, they are entitled to dignity and respect. Second, since God is sovereign, temporal authority is ultimately answerable to a higher authority.

The first truth means that governments may not trample on human rights. In particular, they may not make unlimited claims on their subjects nor circumscribe the people's freedom of conscience. The state's fundamental task is to serve the common good by using public authority to nurture and protect the fundamental rights of citizens.

The second truth—that God is sovereign—means that the state cannot make unlimited claims. Since temporal power is subject to divine judgment, the boundaries of state authority are circumscribed by a higher law. This does not mean that the state should not exert final authority in temporal affairs; rather, it means that the sphere of government must be constrained. The idea of a strong but limited state is consistent not only with biblical faith but also with modern democratic practices that emphasize the role of an energetic civil society. Civil society—comprising such mediating institutions as churches, professional associations, unions, advocacy networks, and other nongovernmental organizations—is important because it nurtures cooperation and trust (social capital) and thereby fosters communal solidarity. Indeed, the efficacy of the state is as dependent on its own institutions as it is on the values, habits, and nongovernmental institutions that provide the foundation for a vigorous society.

Evangelicals also believe that the power of the state must be constrained because of human sinfulness. Indeed, the constitutional tradition began to emerge in the sixteenth and seventeenth centuries in response to European monarchs' abuses of power. It was later refined in the social contract theories of John Locke and Jean Jacques Rousseau, and developed into a political doctrine with the eighteenth-century writings of thinkers like David Hume, Jeremy Bentham, and James Mill. Lord Acton, the nineteenth-century British politician, captured the moral danger of political power with his famous aphorism: "Power tends to corrupt and absolute power corrupts absolutely." The historical record shows that governmental tyranny and oppression have resulted in great human suffering. Such injustice has been perpetrated by deliberate government policies, such as genocide and ethnic cleansing, and as the result of misguided policies, such as forced industrialization or ethnic and religious discrimination.[40] Indeed, more people died in the twentieth century from governments' abuse of power against their own citizens than in interstate wars.[41] James Madison, the father of the American Constitution, captured the central moral challenge in devising an effective yet limited government in *The Federalist*. In his essay Number 51, he wrote: "In framing a government which is to be administered by men over men, the great difficulty is this: you must first enable the government to control the governed; and in the next place oblige it to control itself."[42]

One way of delimiting the state is to view it as one of several institutions directly accountable to divine authority. In his famous Stone Lectures, Abraham Kuyper argued that although God was sovereign over all the earth, his authority in the temporal realm was expressed through differentiated institutions, including the family, church, economic life, politics, and work. According to Kuyper, God entrusts direct responsibility for human welfare in each distinct sphere. Thus, the state is responsible for governmental life, while the church and family are responsible for religious and familial life.[43] By asserting its responsibility in the religious sphere, the church can help prevent the state from encroaching on its domain of service. By the same token, a state that nurtures human freedom and protects religious freedom in particular will benefit from stronger religious communities that can, in turn, foster the renewal of public morality.

In his important statement "Christianity and Democracy," the late Richard John Neuhaus observes, "the first and final assertion Christians make about all of reality, including politics, is 'Jesus Christ is Lord.'" He goes on to note that because the church's major task is to proclaim this message, it must maintain a critical distance from all actual or proposed temporal initiatives. "Christians betray their Lord," he writes, "if, in theory or practice, they equate the Kingdom of God with any political, social or economic order of this passing time."[44]

If the church is to fulfill its obligation in proclaiming the lordship of Christ, it must protect its independence from the state. This means that it must be careful not to engage in partisan politics. As Alexis de Tocqueville noted long ago, "the church cannot share the temporal power of the state without being the object of a portion of that animosity which the latter excites."[45] The church must therefore not become identified with a political leader, party, or nation, since a close political affiliation will call into question the church's autonomy and impair its ability to bring judgment to bear in public life. Most important, if the church ceases to focus on its fundamental spiritual tasks, it will lose its capacity to identify and apply biblical and moral principles to temporal affairs.

Although other elements could undoubtedly be included in this overview of Evangelical political ethics, the five principles examined above represent important features of contemporary Evangelical political theology. [46] How these norms are applied in particular circumstances will, of course, vary greatly and depend significantly on how issues and problems are defined. Still, these shared Evangelical norms can help to illuminate and guide political reflection in the task of engaging important issues in global affairs.

Whither Evangelical Political Ethics?

Historically, Evangelicalism has been a conservative religious tradition. Theologically, it has been conservative because it has emphasized revelation over reason, the authority of Scripture over church teachings. And it has been a conservative political tradition because of the emphasis placed on core moral values, individual responsibility, a limited state, and skepticism about the role of government. Consequently, it is not surprising that when Evangelicals increased their level of public engagement in the 1970s and 1980s, they did so in support of conservative political causes. Beginning in the 1980s with the rise of the Moral Majority, spearheaded by Reverend Jerry Falwell, followed by the establishment of the Christian Coalition, led by Pat Robertson, Evangelicals developed strong ties to the Republican Party. This close association was especially evident in Evangelicals' staunch electoral support during the presidential campaigns of Ronald Reagan in 1980 and 1984 and of George W. Bush in 2000 and 2004.

The reason for this close affinity between party and religion was not solely ideological. It was grounded in shared social values and moral principles. Some of the salient issues that led to strong bonds between Evangelicals and many Republican Party politicians included support for prayer in public schools, opposition to abortion, and opposition to same-sex marriage. For some Christians, however, the close association of Evangelicals with the Republican Party was deeply problematic. They believed that it could potentially compromise the prophetic, transcendent role of the church. As a result, in recent years some Evangelical leaders have tried to broaden the church's social agenda. This was undoubtedly the reason why a group of leading Evangelicals issued "An Evangelical Manifesto" in 2008, declaring that "the Evangelical soul is not for sale." Since the Christian faith demands "an allegiance higher than party, ideology, economic system or nationality," the manifesto calls on believers to rethink their approach to public life, challenging them to demonstrate a stronger commitment to spiritual values than to temporal concerns. The manifesto then states: "we Evangelicals see it our duty to engage with politics, but our equal duty never to be completely equated with any party, partisan ideology, economic system, or nationality."[47]

Since Evangelicals give precedence to personal responsibility in both spiritual and temporal life, Evangelicals will continue to emphasize the role of individual beliefs and actions and remain skeptical of government-centered approaches to political and social life. To be sure, many problems can only be addressed on a society-wide basis. But to the extent that concerns like poverty, religious persecution, human rights abuses, and climate change dominate domestic and international policy debates, Evangelicals are likely to favor personal, small-scale initiatives to address them. Thus, even if Evangelicals were to become convinced that the reduction in carbon emissions was necessary to protect the environment, it is unlikely that they would enthusiastically support a large-scale, transnational climate change initiative. Instead, Evangelicals would be far more likely to support personal initiatives that foster energy conservation at home and at work. Similarly, to the extent that world hunger and poverty remain major public concerns, Evangelicals are likely to favor decentralized initiatives, such as microfinance and microenterprise, and to resist large-scale government-to-government loans and grants.

For Michael Gerson and Peter Wehner, two former senior White House officials in the George W. Bush administration, the major shortcoming of the Religious Right was theological: many of its followers identified the nature and destiny of America with the nature and destiny of biblical Israel. While recognizing that the view of the New World as the "new Israel" has a long history, Gerson and Wehner wisely observe that such a tradition is not theologically or historically compelling.[48] Indeed, they claim that America was not founded as a Christian nation but rather as a country where all faiths are welcome. Gerson and Wehner write that the disestablishment of religion has served the Christian religion well since it has helped to prevent it from "being corrupted and tainted by political power." Charles Marsh, a religion professor, is even more critical of the political actions of the Religious Right. He argues in *Wayward Christian Soldiers* that Evangelicals' politicized faith has distorted the gospel. He writes:

> American [E]vangelicals have resolved to serve a political agenda with the passion we once gave to personal soul-winning, Bible study, the disciplines of Christian holiness, and worship. We have done so at the cost of cheapening our mission to proclaim the love of God for all nations, which is the obligation of every church in every nation; we have done

so by compromising our commitment to the crucified and resurrected Christ, and the cost of retreating from the shattering truth of the first commandment: "Thou shalt have no other gods before me."[49]

For politically progressive Evangelicals like Ronald Sider, a theology professor at Eastern Seminary and founder of Evangelicals for Social Action, and Jim Wallis, the editor of *Sojourners*, the problem with the Religious Right was not its political advocacy but, rather, its support for unjust public policies. Rather than promoting greater domestic and international justice, the Religious Right encouraged war, fostered economic inequality, and failed to care for the poor. During the 2004 election, Wallis and his supporters took out advertisements that trumpeted that "God is not a Republican," and in smaller print pointed out that "God is not a Democrat." In the 2008 presidential campaign, Wallis was an adviser to the campaign of Barack Obama.

Evangelical political engagement has resulted in growing concerns over the politicization of religion. One group of believers has simply called for retrenchment from politics. In their book *Blinded by Might*, Reverend Ed Dodson, a pastor and former adviser for the Moral Majority, and Cal Thomas, a syndicated columnist and former communications director for the Moral Majority, set forth the case that excessive political engagement not only failed to contribute to a more moral and just America but also distorted the priorities of believers. By indulging in political combat, Christians neglected the more important spiritual tasks of the church.[50]

James Davison Hunter, a sociologist at the University of Virginia, offers a similar but more sophisticated critique of the politicization of faith. According to Hunter, the dominant public witness of Christian churches in the United States since the early 1980s has been a "political witness."[51] Although the various efforts of Christians to influence civic life—whether that of the conservative Christian Right, the progressive Christian Left, or the progressive, countercultural neo-Anabaptists—emphasize different strategies, they fundamentally share the common goal of influencing culture and the decision-making processes of the state. According to Hunter, however, the quest by Christian groups to pursue cultural change is both ineffective and counterproductive. It is ineffective because cultural and social change do not occur the way most Christian groups have assumed—namely, as a result of cumulative change in the hearts and minds of ordinary individuals. Rather, such change comes about through "dense networks of elites operating in common purpose within institutions at the high-prestige centers of cultural production."[52] Since Evangelicals are not part of elite structures, their capacity to influence civic life has been negligible. More significantly, the quest to influence culture and political life distorts the church's fundamental mission. Instead of seeking to influence public policies, Hunter calls on believers to carry out an incarnational task that he terms "faithful presence." They should not aim to influence the institutions of government and the centers of cultural and commercial life but instead to bear witness to the love of Christ. Christians, he thinks, should give up on such ideas as "transforming the world," "reforming culture," or "advancing the kingdom." Instead, believers should "be silent for a season and learn how to enact their faith through acts of shalom rather than to try again to represent it publicly through law, policy, and political mobilization."[53]

Although this may not be his intention, Hunter's argument implies a call for decreased cultural and political engagement. For the late Charles Colson, the founder of Prison Fellowship, Hunter's argument was problematic because it suggested "an abdication of responsibility." In his view, believers had a responsibility to bring Christian values and perspectives to bear on all aspects of social, economic, political, and cultural life. The call for a restrained public engagement, he claimed, could lead Christians to disregard injustice and suffering.[54] Therefore, to the extent that the strategy of "faithful presence" disregarded civic life, it could lead to a return to the political passivity and cultural indifference that characterized pietistic fundamentalism during the first half of the twentieth century. A return to such pietism, Colson believed, would be regrettable.

The gospel is not simply about personal salvation; it is also about living life in accordance with God's righteousness. Theologian Richard Mouw writes that evangelism is in part political because the gospel is also concerned with demonstrating the effects of salvation in both personal and collective life. "A purely individualistic understanding of the Christian life," he writes, "is a serious distortion of New Testament Christianity."[55] If the church is to be faithful to its calling of proclaiming and modeling the good news, it must demonstrate how Christ's atonement results in the renewal of culture and the creation of new social, economic, and political relationships. Of course, in carrying out its work of redemption and reconciliation, the church relies not on its human resources but on Christ, the head of the church. Mouw writes: "It is because we have known his power in the church that we can proclaim his power in the world. Having been healed, we are sent to do a healing work among men."[56]

The ongoing debates among Evangelicals over the extent and manner of political engagement are unlikely to subside. The challenge for believers is how to bring the salt and light of the gospel to the realm of public affairs without compromising the gospel message. As John notes in his gospel, believers are called to be "in" the world but not "of" the world. This is always a difficult task. The easiest strategies are those that call either for strict separation between the community of faith and the temporal responsibilities of the state or for complete correspondence between faith and social and political action. The first approach, practiced by Fundamentalists, was rejected by a group of traditional Protestants, giving rise to the new Evangelicalism of the mid-1940s. The second approach was practiced by the medieval Catholic Church when religious and secular authority were fused. The challenge for Christians has remained the same throughout time—namely, how to be in the world but not of it. The challenge for Evangelicals is, therefore, to proclaim the centrality of Christ's redemption while expressing that message in tangible cultural, social, economic, and political deeds.

Even though Evangelicals have not established a fully developed political doctrine to structure thought and action, they have devised a body of principles that collectively constitute a rudimentary political theology. If these basic norms are to contribute to ongoing political analysis, they must be supported by careful, discriminating analysis by competent social scientists. It is not enough to have sound biblical and theological knowledge. A political theology must also be rooted in competence in political, economic, and social analysis. Thus, if Evangelicals are to address an issue like immigration reform, they must understand the legal and political character of the existing Westphalian international order on which the United Nations is based. A sound political theology will thus presuppose competence in both theology and politics.

Some observers have suggested that Evangelical political ethics are underdeveloped because of an incomplete theology. But perhaps the major shortcoming is a lack of competence in the affairs of the world. This limitation is evident in the tendency among Evangelicals to address social and political concerns, including global issues, without sufficient knowledge of the social and political issues themselves. The late Congressman Paul Henry called attention to this shortcoming. He observed that Evangelical Christianity often pursued issues with an anti-intellectual perspective, writing:

> Its social and political ethic, rather than being clearly thought out and systematically stated, is a collection of moralisms which tends to romanticize concrete social and political problems as if they were nothing more than vaguely "spiritual" in character....So long as Evangelicals engage...in prescribing only moral clichés to difficult social and political problems, they are in fact avoiding any direct interrelating of their faith with the sociopolitical world around them.[57]

Nearly forty years later, Henry's call for the development of a competent, sophisticated approach to Evangelical political engagement remains only partially fulfilled.

EVANGELICALS AND GLOBAL POVERTY

While Evangelicals have generally assumed that meeting human needs is a biblical imperative, they have developed few conceptual resources to guide reflection and action on the problem of global poverty. Unlike mainline Protestant denominations and the Roman Catholic Church, which have issued numerous declarations and teaching documents to guide moral reasoning about poverty, Evangelicals have developed limited resources to illuminate the nature and causes of global poverty and to identify institutions and policies that might alleviate human suffering and foster long-term economic development.

Evangelicals nonetheless have played a crucial role in fostering human dignity. Their efforts include promoting education, building clinics, distributing food and medical supplies, teaching agriculture, and modeling behaviors essential to civic life. Since meeting global human needs is a distinctive feature of the social and political ethics of Evangelicalism, this chapter highlights the important role of American Evangelicals in global humanitarianism.

The Nature of the Problem: Poverty or Inequality

How should poverty be conceptualized? Is it an economic, spiritual, or social concept? In May 2010, a group of Evangelicals gathered in Wheaton, Illinois, for a two-day consultation on global poverty, and they issued a statement titled "Government, Global Poverty and God's Mission in the World: An Evangelical Declaration." The statement defined poverty as follows:

> Poverty is one disastrous aspect of human sin. Emerging from a variety of conditions and causes, poverty manifests itself in dignity-stripping and life-destroying realities of all types—including hunger, disease, sexual exploitation, lack

of education, and premature death—and the misery and hopelessness that follow. Poverty violates right relationships among human beings and with God. Poverty is harmful. Poverty is violence against the poor. Poverty is systemic injustice. Poverty is an affront to God.[1]

Although such a broad, all-inclusive definition may be helpful in inspiring moral concern, a more narrowly focused approach is likely to foster a more effective strategy—one that can contribute to the development of specific public policies to help improve living conditions for those suffering from hunger, malnutrition, disease, and lack of shelter. From an economic perspective, poverty is often approached either as absolute deprivation or as a relative deprivation. The first approach views poverty as a failure to achieve specific social and economic standards of living; the second approach, by contrast, regards poverty as the maldistribution of economic resources. If poverty is defined in relation to the living conditions of others, then poverty can be addressed through the redistribution of economic resources within a community, a society, or the entire world. The moral pursuit of justice will necessarily involve redistribution.

By contrast, if poverty is defined in absolute terms—namely, as the failure to provide essential services to meet basic human needs—then improving the standard of living becomes the primary moral concern. In this case, poverty reduction need not focus on redistribution. Indeed, the welfare of the poor can improve when inequalities persist, or even if they increase. What matters is whether the standard of living improves for those at the bottom of the economic ladder. When he was president of the World Bank, Robert McNamara approached the problem of poverty from this perspective. In the late 1960s, he coined the term "absolute poverty" to describe the condition of life characterized by illiteracy, malnutrition, and disease as beneath any reasonable definition of decency.[2] The challenge for modern societies, he believed, was to help eradicate this condition, which existed in many nations in Asia, Africa, and Latin America.

In 2000, the UN General Assembly adopted a series of goals—the so-called Millennium Development Goals (MDGs)—to help eradicate extreme poverty. These include such aims as ending malnutrition and hunger, reducing infant mortality, advancing universal education, and eliminating gender inequality in schools. According to the UN Millennium Campaign, contemporary human suffering is manifested by:

• The annual death of more than 10 million children from hunger and preventable diseases
• Over 1 billion people living on less than one dollar a day

- Six hundred million children living in absolute poverty
- Per capita income in Africa's poorest countries falling by a quarter in the past two decades
- Eight hundred million people suffering from chronic hunger
- The annual death of nearly 11 million children before their fifth birthday[3]

Since Christians believe that all persons bear the image of God and are therefore entitled to dignity, they view absolute poverty as contrary to divine will. However, like most informed citizens, Evangelicals have not achieved consensus either on the nature and causes of poverty or on what strategies are most likely to eradicate it. Indeed, the analysis of global poverty is often pursued from a simplistic and moralistic perspective, and frequently is based on misinformation and unfounded beliefs. Three myths that often characterize religious actors' perspectives on global poverty are: (1) Third World poverty is a direct by-product of the modernization and economic growth of the rich, developed nations; (2) poor countries have achieved little progress in improving living conditions; and (3) rising economic inequality between countries is a major source of human suffering in the poor countries.

The first myth—often captured by the saying "the rich get richer and the poor get poorer"—is that the poverty of the Third World is a direct result of the economic growth of the rich countries. According to this perspective, economic life is static. Total wealth is fixed, and increases in income for some can only occur through a decline in income for others. Although this view is not corroborated by empirical data, it was widely accepted during the Cold War years and often referred to as the North–South conflict. According to the defenders of this myth, the poverty of developing nations was due in great measure to the unfair rules and practices imposed by powerful developed nations. Multinational corporations have invested in poor countries but have failed to compensate workers fairly. Additionally, foreign firms have exploited natural resources in poor countries without providing just compensation. Supporters of this myth have also claimed that the existing institutions and international financial and commercial rules of the global economy are discriminatory. Based on this myth, developing nations carried out a campaign in the 1980s to develop an alternative international economic order, one that would offer poor countries trade preferences, greater access to capital and economic aid, and increased influence at such institutions as the World Bank and the International Monetary Fund.

Although powerful states undoubtedly pursued economic exploitation in past centuries, modern economic growth is not necessarily exploitative.

According to the theory of modern wealth creation, sound national economic expansion can benefit all members of society. Economists call wealth creation a positive-sum process, as distinguished from a zero-sum process, where the gain of one country must involve a loss to another. The best evidence against the zero-sum myth is that, despite the alleged unfairness of the world economy, many poor countries have achieved significant economic growth in the past three decades. Indeed, low- and medium-income countries have been growing at a faster overall rate than the rich nations. China and India—the two most populous countries—have achieved record economic growth rates of 7 to 9 percent per year in the new millennium. Recent experience indicates that when countries—regardless of their level of development—adopt policies favorable to job creation, most citizens will experience improved living conditions.

The second myth alleges that participation in the modern international economy has increased global poverty. To a significant degree, this claim is based on the belief that modern economic growth is unjust because it exacerbates economic inequalities within and among countries. But the history of modern economic growth does not support this claim. Indeed, the overall quality of life in most poor, developing nations of Asia, Africa, and Latin America has improved dramatically over the past half-century. For example, fifty years ago almost 20 million children under the age of five died each year. By 2010, however, that number had fallen to 7.6 million—a 60 percent reduction. The increase in longevity throughout the world—made possible by better nutrition and medical care—provides another measure of the rise in living conditions. According to the UN Development Programme, developing nations increased life expectancy from an average of forty-six years in 1960 to an average of sixty-two years in 1987.[4]

Perhaps the best measure of poverty reduction is the rise in the human development index (HDI)—a United Nations index that measures longevity, education, and per capita income based on purchasing power.[5] Mali and Nepal, for example, experienced average annual HDI growth of 2.28 percent and 2.08 percent, respectively. When the world's countries are divided in terms of development levels, the average annual HDI growth rates range from 0.48 percent for the very high human development countries to 1.31 percent growth for the medium human development countries. Significantly, the countries in the low human development category had an average growth rate of 1.19.[6] Thus, contrary to myth, the poor have not been getting poorer. Indeed, the physical quality of life in low- and medium-income countries, based on HDI data, has improved more than in high-income countries.

Notwithstanding these improved living conditions in the developing nations, a large segment of the world's population continues to live in abject poverty. While the percentage of the world's population living in extreme poverty has declined markedly in the past thirty years, the total number has not declined significantly. This is because the population growth rate of the poorest countries is nearly double that of the developed nations. As a result, of the world's 7 billion people, nearly a billion continue to suffer hunger, deprivation, and abject poverty.

The third myth is that economic modernization fosters income inequality and that such inequality is harmful to those living in poor countries. There can be little doubt that economic development in the past century has increased income inequality among nations. According to economist Martin Wolf, the ratio of per capita income between the richest and poorest countries in 1913 was 15 to 1; by 1950, the ratio had increased to 26 to 1; and by 2000, it had grown to 71 to 1.[7] Is the rise in global inequality harmful, and has it contributed to the poverty in low-income countries? Although global inequality involves concerns about distributive justice, the expanding international inequalities would be especially morally troubling if increased income in the rich countries came at the expense of the poor nations. This, of course, is not the case. Since economic growth is potentially beneficial to all members of society, it does not necessarily cause poverty. Indeed, without economic modernization, the living conditions of the poor would be even worse. As noted above, modernization has improved the standard of living of most people throughout the world. Longevity has risen and infant mortality has declined in nearly all countries. Thus, despite rising economic inequality, the overall quality of life for most people, in both rich and poor countries, has improved.

The core moral challenge posed by the contemporary global economic system is not economic inequality, however troubling such disparities may be. Rather, the fundamental task is how to reduce poverty, how to uplift people living in degrading, inhumane conditions. Despite significant improvements in living conditions among most of the world's people, a large portion of the world's population continues to suffer from absolute poverty. While more than 5 billion people have benefited from globalization and economic growth, more than 1 billion people live in societies plagued by violence, disease, ignorance, and hunger. In his compelling book *The Bottom Billion*, economist Paul Collier argues that roughly 1 billion persons live in countries that are "stuck at the bottom."[8] They are stuck not because they are poor but because they are unable to overcome fundamental "traps" that impede economic development. According to Collier, four major obstacles impede growth in the poorest countries: conflict, including ongoing civil war; a land-locked location next to bad neighbors; abundant natural resources, resulting in distorted economic priorities; and bad government.

Poverty is not caused by modernization's inequalities. Indeed, the problem of the poor is that they are not benefiting from integration into the modern global economy. Martin Wolf argues convincingly that modernization does not foster global poverty. Rather, poverty persists because societies are unable to take advantage of economic modernization. Wolf writes:

The proportion of humanity living in desperate misery is declining. The problem of the poorest is not that they are exploited, but that they are almost entirely unexploited: they live outside the world economy. The soaring growth of the rapidly integrating developing economies has transformed the world for the better. The challenge is to bring those who have failed so far into the new web of productive and profitable global economic relations.[9]

Perhaps the most powerful illustration of the effect of economic growth on poverty is the dramatic reduction in the proportion of Chinese people who are poor. According to some estimates, China's annual economic growth rate of nearly 9 percent over the past thirty years has helped to bring more than 600 million people out of poverty.[10] This development is surely one of the most significant humanitarian achievements of the modern world. Recent rapid economic growth in India has similarly uplifted tens of millions out of poverty.

In sum, the international community's chief economic challenge is to uplift those at the bottom. If Evangelicals are to participate in reducing global poverty, they must encourage economic growth, especially in those low-income countries "stuck at the bottom," to use Collier's conceptualization.

Alternative Approaches to Poverty Reduction

Despite significant reductions in the percentage of the world population that is poor, the total number of people who suffer from absolute poverty has not declined significantly in the past half-century. As noted, roughly 1 billion people continue to live in extreme poverty. How should people in high-income countries respond to the needs of poor societies? What perspectives and principles should guide poverty-reduction initiatives?

Although public policy advocates and public officials have used a variety of initiatives to improve living conditions among those suffering from extreme deprivation, two approaches have dominated the public discourse on global poverty over the past fifty years. The first model, which I call the *structural thesis*, approaches poverty chiefly as a distributional issue. Fundamentally, this approach is rooted in the ideology of socialism and favors strict regulation of economic and social life. This approach regards meeting the needs of all members of society as the most significant economic problem and assumes that this goal can best be realized through governmental intervention in the production and distribution of goods and services. The second model, the *free enterprise thesis*, is based on the ideology of capitalism. Unlike the structuralist perspective, market economics regards poverty as a by-product of limited productivity. Accordingly, the primary task in economic life is to create work in order to generate income and thereby improve living conditions. If a society is to create jobs, however, government must ensure a stable legal and financial structure while avoiding excessive entanglement in the production and distribution of goods and services. In effect, supply and demand for goods and services should be the primary basis for allocating scarce economic resources.

The structural thesis is based on three core assumptions. First, structuralism is rooted in the conviction that the basic condition of humankind is sufficiency, not poverty. As one radical economist put it, traditional societies were originally primitive, "undeveloped" communities, but after modern capitalism was introduced some countries became developed while others became "underdeveloped."[11] Underdevelopment was viewed as a direct by-product of the economic dislocations and disparities arising within and among capitalist countries. From the structural perspective, the global expansion of capitalism in the nineteenth and twentieth centuries exacerbated the suffering of many peasants and workers, since the gains from production were distributed unfairly and unequally within and among countries.

A second key element of the structural approach is its view of economic growth. According to the structural thesis, economics, like politics, is a zero-sum game in which the economic benefits of one group or nation result in losses for another. Since the total value of wealth is fixed, gains in business and commercial life must inexorably result in the economic loss of another firm, group, or nation. Net wealth creation is difficult, if not impossible. The economic development of some nations has necessarily led to the decline of other nations. In short, the emergence of global poverty is a direct result of economic modernization.

A third claim of structuralism is that domestic and world capitalist institutions are the chief causes of poverty. Because extreme poverty stems directly from the application of capitalist structures, the world economy is fundamentally unjust, favoring the rich, powerful nations in the global North. Accordingly, the best strategy is to reform domestic and international institutions to distribute the gains from economic production more justly. In the short term, economic transfers from the rich to the poor, both domestically and internationally, represent the most effective strategy to curb poverty.

Contrary to conventional wisdom, the free enterprise model does not assume that "the best government is that which governs least." Indeed, a successful capitalist economy presupposes a strong state, where government maintains the rule of law, ensures a stable monetary system, protects property rights, and ensures a free, competitive environment among diverse economic interests. Three core assumptions characterize the free enterprise model. First, it assumes that the basic condition of life is scarcity and poverty. The major economic challenge is to generate wealth through increased productivity, which is the only effective way to reduce poverty and improve physical quality of life. To be sure, not all economic expansion necessarily benefits the poor or society at large. Some modernization has resulted in human misery and environmental degradation, including crime, pollution, economic exploitation, human insecurity, and impersonal work conditions. But without economic growth, the standard of living cannot improve. Thus, rather than causing human misery and hunger, as the structuralists allege, economic development increases longevity and overall human welfare. The people of both developed and developing nations benefit from economic growth.

Another important feature of the free enterprise model is its assumption that wealth creation is a positive-sum process whereby an increase in the welfare of one nation or group does not necessarily come at the expense of another. According to this perspective, economic production is a job-producing, wealth-enhancing process. However, while the invention, production, and sale of goods and services benefit both producers and consumers, the gains from business enterprise will not necessarily be distributed evenly. Rather, the rewards from production and trade go to the individuals, enterprises, associations, and nations that are most economically efficient in providing goods and services that people want. Such results, however, are not a consequence of exploitation but of different productive capacities. The late Steve Jobs, founder of Apple Inc., was a successful entrepreneur because he conceived, developed, produced, and sold sophisticated technological products craved by people throughout the world. Jobs's wealth, and that of his corporate stockholders, did not come from exploitation but from producing technological products that people found useful and desirable.

A third key claim of the free enterprise model is that the liberal international economic order that emerged after World War II is relatively neutral. Global capitalism has not predetermined wealth and poverty in the international economy. Rather, the economic rise and fall of nations is a direct result of the policies and institutions that governments establish. Those with market-friendly policies have achieved higher rates of economic growth than those that have sought to guide production and distribution through government regulations. The rapid economic rise of East Asian states in the 1980s and 1990s was a direct consequence of the adoption of export-based trade policies. Similarly, the rise of modern China is due to its communist government's shift in domestic economic policies from state socialism to free enterprise.

To a significant degree, the conflict between these two approaches to economic life is over. While the dispute between socialism and capitalism was intense during the Cold War, by the time the Soviet Union collapsed in 1991, its system had been totally discredited. Free enterprise became the dominant model simply because it was more effective in generating wealth than the alternative. In 1989, as the Cold War was ending, economist Robert Heilbroner wrote of the victory of capitalism over socialism as follows:

> Less than seventy-five years after it officially began, the contest between capitalism and socialism is over: capitalism has won. The Soviet Union, China and Eastern Europe have given us the clearest possible proof that capitalism organizes the material affairs of human kind more satisfactorily than socialism: that however inequitably or irresponsibly the marketplace may distribute goods, it does so better than the queues of a planned economy; however mindless the culture of commercialism, it is more attractive than state moralism; and however deceptive the ideology of a business civilization, it is more believable than that of a socialist one.[12]

In the two decades since the collapse of the Soviet Union, most developing nations have shifted from a government-controlled economy toward a freer, private-enterprise approach. Rather than seeking to reform global structures and demanding greater foreign aid, many developing nations—led by such emerging countries as Brazil, Chile, China, India, and Indonesia—adopted market-friendly policies, resulting in significant economic growth. Indeed, from 1990 to 2005, the world's low and medium human-development nations grew faster than the high human-development nations. According to the UN Human Development Report, developing nations had an annual per capita growth rate of 3.1 percent during the 1990–2005 period, whereas developed nations had a growth rate of 1.8 percent. To be sure, the average rates fail to illuminate important differences among countries and regions. Additionally, it is important to stress that the high rate of average growth in the developing nations was due to the exceptional performance of East Asian and Pacific economies, which grew at an annual rate of 5.8 percent annually, while sub-Saharan African states grew at only 0.5 percent. Indeed, from 1975 to 2005 sub-Saharan Africa experienced an average annual economic decline of 0.5 percent.[13]

Despite these noteworthy changes in the global economy, American churches and religious groups have continued to identify with the structuralist/distributional model. To a large degree the preference for the structuralist approach is due to the belief that egalitarianism and socialism are more consistent with biblical justice than are the inequalities generated by free enterprise. But does the structuralist approach offer an effective strategy for poverty reduction?

To begin, structuralism does not provide a long-term solution to the problem of global poverty. There are two reasons why resource transfers fail to meet the world's rising needs, including the needs of those suffering from extreme poverty. First, since the population of many poor nations continues to grow at 2 to 3 percent per year (largely because of better nutrition, hygiene, and medical care), improved living conditions can only be realized when economic growth exceeds the population growth rate. It is not enough to give poor people bread and fish; the only effective strategy is to teach them how to fish. Historian Philip Jenkins, in a foreword to a short study on wealth and justice by Peter Wehner and Arthur Brooks, writes that there is no reason to conclude, as some Evangelical activists have, that the Bible supports state intervention and socialist policies, especially when they often clash with other fundamental values, including the priority of the family. Jenkins writes: "Historical experience leaves not the slightest doubt of the superiority of free-enterprise capitalism as the best means of helping the poor—or rather, of making them self sufficient, so that they no longer need help."[14]

A second shortcoming of structuralism is that it approaches poverty chiefly from a materialist or monetary perspective. To be sure, poverty results from a lack of resources to sustain a humane standard of living. But poverty, as economist Amartya Sen has noted, is much more than material deprivation.

In his compelling book *Development as Freedom*, he argues that what impairs human flourishing is not simply low income or insufficient resources but, rather, barriers to the development of human capabilities. For Sen, freedom to develop and use human capabilities is both the means and the end of development.[15]

As Don Eberle has noted, government foreign aid programs have generally approached the problem of Third World poverty as an issue of limited financial resources.[16] As a result, governments tend to emphasize the transfer of money to poor countries. Approaching poverty as a lack of monetary resources is appealing because it provides an easy way to measure the extent of the donor country's generosity. But if poverty is not simply a lack of money but also a sign of insufficient human capabilities, then poverty reduction will demand much more than financial transfers.

An irony of the studies and declarations on global poverty by Christian groups is that they overemphasize material wants and needs, neglecting the spiritual and moral values and practices that must undergird a creative and productive economic society. In particular, these statements neglect the important task of job creation. One of the important biblical themes is the mandate to create. The human task of managing and controlling the earth derives from the special place that God has entrusted to humans in his created order. In his encyclical *On Human Work*, Pope John Paul II eloquently called attention to the creation mandate: "Man is the image of God partly through the mandate received from his Creator to subdue, to dominate the earth. In carrying out this mandate, man, every human being, reflects the very action of the Creator of the universe."[17] Work is important because it allows people to express themselves in society and to develop and realize their human potentialities. Even more significantly, work allows people to participate in the divine process of creation. As a group of Catholic thinkers and business leaders noted in *Toward the Future*, a study of Catholic social thought and the U.S. economy, "Creation is not finished.... Humans become co-creators through discovery and invention, following the clues left by God."[18]

Regardless of how one approaches the problem of global poverty, participating in economic life is both a right and a moral responsibility. It is a right because human dignity depends in part on work. It is a responsibility because the need to work derives from the need to care materially for ourselves and for others. Theologically, this responsibility derives from the biblical command to be stewards of the gifts and talents that God has entrusted to us. Because we are called to be co-creators with God, we have a responsibility to continue the divine process of creation.

Evangelical Thought on Global Poverty

As noted earlier, unlike Protestants and Catholics, Evangelicals have made few noteworthy contributions to the analysis of global poverty or to the process of job creation as a way to alleviate human poverty. Because of the activist, action-oriented nature of Evangelicals, their chief contribution to advancing human dignity has come through charitable actions to meet basic human needs, both domestically and internationally. As I noted earlier, Evangelical missionaries not only carried the message of salvation but also instituted important educational, nutritional, medical, and humanitarian initiatives throughout the world. Nonetheless, Evangelical thinkers and activists have written articles and books and have sponsored colloquia that collectively illuminate important beliefs and perspectives about the nature, causes, and impact of global poverty.

The first noteworthy book by an American Evangelical to address global poverty from a biblical perspective was Ronald Sider's *Rich Christians in an Age of Hunger*, published in 1978. Sider, a theologian, approached the problem of poverty as a distributional issue, emphasizing the dangers of materialism, excessive concern with wealth, the priority to care for the poor, and the injustice of extreme economic inequalities. In his view, "the rich neglect or oppose justice because justice demands that they end their oppression and share with the poor." He therefore concluded that "God actively opposes the rich."[19] But while Sider argued that God took the side of the poor, he also claimed that God was not partial. Contrary to the Roman Catholic teaching of "the preferential option for the poor,"[20] he believed that God was concerned equally for all persons. Thus, Sider claimed that while God cared as much for the weak as for the strong, "[t]he God of the Bible is on the side of the poor just because he is not biased, for he is a God of impartial justice."[21]

Although Sider called attention to the absolute needs of those suffering from deprivation, his chief concern was with the maldistribution of wealth. In particular, he was concerned with unfair economic and social systems that fostered and perpetuated exploitation and oppression. For him, injustice, oppression, and poverty largely referred to the same human condition.

Since poverty was not the natural condition of human life, it emerged in great part from unjust practices and institutions. Sider called attention to the unfairness of economic systems that condoned egregious inequalities. He noted that while some poverty was due to laziness, the major biblical explanation for poverty was "calamity and oppression." Drawing on the book of Exodus, he argued that liberation was the appropriate response to the injustice of slavery and oppression. Sider concluded that America was partly responsible for the misery and human suffering in poor societies: "We are all implicated in structural evil. International trade patterns are unjust. An affluent minority devours most of the earth's nonrenewable natural resources. Food consumption patterns are grossly lopsided. And the returns on investment in poor countries are unjustly high. Every North American benefits from these structural injustices."[22]

Sider's book has sold more than 400,000 copies and has gone through several revisions. The fifth edition, published in 2005, includes numerous modifications from the first, shorter edition.[23] But it continues to conceive of poverty from a relational or distributional perspective. "Today's wealth," writes Sider, "is divided in a way that flatly contradicts the Bible."[24] At the same time, the newer version emphasizes the priority of creating work in order to uplift all those suffering from economic and social deprivation. Claiming that "God demands that all people have the opportunity to earn a reasonable living,"[25] Sider now argues that a market system, despite its imperfections, is the preferred economic approach to meeting human needs.[26] Still, rather than identifying the cultural, political, and economic preconditions for job creation, Sider dwells on reforms that can improve the distribution of the world's goods and services. He writes: "We can correct unjust structures. Our challenge today is to take the next practical concrete steps to empower the poor."[27] Some of Sider's public policy recommendations include greater foreign aid, increased availability of capital for poor people, fairer international trade practices, and reducing the foreign debt of highly indebted low-income countries.

A second analysis of global poverty by an Evangelical thinker is philosopher Nicholas Wolterstorff's *Until Justice and Peace Embrace,* a book based on the author's Kuyper Lectures at Amsterdam's Free University in 1981.[28] Although the book devotes only one chapter to international economic relations and global poverty, the study is important because it presents a compelling theological argument for caring for persons suffering from extreme poverty. Wolterstorff, like Sider, argues that poverty is an affront to God. Because humans bear God's image, they must be accorded dignity and respect. Following the teachings of John Calvin and Abraham Kuyper, Wolterstorff argues that Christians should not only care for those in need but also seek to create structures and policies that will foster social and economic justice. The challenge for believers is to develop and apply a "world-formative Christianity" approach to public life.

While Wolterstorff's call to reduce poverty is morally and biblically compelling, his social-scientific analysis of the causes of human misery is not persuasive. This is because he relies on a perspective—dependency theory—that was deeply contested when he wrote the book, and which has been subsequently discredited. The essence of this theory is that poverty is a direct by-product of global capitalism. According to this approach, the international economic order was divided historically between rich, powerful countries (the core or metropolis) and poor, weak countries (the periphery or satellites). The theory claimed that the gains from economic interaction between core and periphery states necessarily accrued to the core or center. The international economic system was thus structurally flawed, contributing to international inequality and to Third World poverty in particular. Reflecting this structural paradigm, Wolterstorff asserts that the modern international economic order is one "in which the core dominates the periphery, characteristically out of greed and a lust for power." He amplifies his argument as follows:

> The mass poverty of the Third World is...not some sort of natural condition that exists independent of us [the United States and other states in the core]; quite the contrary, a good deal of it is the result of the interaction of the core of the world-system with the periphery over the course of centuries. In many areas there has been a development of underdevelopment, and we in the core have played a crucial role in that development. Underdevelopment has a history, a history inseparable from ours.[29]

I have focused on Sider's and Wolterstorff's accounts of poverty because they reflect the general sentiments and perspectives prevalent among American church leaders in the 1980s. For them, as for many progressive Evangelical thinkers, the dominant approach to global poverty was based on a belief that global capitalism was responsible for unjust economic institutions and that a dramatic restructuring of the global economy, coupled with vigorous redistribution of income, was essential to combat poverty. To be sure, some Evangelicals, such as economist Brian Griffiths and historian Herbert Schlossberg, challenged this account.[30] But the prevalent approach among American religious elites was consistent with Sider's and Wolterstorff's analyses.[31]

What accounts for the widespread belief among Christians, including many Evangelicals, that redistribution of economic resources is the most effective way to care for the poor? One explanation is that socialist ideals retain significant influence.[32] Since socialism emphasizes meeting the human needs of all members of society, its goals appear at first glance more compatible with human dignity than the emphasis on individual agency found in the competitive capitalist ethos. Indeed, the allure of socialist thought for many

Christian idealists is undoubtedly rooted in socialism's mythic claim to justice and its alleged capacity to care for the needs of the poor. Theologian Clark Pinnock explains the appeal of socialism as follows:

> The alignment of some Christians with Marxism can be explained by invoking the category of utopian myth. Human hope for salvation in history—the millennial longing for a world purified of evil—is immense. Christianity provides a solution, but those who want change according to their timetable, not God's, sweep aside even developed critical judgment in their rush to force open the gates of Eden. In this respect socialism possesses a clear "advantage" over capitalism. Socialism is one of the most powerful myths of the modern era, and the fact that it is nowhere realized only adds to its appeal.[33]

In Pinnock's view, religious elites failed to effectively address the problem of wealth creation because they were trapped by ideology. This led them to uncritically accept utopian socialism as a framework of analysis, even when evidence suggested that such strategies were unlikely to contribute to poverty reduction. Pinnock writes that, had Christians been serious about God's preferential option for the poor, they would have been unwise to "side with an ideology which...has such a bad record in regard to reducing the misery of poor people."[34]

Lawrence Mead, a leading scholar of public policy, offers an alternative explanation rooted in religious thought. He claims that the emphasis on redistribution has been influenced by an overreliance on biblical prophetic teachings. Although prophetic claims are part of the biblical narrative, they alone do not provide a sufficient account of how to care for the poor. What is needed is a more complete understanding of the Scriptural tradition—one that takes into account the Old Testament teachings from ancient Israel as well as the New Testament teachings of Jesus. According to Mead, Jesus emphasized the restoration of relationships, not simply the transfer of resources. "The duty of those who follow him," he writes, "is not simply to bail out the poor but to *relate* to them on an ongoing basis—to welcome them into mainstream society but also to expect from them the normal civilities of that society."[35] Mead argues that when policymakers rely chiefly on prophetic teachings, the result is an overemphasis on distributive justice and a neglect of social relationships and community. Mead writes:

> In the New Testament, like the Old, helping the poor is a priority, but helping means primarily to restore the poor to community rather

than simply to subsidize or liberate them. The community is based on mutual expectations about good behavior. Poverty represents a breakdown where, typically, the society has neglected the needy, but the latter have also infringed social norms in ways that alienate others. The commandment is to rebuild community through doing more to help but also by expecting better behavior from those aided. Assistance is not a substitute for engagement. The answer to poverty is not redistribution but the rebuilding of relationships with the poor where both sides give and receive.[36]

How, then, should Christians respond to poverty? For Mead the answer is set forth in the title of his short book *From Prophecy to Charity*. We should help the poor not because they have a right to social justice but, rather, because God commands humans to care for those in need. In meeting the needs of the poor, the aim is not the restoration of a fairer, more just economic order; rather, the goal is compassionate action toward those in need according to God's commands.[37]

A group of Evangelical leaders, academics, and relief and development workers gathered in Villars, Switzerland, in 1987 to develop an alternative approach to global poverty. After several days of dialogue and discussion, the participants issued "The Villars Statement on Relief and Development." This declaration challenged prevailing assumptions about Third World poverty and encouraged Evangelical thinkers to develop perspectives that were more consistent with a Christian anthropology, and with a deeper understanding of persons as responsible moral agents. Some of the key concerns expressed in the statement include:

- "the tendency to focus on meeting material needs without sufficient emphasis on spiritual needs"
- "the emphasis on redistribution of wealth as the answer to poverty and deprivation without recognizing the value of incentive, opportunity, creativity, and economic and political freedom"
- "the attraction to centrally controlled economies and solutions"
- "the need to make conversion and discipleship an essential component of Christian relief and development work"
- "the need to reaffirm the Biblical support for the family as the basic social and economic unit and its right to own and control property"[38]

Three years later, some one hundred Evangelical leaders gathered in Oxford, England, for a groundbreaking conference on Christianity and economics.

Prior to the conference, groups of scholars and theologians gathered in regional meetings to carry out preliminary studies on different topics and themes. Thus, when the leaders met in January 1990, they were able to issue a consensus document titled "The Oxford Declaration on Christian Faith and Economics." Although relatively brief, the statement covers four major themes relevant to Christianity and economic life: creation and stewardship, work and leisure, poverty and justice, and freedom and governmental systems.[39]

The Oxford Declaration is careful not to attribute the problem of global poverty to international economic relations. Instead, it suggests that the best solution is a strategy that combines economic growth and some redistribution. The statement declares:

> We recognize that poverty results from and is sustained by both constraints on the production of wealth and on the inequitable distribution of wealth and income. We acknowledge the tendency we have had to reduce the causes of poverty to one at the expense of the others. We affirm the need to analyze and explain the conditions that promote the creation of wealth, as well as those that determine the distribution of wealth.[40]

Most significantly, the Oxford Declaration emphasizes the important role of stewardship in using human capacities and natural resources effectively. "Production is not only necessary to sustain life and make it enjoyable," it states, but "it also provides an opportunity for human beings to express their creativity in the service of others."[41]

Although the Oxford Declaration provided few public policy insights on how to address global poverty, it represented a shift away from the structuralist perspective dominant among religious elites and toward a more balanced account based upon both socialist and capitalist principles. In effect, the declaration offered a more comprehensive account of the tasks of promoting economic expansion and meeting global needs. Despite this, some social scientists thought that much work still remained to be done on this subject. James Skillen, for example, writes that the declaration "does not go very far in articulating a Christian understanding of economics, production, business, labor, public policy and the responsibilities of multiple institutions of our society for economic justice." In his view, it would have been preferable if the signers had "affirmed their confessional agreement as Christians" and then outlined the tasks yet to be done to develop a more complete economic approach to contemporary problems.[42]

While Evangelicals contributed to an awareness of global poverty and to a compassionate response to those in need, they were much less effective in assessing the nature and causes of global poverty and in providing suggested remedies. Interestingly, the NAE did not adopt a single resolution or declaration on global poverty either during or after the Cold War. Perhaps one reason for this silence is that Evangelical leaders, like specialists in economic development, hold widely different views on this complex, contested subject. Still, when Christian leaders, including Evangelicals, sought to address the subject of global poverty from a biblical perspective, they relied chiefly on structuralism—a flawed paradigm that was unable to adequately explain how wealth is created in the modern economy or how to help alleviate human suffering in poor countries.

Following the end of the Cold War, however, high-level international agreement emerged among scholars and public officials that the most effective way of addressing global poverty was through national economic growth, and that such growth could be realized most effectively through free enterprise domestically and free trade internationally. Whereas Cold War ideologies had divided government officials and academics, the emerging consensus—often referred to as the "Washington Consensus" because it reflected not only the prevailing views of major Western economic powers but also those of leading international organizations like the World Bank and the IMF—was rooted in the belief that market economics was a more effective approach to job creation than state-regulated and state-owned enterprise. To a significant degree, the new consensus was based on the empirical record of a growing number of countries—including Chile, China, Hong Kong, Indonesia, Singapore, and South Korea—that adopted free enterprise and encouraged international trade to foster economic growth.[43] Although scholars continued to debate how best to transform poor countries, a significant level of consensus existed in developed and emerging economies that growth was ultimately the only effective way to meet the rising needs of societies. Foreign aid could provide temporary relief, but it could not establish the social, political, and economic preconditions necessary for efficient production.[44]

In sum, throughout the Cold War years, the analysis of global poverty by religious elites was deeply influenced by the ideological debate between capitalism and socialism. As a result, reflections about global poverty were based more on secular socialist thought than on such biblical ideas as human dignity, family, generosity, consumption, vocation, and stewardship. Although modest initiatives to offer alternative perspectives were undertaken in the late 1980s, the nature of the religious debate on poverty did not change decisively until China's economy began to thrive after adopting free enterprise in the

1980s and the Soviet Union ceased to exist in 1991. These two developments provided the tipping point for the free enterprise model to become the dominant approach to economic growth and poverty reduction.

Evangelical Humanitarianism

How have Evangelicals helped people suffering from absolute poverty? Because of Evangelicals' preference for local, small-scale initiatives, they tend to be skeptical of the role of central government in promoting economic growth. As a result, support for foreign aid has been mixed, favoring disaster relief, for example, but skeptical of official aid geared toward large-scale economic growth projects. Instead, Evangelicals have been strong proponents of microenterprise, especially projects associated with religious organizations and designed to empower women and children. In 1995, the NAE leadership passed a resolution in support of U.S. foreign aid that reflected some of these concerns. The resolution called for continued economic assistance to poor countries, provided efforts were made to eliminate waste and corruption and to encourage programs that "have demonstrated the ability to make a real difference in the lives of those in need."[45] In addition, the resolution called for continued use of private voluntary organizations (PVOs) in meeting human needs in poor societies.

Evangelicals have acted principally through global humanitarian initiatives. While Evangelical missionaries were at the forefront of humanitarian efforts, such projects remained relatively small until after World War II. The rise of postwar Evangelical humanitarianism was led by Reverend Bob Pierce, a Far East war correspondent, who began World Vision in 1953 to help meet the needs of children orphaned by war. Although the organization was created to care for foreign children in crisis, Pierce subsequently expanded the program to include relief and development. Throughout the 1960s and 1970s, Evangelical denominations and associations established numerous humanitarian organizations, such as the Adventist Development and Relief Agency, the Christian Reformed World Relief Committee, Food for the Hungry, Opportunity International, Samaritan's Purse, and World Relief. In 1978, leaders of these humanitarian organizations established an umbrella organization—the Association of Evangelical Relief and Development Organizations (AERDO)—in order to disseminate information about successful humanitarian practices. The association, which recently changed its name to Accord, holds periodic meetings that have contributed to the growth and professionalism of Evangelical humanitarian organizations. Currently, seventy-five relief and development organizations and institutes are members of Accord.[46]

According to Rachel McCleary, who has compiled the most exhaustive data on humanitarian PVOs, the most notable change in relief agencies in the postwar era is the significant growth of Evangelical and faith-based nongovernmental organizations. Whereas Evangelicals accounted for only 16 percent of all humanitarian PVOs in 1946, by 2005 that number was 49 percent. This was significantly higher than the percentages for Catholic and mainline Protestant PVOs, which accounted for 8 and 7 percent, respectively.[47]

The expansion of Evangelical humanitarianism is seen most clearly in the growth of World Vision. By 2011, World Vision International (WVI) had become the largest religious relief and development organization in the world, with an annual budget of over $2.5 billion and 40,000 employees serving in nearly 100 countries.[48] Despite the organization's increased global funding and operations, the foundation of its support network remains in the United States, with American donors contributing more than $1 billion in 2010.[49]

Another organization that illuminates the pioneering role of Evangelical humanitarianism is Opportunity International (OI), an organization that fosters small business enterprise through small-scale, short-term loans. Established in 1971 by two former business executives who believed that job creation was essential to reducing Third World poverty, OI was one of the first nonprofit organizations to recognize the importance of small business loans in poor countries. Because of its success in microenterprise, OI has been a model for other secular and religious PVOs. And because OI emphasizes training and moral responsibilities, the loan repayment rate is an astounding 95 percent. In 2010, OI had 1.5 million active loans in twenty-four countries, with an average loan of $138.[50]

A significant part of Evangelical PVOs' humanitarian work is disaster relief. For example, after a destructive Indian Ocean tsunami hit Indonesia, Thailand, and Sri Lanka in December 2004, leaving some 230,000 persons dead or missing and hundreds of thousands without water, food, or shelter, Christian charities lent aid to tens of thousands of victims. It is estimated that nongovernmental U.S. emergency relief for the devastated areas was more than $1.6 billion, far exceeding aid appropriated by Congress.[51] Similarly, religious PVOs played an important role in the aftermath of Haiti's devastating earthquake in January 2010—an event that destroyed much of Port-au-Prince, the country's capital, and killed an estimated 200,000 people. Again, Evangelical NGOs responded immediately, providing significant financial and material assistance to victims in this impoverished country.

Since the late 1940s, the U.S. government has collaborated with religious organizations to meet humanitarian needs overseas.[52] In his fine study on refugees, J. Bruce Nichols showed that American religious organizations played a crucial humanitarian role following World War II. Although church-state constitutional concerns constrained government support for domestic social and economic programs administered by churches and religious organizations, Nichols revealed that church-state constitutional constraints placed few limitations on federal funding of religious NGOs. Indeed, such organizations have not only provided specific humanitarian services but have also helped to define "America's ties with the rest of the world."[53]

Whereas official development assistance in the Cold War era emphasized government-to-government loans and grants, in the post–Cold War era the U.S. government has channeled an increasing share of foreign aid through PVOs and local grassroots organizations. For example, roughly 20 percent of the funds allocated for AIDS relief under the President's Emergency Plan for AIDS Relief (PEPFAR) were distributed through religious PVOs. Similarly, educational and medical relief, small-scale enterprise, and other related initiatives have been channeled through American and indigenous nongovernmental organizations. As Don Eberle has noted, the U.S. government is increasingly relying on civil society organizations to advance its humanitarian foreign policy objectives.[54]

While the U.S. government began funding secular and religious humanitarian PVOs in the aftermath of World War II, Evangelical PVOs have varied in their openness to federal funding. Some are eager to receive government grants to carry out their humanitarian services; others, fearful of compromising their independence, have opposed government funding. During the early postwar years (1955–67), government funds accounted for an average of 33 percent of total PVO revenues; since then (1968–2005), government funds have dropped significantly, to an average of only 11 percent of annual budgets.[55] Table 5.1 shows the annual budget size of leading Evangelical PVOs, along with the percentage of the budget that comes from the U.S. government.

Finally, it is important to call attention to the contributions of short-term missionary work that often supplements the work of Evangelical PVOs. Every year tens of thousands of church volunteers travel at their own expense to provide humanitarian services in poor lands. These groups not only transfer financial resources to poor communities but also help to meet human needs in countless other ways, such as providing medical care, protecting children from sexual abuse, supporting orphans, building clinics and sanitation facilities, and constructing shelters, schools, and homes.

Evangelicals' major contribution in confronting the global challenge of poverty has been humanitarianism—that is, the provision of services and resources to alleviate human suffering. Since absolute poverty is an affront to

Table 5.1 Faith-based PVO Budgets, 2010

Organization	2010 Budget (millions of dollars)	U.S. Government Funds (percentage of budget)
Adventist Development and Relief Agency*	62.9	53.5
Catholic Relief Services	918.9	34.0
Christian Reformed World Relief Committee	39.4	7.6
Church World Service	83.0	42.8
Compassion International	507.2	0
Feed the Children	901.8	0
Food for the Hungry**	98.9	37.0
Lutheran World Relief	40.9	5.9
Map International 209.6	0	
Opportunity International	32.8	5.0
Samaritan's Purse	244.1	0
World Relief	67.9	48.2
World Vision	1,041.0	28.0

*Data is for 2009; **USAID funds are not included.

Source: Data compiled in October 2011 by Joshua Steddom from organizations' websites

human dignity, Evangelical thinkers have argued that the church has a responsibility to care for those in need, especially those suffering from abject poverty. One way to meet human needs is through short-term relief to help care for those threatened with disease, hunger, and lack of shelter. Evangelical organizations have played an important role in carrying out this task throughout the past century, but especially since the 1960s. To a significant degree, the preference for relief initiatives over systemic job creation is a reflection of the desire to address human needs immediately and directly. Whereas distributing food and medical supplies and building wells, schools, and clinics can be carried out in the short term, job creation emerges slowly and its effects are less apparent. Not surprisingly, with the exception of microlending initiatives, Evangelical organizations have historically focused on meeting immediate human needs.

But if the aim is to reduce global poverty, more attention needs to be given to fostering conditions that lead to long-term economic development. In the 1970s and 1980s, Evangelicals, along with other religious elites, contributed little to this task—in great part because they focused on the redistribution of income within and among countries rather than on economic growth itself.

Evangelicals can make an important contribution to job creation if they seek to nurture the moral habits and values that are conducive to work, service, and personal integrity. Since Evangelicals emphasize individual spirituality and personal responsibility, perhaps the church should worry less about devising sound economic policies and institutions, and give greater emphasis to the development of moral and cultural values conducive to trust, integrity, and diligence.

Central to Evangelicals' strategy on global poverty is the belief that people's spiritual and temporal needs both must be addressed. For Evangelicals, Christian mission and Christian service are simply different elements of the church's overall task. The problem is that believers are often tempted to give priority to either religious proclamation or to loving service. Both, however, are necessary parts of authentic Christian discipleship. Andrew Walls, the noted scholar of Christian missions, has written wisely about the need for balance:

> Christian mission and Christian service can neither be identified nor separated. Identify them—equate the Church's mission with acts of loving service to the community—and we may produce a Church which, instead of being Christ-centered, has become problem-centered.... If we confine Christian mission to the solving of problems, we will be in for frustration and disappointment, because there is not always the guarantee of a solution. But we will also be untrue to our commission: for the redemption which Christ effected is concerned with sin.... To absorb ourselves in problems, then, and hide away the word about forgiveness through Christ is not to serve the world, but to betray it. But to separate service from mission, to treat it as a distraction from that mission, or as a sort of bribe to get a hearing or ingratiate ourselves—this could be even worse. If we settle down and say "All we have to do is preach the Gospel and all other things will come right," we deceive ourselves. They do not.[56]

Both proclamation of Christ's forgiveness of sins and care for human needs are necessary to authentic faith. Although many historic Protestants in America became excessively pietistic in the early twentieth century, the rise of the "new" Evangelicals after the Second World War helped to restore a more authentic Evangelical faith, where mission and service, preaching and caring, regained a more satisfactory balance.

6 EVANGELICALS AND U.S. FOREIGN POLICY TOWARD ISRAEL

Among the many international issues that concern American Evangelicals, few are more important than the well-being of the Jewish people and the security of the Israeli state. Polling data have shown repeatedly that Evangelicals have a strong commitment to the Jewish nation. A Pew Research Center poll in 2003 found that 55 percent of white Evangelicals identified with Israel, whereas only 34 percent of mainline Protestants and 39 percent of Roman Catholics did so. Amazingly, public opinion surveys indicate that, after Jews, no other group in the United States identifies as strongly with Israel as Evangelicals do.

What explains Evangelicals' strong commitment to the Jewish people and to Israel? When and how did this deep support emerge? Is religious belief the primary, if not sole, source of political commitment? And if so, what are the beliefs that give rise to such strong sympathies toward Israel? Moreover, since tensions in the Middle East center on the quests of two peoples—Jews and Palestinians—to own the same land, is there a biblical basis for prioritizing Jewish interests over those of Palestinians? If religious beliefs justify support for Israel, should Evangelical support be conditional on just, peaceful, and humane behavior by the Israeli government?

Perhaps the most fundamental reason why Evangelicals are concerned with the Middle East is that Palestine is the Holy Land—the territory from which both Judaism and Christianity emerged. The Jewish faith began and developed in this region, where Abraham and his descendants learned to trust God's promises and to follow his law. Palestine is also important to Judaism because it provides a specific territorial context where God guided, sustained, protected, and judged his chosen people. For Christians, the Holy Land is doubly important since it provided not only the religious environment that gave rise to the Christian faith but also the territory in which the birth, death, and resurrection of Jesus took place.

Timothy Weber writes: "Evangelicals' view of the Bible gives them a proprietary interest in Israel. It is the Holy Land, the site of God's mighty deeds. In a way, they think the Promised Land belongs to them as much as it does to the Israelis."[1] American Evangelicals and Fundamentalists have traveled in great numbers to Israel, making Holy Land tours a significant source of foreign exchange for Israel.

Religious beliefs are also important to Evangelical support of Israel. Fundamentally, Evangelicals use the Bible to justify their support of Israel in two ways: first, by relying on the teachings and promises of Scripture about the Jewish nation; and second, by giving priority to the prophetic teachings of Scripture about events surrounding Jesus's Second Coming. According to the first perspective, God used a nation—the Jewish people—to carry out his plan of redeeming humankind. God not only made the Jews his chosen nation to serve as an instrument of divine redemption, but he also granted them title to the land of Canaan, a territory extending from the Nile in Egypt to the Euphrates in Iraq. According to this theological perspective, God made two covenants with Abraham: first, he promised to bless the world through his seed (Gen. 12:1–2); and second, he promised to deliver Canaan to his natural descendants as an "everlasting possession" (Gen. 17:8). Many Evangelicals believe that these promises are unconditional and timeless, and thus remain valid. Moreover, Scripture teaches that divine blessing will be bestowed on those who care for Jews. God's promise to Abraham, recorded in Genesis 12:3, is: "I will bless them that bless thee, and curse him that curseth thee: and in thee shall all families of the earth be blessed."

Some Evangelicals also base their support of Israel on eschatology. Those who do so claim that, while the manner and timing of Christ's Second Coming cannot be fully known, Scripture provides numerous clues to how God will complete his work of salvation. According to prophetic teachings of the Bible, the Jewish people will play a key role at the end of time. Prior to Christ's return, they will return to Israel and confront the forces of evil in an epic conflict—a battle (Armageddon) that will be fought on the plains of northern Israel. Only after the forces of evil (led by the Antichrist) have been destroyed will Christ return. Evangelicals of the prophetic persuasion thus identify strongly with the political aspirations of the Jewish people. Indeed, because the full restoration of Israel is a necessary precondition for Christ's return, prophetic Evangelicals strongly identify with Jewish interests and offer political support for a secure and prosperous Israeli state.

When taken together, these spiritual and biblical claims provide a strong religious explanation for Evangelicals' support of Jews and Israel. New

Testament professor Gary Burge describes this widely accepted perspective—the conventional wisdom on Evangelicals and Israel—as follows:

> [T]he vast majority of Evangelicals instinctively believe that a vigorous support of Israel is the only appropriate response to the conflicts in the Middle East. Their stance has little to do with history, less to do with politics. The average believer sitting in the pew is persuaded that such support is God's will: the Jews are God's people, and they are returning to the land God promised to them.[2]

While religious beliefs, such as those noted by Burge, play an important role in Evangelicals' support for Israel, they are not the whole story. Other elements, especially liberal political ideals, matter as well. American Evangelicals, like the general U.S. population, support Israel because of its democratic institutions, commitment to human rights, and shared moral ideals. In social science parlance, while religious beliefs may be a necessary condition for Evangelical support for Israel, they are not a sufficient condition.

The Bible and Israel

To gain an understanding of the nature and depth of Evangelicals' support for Israel, we must begin with the Bible. Scripture, after all, is for Evangelicals the fundamental guide to religious belief and action. Indeed, ever since the Reformation gave rise to the principle of *sola scriptura*, Protestants have regarded the Bible as the sole and sufficient source of revealed truth.[3] Although Protestantism has encouraged Bible reading, it also has fostered the notion that believers could interpret Scripture apart from established churches. As a result, Protestantism has spawned a proliferation of doctrinal and theological beliefs.

Biblical interpretation is not a simple task. Although some parts of the Bible present few hermeneutical challenges to Christian laypersons, others are far more challenging. Interpretation becomes even more difficult when confronting major theological issues, such as the relationship of Old Testament law to the good news of the gospel or the validity of God's covenants with the Jewish people. Does the fact that Canaan was given to Abraham and his descendants mean that Jewish sovereignty over Israel is based on a divine claim, unlike the natural political claim of other contemporary sovereign states? Moreover, how should God's covenants with the Jewish people be interpreted—as irrevocable and binding, or as superseded by a new covenant under Christ? And finally, what role, if any, should biblical prophecy play in preparing believers for current and future political and economic developments and challenges? In particular, how should prophetic insights affect perspectives and views on Israel and the Jewish nation?

Since Christians throughout the ages have interpreted Scripture in manifestly different ways, especially in confronting nettlesome and complex issues like those posed above, it is unlikely that Evangelicals will hold uniform, coherent answers to such questions. Indeed, Evangelicals remain deeply divided over the place of Jews in God's redemptive order, the validity of God's promises to Abraham and his descendants, and the role of biblical prophesy in Christ's Second Coming. If we are to better understand the various Evangelical views on the Middle East, it is helpful to sketch some of the major theological perspectives that structure biblical interpretation on the Jewish people and their nation-state.

A variety of theologies have influenced recent Evangelical views on Israel and the Jews. The three most widely accepted theological approaches are replacement theology, covenantal theology, and premillennial dispensationalism. The first two assume that Scripture presents a single, unified story of divine redemption, whereas the third assumes two different redemption plans—one for Jews and the other for Gentiles. For replacement and covenantal theologies, the Bible is a coherent story that begins with Abraham and his descendants and is completed in the work of Christ. In this integrated narrative, Old Testament law is not disregarded but, rather, fulfilled by Jesus's death and resurrection. In effect, Judaism provides the ethical foundation for Christ's redemption on the cross. Dispensationalism, by contrast, interprets Scripture as offering two covenants: the Old Testament legal covenant for Jews and the New Testament covenant of grace for all who believe in Jesus. The dual-covenant approach is a minority perspective not only because it calls into question the coherence and unity of biblical revelation but also because it tends to justify two strategies of salvation—one for Jews and the other for Gentiles. More significantly, it shifts the focus away from the redemptive work of Christ.

Replacement Theology

Historically, the most widely accepted view of Israel among Christians is replacement theology, or supersessionism—the belief that the good news of the gospel supersedes Old Testament law. According to this approach, when Christ, the long-awaited Messiah, arrived, God stopped exercising special care for the Jewish people and their land. Under the new covenant, Israel was replaced with the "new" Israel, the Christian church, comprising all who believe in Jesus as Savior and Lord. Thus, the land of Israel ceased to play a critical role in Christianity, leading Gerald McDermott to observe that "most Christians for most of the last two millennia have believed that the land has no theological importance."[4] Supersessionists believe that Israel was important in ancient times in establishing the legal and moral context in which Christ was to emerge, but with the arrival of Jesus, the Jewish people and the land no longer played a decisive role in God's divine plan. Some supersessionists even claim that the Jews ceased to play a favored role in God's plan because of their rejection of Christ. This so-called punitive supersessionism is supported by Saint Augustine, who believed that the Jews lost title to the Promised Land when they crucified Jesus.[5]

Replacement theology has been popular among believers for a number of reasons. First, its focus is Christological, emphasizing the completed and sufficient work of Christ through his suffering on the cross, his atoning death, and his resurrection on behalf of all people. Second, it emphasizes the unity and singleness of God's plan of redemption, proclaiming one covenant, one plan of redemption, and salvation based on Christ alone. Since salvation is available to anyone who believes, and since believers are one in Christ, differences and divisions among people, especially between Jews and Gentiles, cease to be important. Third, it presumes that the Old Testament promises given to Israel have been, or are being, fulfilled in Christ's church.

In the past century, replacement theology has declined in influence among Christians. Some critics argue that this perspective, while claiming that Scripture is a unified and integrated account of God's redemption, fails to adequately incorporate Old Testament teachings. Critics also note that supersessionists not only disregard the special place of Jews in God's redemptive order but also fail to acknowledge adequately the Judaic roots of Christianity. Finally and most importantly, a large number of Bible scholars now interpret Scripture, especially Paul's letter to the Romans, as reinforcing the validity of the Abrahamic Covenant.

Covenant Theology

The second major approach influencing Evangelical opinions on Israel is covenant (or Reformed) theology, which views Scripture as a unified, coherent revelation of God's sovereign plan of redemption. John Calvin and his followers believed that to fully appreciate the work of Christ, it was important to understand how God had revealed himself to Abraham and his descendants and how his covenants with them illuminated his loving, righteous, and just character. Reformers not only placed great emphasis on the Hebrew Bible, but they also encouraged regular use of the Psalms of David in worship. Since it considers both the old and new covenants valid, covenantal theology affirms that the Jews are God's chosen people and that his promises to them remain intact, even while salvation history is being fulfilled through the church. Law and grace, the old covenant of Israel and the new covenant of the church, function as integral parts of God's redemptive plan. In defending this perspective, Richard Mouw, president of Fuller Theological Seminary, argues that Paul (in Rom. 11) suggests that the Jewish people are the "natural branches" that will eventually be grafted back onto God's tree.[6] The relative standing and role of Gentiles and Jews, however, is not settled, for Paul ends his analysis of law and grace by affirming the mystery of God's ways: "How unsearchable are his judgments, and his ways past finding out!" (Rom. 11:33).

Unlike replacement theology, which gives precedence to the New Testament over the Old Testament, covenant theology regards the old covenant of law and the new covenant of grace as distinct but interdependent elements of God's plan of redemption. Moreover, whereas replacement theology emerged as a response to the challenge of reconciling the legal and prophetic teachings of the Old Testament with the life and witness of Jesus Christ, as recorded in the four Gospels and amplified in Paul's Epistles, the covenantal perspective arose out of a commitment to view the entire biblical narrative as God's revelation to humans. Thus, since the covenantal perspective emphasizes the interrelationship of the Old and New Testaments, it offers specific biblical resources for addressing issues about Israel and the Jewish people.

Dispensationalism

The third tradition that influences Evangelicals' views of Israel is premillennial dispensationalism, generally referred to simply as dispensationalism. Dispensationalists use a literalist hermeneutic that focuses on biblical prophecy to interpret "end-times" developments, especially those surrounding Christ's Second Coming. A fundamental assumption of this approach is that Christ's Second Coming will occur prior to the millennium—Christ's one-thousand-year reign on earth.[7]

The dispensationalist movement emerged in Britain in the mid–nineteenth century with the work of John Darby and expanded significantly in the United States in the late 1900s.[8] Up until the mid–twentieth century, the movement continued to expand but remained largely a Bible-centered perspective. This changed, however, when political developments in the Middle East—especially Israel's emergence as a state in 1948 and its acquisition of Jerusalem in the 1967 Arab-Israeli War (Six-Day War)—were interpreted as the fulfillment of biblical prophecy. In recent decades, dispensationalism has been taught in nondenominational Evangelical and Fundamentalist churches, popularized by pastors like Jerry Falwell, Pat Robertson, and John Hagee, and taught at educational institutions like Moody Bible Institute, Biola University, and Dallas Theological Seminary. Perhaps the most influential promulgators of this approach have been Tim LaHaye and Jerry Jenkins, whose *Left Behind* series of novels on eschatology have sold more than 60 million copies.

Some scholars contend that the strong affinity between Evangelicals and Israel is due to the influence of dispensational theology. For example, in his book *On the Road to Armageddon: How Evangelicals Became Israel's Best Friend,* Timothy Weber attributes Evangelical support for Israel to the pervasive influence of dispensationalism.[9] He rightly questions the appropriateness of addressing complex political issues based on such a hermeneutic. "When [E]vangelicals force all the complicated issues in the Middle East through the tight grid of their prophetic views," he writes, "they can lose the ability to think critically and ethically about what is really going on there."[10] But Weber greatly overestimates the number and influence of dispensationalists. Although this perspective is popular among some Evangelicals, it is much less influential than the first two approaches. *Christianity Today* estimates that about 10 percent of Evangelicals are dispensationalists.[11] Even though they are a small percentage of Evangelicals and their influence on public affairs is comparatively limited, dispensationalists nevertheless receive a disproportionate amount of media coverage.

Malcolm Hedding, the executive director of the International Christian Embassy in Jerusalem (ICEJ), an organization that represents millions of Evangelicals worldwide, says that his support for Israel is based on God's promises to Abraham, not on prophetic schemes and end-times scenarios. Reverend Ted Haggard, the former head of the NAE, also echoes this view when he states: "I am a Christian Zionist. But I am not a Christian Zionist because of eschatology."[12] Stephen Spector, who carried out extensive interviews of leading Evangelicals for his excellent book *Evangelicals and Israel,* similarly found limited support for eschatological justifications for pro-Israel sentiments. He writes, "Not one of the prominent Evangelical leaders I talked with gave hastening the end-times as his reason for championing

Israel."[13] Moreover, in carrying out his research, he expected to find "a theological rigidity, especially about the end-times, that issued in political obduracy. . . . I found instead an unexpected pragmatism, flexibility, and nuance in evangelicals."[14]

It is difficult to overstate the importance of Evangelicals' biblical hermeneutics to their views on international affairs. If the Bible is regarded as a direct guide to foreign policy issues, believers are likely to define global issues like the Middle East peace process in simplistic ways. On the other hand, if the Bible is viewed not as a manual on international relations but as a source of foundational principles that must be applied skillfully and judiciously to intractable interstate problems, then Evangelicals are likely to interpret problems pluralistically and devise multiple strategies for addressing them. The vast majority of Evangelicals identify with the second approach.

But even if Scripture is regarded as a source of principles rather than a catalog of mandates, the role of different theological approaches is unlikely to yield a common approach to foreign affairs. While the prevalence of multiple theological perspectives has fostered a diversity of perspectives on the Bible and Israel, a significant consensus has emerged nonetheless on important biblical principles relevant to Israel and the Jewish people. Evangelicals:

1. Believe that even though Jews rejected the Messiah, they are God's chosen people and remain an important part of his plan of salvation.
2. Believe that they should honor and support the Jewish people.
3. Interpret Scripture as a coherent, unified account of God's redemptive order, with significant continuity between the Old and New Testaments.
4. Are divided on how to regard Israel and the church: some believe that the old covenant has been replaced by the church, the "new" Israel, while others believe that the church and Israel remain distinct and will be unified only at the end of time.
5. Tend to believe that God's promises to the Jewish people remain valid, but interpret these promises, especially those relating to the land of Canaan, differently.
6. Hold different views on the role of prophecy: some interpret biblical prophecy literally, while others view it figuratively.
7. May rely on a literalist prophetic hermeneutic that emphasizes the role of Jews and Israel in the end-times, but most emphasize Israel and the Jewish nation without relating such concern with Christ's Second Coming.

Christian Zionism and the Making and Sustaining of Israel

Zionism is the movement for the return of the Jewish people to their ancient homeland. Although small Jewish communities have always existed in Palestine, the vast majority of Jews lived elsewhere, having been exiled on numerous occasions, first in the sixth century B.C., when Babylonians forced Jews from Israel, and again in A.D. 132–35, when the Roman Empire expelled them from Judea. Zionism is the longing to return to Zion, the Temple Mount in Jerusalem on which the Jewish Temples had been built.

Prior to the middle of the nineteenth century, Zionism was essentially a religious longing, devoid of a specific political program. But as secular ideals from Enlightenment thought spread throughout Europe, Jews were challenged to reconcile their religion with the demands of modernity. This resulted in an increasingly secular, political Zionism.[15] By the end of the nineteenth century, political Zionism had gained an increasing number of prominent British and American supporters. In 1917, in the Balfour Declaration, the British government publicly affirmed its commitment to the creation of a political home for the Jewish people in Palestine, the first official government declaration to support the Zionist political dream.[16] This declaration was especially significant since the British government, which held governing authority over Palestine after World War I, oversaw the migration of a growing number of Jews to Palestine. When Britain ended its mandate in 1948, Israel immediately declared statehood.

Christian Zionism, by contrast, is a belief among Christians that Jews should be able to return to their ancestral homeland. This movement arose in the sixteenth and seventeenth centuries when Protestants developed an interest in the Hebrew Bible and the place of the Jewish people in God's plan of redemption. During the seventeenth century, Puritans in particular began calling for a return of Jews to Israel. Although some Christian Zionists based their views on eschatology, the primary motivation was the belief that God had given the Promised Land to the Jews, his chosen people.[17]

Some of the central tenets of Christian Zionism include that: (1) God's promises to the Jews are irrevocable and eternal, (2) the Promised Land belongs to the Jews, (3) Christians should care for Jews because God does, and (4) Christians should support the restoration of a Jewish homeland. According to Stephen Sizer, a British Anglican priest, one of the foundational claims of Christian Zionism is that "the Jews remain God's chosen people, enjoying a unique relationship, status and eternal purpose within their own land, separate from any promises made to the church."[18]

Christian Zionists contributed significantly to American political support for the creation of the state of Israel. Although Protestant believers began to assert Zionist claims in the seventeenth and eighteenth centuries, the movement did not begin to take shape until the middle of the nineteenth century in Britain and America. For example, Lord Shaftsbury—who worked quietly but effectively in propagating Zionism in Britain with the slogan "A land without a people for a people without a land"—was instrumental in 1938 in establishing a British consulate in Jerusalem, the first diplomatic representation in Palestine.[19] And in America, William Blackstone, a Methodist preacher and author, was successful in coordinating a presidential petition, signed by more than 400 leading American political, civic, business, and religious leaders, calling on President Benjamin Harrison to convene an international conference to facilitate the creation of a Jewish state in Palestine. Walter Russell Mead observes that by the end of the nineteenth century, public support for the creation of a Jewish state was growing. While the American Jewish community was neither large nor powerful, he writes, "The pillars of the American gentile establishment went on record supporting a U.S. diplomatic effort to create a Jewish state in the lands of the Bible."[20]

Christian Zionism has three strands—covenantal, prophetic, and progressive. *Covenantal Zionism*, the most influential strand, is based on the Old Testament promises to the Jewish people. These divine promises include the claim that God will bless those who bless his chosen people, the Jews, and that the Promised Land belongs to them. Ever since Saint Augustine, a large segment of the Christian church has believed that the Jews ceased to be God's chosen people and lost title to the land because they rejected Jesus. The theology that dominated much of Christendom thus emphasized the gospel over Judaism, grace over law. According to this theological approach, the Jews were replaced by the church (the new Israel) as God's agent of redemption. Covenantal Zionism challenges this replacement theology by reaffirming the claims and promises of the Old Testament and, in particular, by reaffirming the Jews as God's chosen people. Its distinctive features include an emphasis on the continuity of the Old and New Testaments, the continued importance of Jews in God's redemptive order, the continuing validity of God's promises to Abraham and his descendants, and the refusal to accept the supersessionist claim that Israel has been replaced by the church. Gary Anderson, an Old Testament scholar who advocates this view, writes: "Christians must also insist that the promises of scripture are indeed inviolable and that Israel's attachment to this land is underwritten by God's providential decree."[21]

Prophetic Zionism, the second strand, is based chiefly on a dispensational hermeneutic. According to this perspective, God's redemption of the world has proceeded through distinct epochs, or dispensations, and will culminate in the "millennium," Christ's unchallenged reign over the earth for one thousand years. This last epoch is preceded, however, by a period of great suffering known as the "tribulation." Dispensationalists also teach that just before the era of tribulation begins, Christ will suddenly remove ("rapture") all believers from the earth, thereby sparing them the cataclysmic suffering that will engulf all nations as the Antichrist carries out his quest for dominion. The influence of this theological approach increased after Israel gained statehood in 1948, and especially after it took control of Jerusalem following the 1967 Six-Day War, since both developments were regarded as fulfillments of biblical prophecy. Although this strand of Zionism remains limited, it is popular among some Evangelicals and many Fundamentalists.[22]

According to Mead, a third strand of Zionism emerged in the nineteenth century from the progressive beliefs of liberal Christians. *Progressive Zionism* was not motivated by the fulfillment of biblical promises and prophecies; rather, it sought to promote a more humane and peaceful world by propagating democratic institutions and political ideals, including the fundamental equality of persons, the priority of education, and human liberty. Because God had blessed the United States politically and economically, Protestant missionaries and public officials were inspired to share American values and institutions in order to spur human progress. This progressive movement extended to a concern for oppressed and persecuted Jews in the Middle East and Europe. Mead writes:

> Some American Protestants believed that God was moving to restore what they considered the degraded and oppressed Jews of the world to the Promised Land, just as God was uplifting and improving the lives of other ignorant and unbelieving people through the advance of Protestant and liberal principles. They wanted the Jews to establish their own state because they believed that this would both shelter the Jews from persecution and, through the redemptive powers of liberty and honest agricultural labor, uplift and improve what they perceived to be squalid morals and deplorable hygiene of contemporary Ottoman and eastern European Jews.[23]

Unlike the other two strands, progressive Zionism, while inspired by Christian ideals, was largely concerned with temporal political and economic issues. But by promoting a better world through tangible human progress, it strengthened religiously motivated Zionism. The different strands of Zionism have reinforced each other, contributing to strong public support for Jews and Israel. Non-Jewish Zionism in the United States has played an important role in encouraging public support for Jews, in facilitating their return to Palestine, and more specifically, in promoting a separate Jewish state. To be sure, Israel would not have been created in 1948 without the persistent and courageous work of Jews themselves. But without international, especially American, support, the Zionist dream would have been delayed or failed altogether.

The American People and Israel

The U.S. government played a critical role in the creation of Israel. When the British government announced that it would terminate its mandate over Palestine, the United States, as the leading democratic power in the world, used its influence to support the partitioning of Palestine—a plan adopted by the UN General Assembly on November 29, 1947. Although Zionist ideas influenced the cause of creating a political homeland for Jews, the most important impetus for a new state was not religion but moral claims to justice. Historian Paul Merkley observes that the United Nations debate over the partition of Palestine was suffused with claims of justice. He writes: "In the long background of this perception that the cause of the Zionists was 'just' was the two thousand years of Jewish Diaspora characterized by many kinds of deprivation and persecution. In the immediate background was the Holocaust. In the foreground was the reality of several hundred thousand homeless European Jews."[24]

In the United States, however, support for partition among government officials was deeply contested, especially in the Departments of State and Defense. Secretary of State George Marshall, who had strongly opposed the partition plan, went so far as to threaten to vote against President Truman in the upcoming presidential election if he supported the recognition of an Israeli state. But after weighing the pros and cons of a new state, the president decided to grant the state official recognition. Thus, within minutes after the Jewish authorities had declared political independence on May 14, 1948, the White House recognized Israel's de facto authority, thereby giving legitimacy to the new nation-state. Shortly before the White House announced its recognition of Israel, Secretary of State Marshall withdrew his threat and agreed to keep his opposition private.

President Truman, a Baptist, believed that the Jewish people and the Holy Land had distinct roles in God's plan. And because of the great suffering that they had endured over two millennia as a dispersed people, he strongly identified with Jews' quest for a homeland, especially in the aftermath of the Holocaust. In these sentiments, Truman reflected the political opinions of a significant segment of the American people. And ever since the U.S. government first pledged its support for Israel in 1948, subsequent administrations have reaffirmed in tangible and intangible ways the close political bond with the Jewish nation. This support does not mean that the U.S. government agrees with all of the Israeli government's actions and policies. Nor does it suggest that Jewish interest groups are especially influential in lobbying the White House and Congress. Rather, it suggests that strong moral and political ties exist between two peoples based, in part, on shared ideals and common values.

Soon after Israel's declaration of independence, a Gallup poll found that American support for Jews was about three times greater than support for Arabs. Subsequent polls have consistently shown that Americans are far more supportive of Israelis than of Palestinians. A Pew Research Center poll in September 1993 found that 45 percent of respondents sympathized with Israelis and 21 percent with Palestinians, while a subsequent poll in May 2006 found that support for Israelis and Palestinians was 48 percent and 13 percent, respectively. Similarly, a Gallup poll in February 2010 found that support for Israel was at near-record levels at 63 percent, while support for Palestinians was only 15 percent.[25]

What explains the strong, continuous bond between Americans and Israelis and between the U.S. government and the government of Israel? The most persuasive answer is that Israelis and Americans share similar values and common security concerns. Middle East observers and religious and political commentators have offered a number of other explanations, however. One explanation that has received significant attention in recent years is the argument that a set of interest groups—the so-called Israel lobby—has dictated U.S. policy toward Israel. Observers have also offered religions explanations—namely, the role of Christian Zionism and the influence of prophetic Christianity.

Shared Values

As noted above, the American people have consistently and overwhelmingly supported Israel. The major reason why Americans identify more with Israelis than with Palestinians is a deep bond between Israelis and Americans rooted in shared religious values, common humanitarian and political aspirations, and similar strategic interests. To begin with, the roots of the friendship can be found in the shared elements of the Judeo-Christian religion. Christianity is rooted in the Jewish faith. The Hebrew Bible is viewed as an essential element of God's revelation of humankind. In *On Two Wings*, Michael Novak argues that America's founding is rooted in two major sources—Enlightenment principles that emphasize natural law, reason, and individual rights, and faith in the God of Israel.[26] Novak claims that while scholars and pundits typically emphasize the role of John Locke and individual rights in the establishment of the United States, they underestimate the role of religion. According to Novak, Jewish metaphysics played a crucial role in the founding of the United States. In particular, biblical notions of justice, righteousness, law, the sanctity of persons, the priority of covenants, the role of mercy and compassion, and the need to care for the weak and poor influenced the thought of the Founding Fathers. In view of the important role of the Judeo-Christian tradition in American society, it is not surprising that Americans continue to identify with the faith, geography, and people of the Hebrew Bible.

A second element of the shared-values thesis is the common political aspirations of the two countries. Israel is a democratic state with a strong constitutional tradition. The legitimacy of the Israeli government is rooted in consent. The fact that Israel has regular elections and follows constitutional traditions in protecting human rights is especially significant because of Israel's nondemocratic neighboring states. Not surprisingly, the American people sympathize with Israel because it shares democratic institutions and constitutional traditions that contribute to limited government and the protection of human rights.

Finally, America identifies with Israel because the two countries share numerous security concerns. From its inception, the United States has provided military aid to Israel to ensure its security from the threats of its Arab neighbors. This assistance was increased significantly in 1979 after Egypt and Israel restored peaceful relations as a result of the Camp David Accords. Shared strategic interests were further reinforced after Muslim terrorists carried out the deadly attacks on New York City's World Trade Center and the Pentagon on September 11, 2001. The continuing threat of terrorism from radical Islamists has further intensified cooperation between U.S. intelligence organizations and Israeli security agencies. Additionally, since the United States and Israel continue to oppose Iran's quest for nuclear arms, this shared strategic concern has also strengthened military cooperation.

In short, overwhelming American support for Israel derives from shared religious values, democratic traditions, and strategic interests. In her book *The Mighty & The Almighty*, former Secretary of State Madeleine Albright echoes this conclusion, claiming that the most persuasive account of why the United States consistently supports Israel is that the United States and Israel share a common commitment to human rights and democracy. She writes: "Americans from across the ideological spectrum support Israel because we see in that society qualities with which we identify and that we admire."[27]

The Lobby

An alternative explanation for the strong U.S. governmental support of Israelis is offered by John Mearsheimer and Stephen Walt in their controversial book *The Israel Lobby and U.S. Foreign Policy*. Mearsheimer and Walt claim that U.S. foreign policy toward Israel is dictated by a broad coalition of pro-Israel groups—the so-called Israel lobby—that undermines the United States' fundamental interests in the Middle East. Like all interest groups, the Israel lobby seeks to advance the particular interests of its members. But, according to Mearsheimer and Walt, whereas lobbies generally compete with other groups to advance desired goals, the Israel lobby, because of its extraordinary effectiveness and broad impact, not only stifles debate but also distorts American foreign policy priorities.

The Mearsheimer-Walt book has been critiqued widely for its questionable scholarship, unclear conceptualization of key terms, and inadequate empirical data.[28] For our purposes, however, its major shortcoming is its simplistic and reductionistic single-factor analysis. It claims that a single condition—lobbying by one coalition—explains America's foreign policy toward Israel. Dennis Ross, the chief negotiator for the Middle East under Presidents George H. W. Bush and Bill Clinton, challenges this simplistic assertion. He writes: "Never in the time that I led the American negotiations on the Middle East peace process did we take a step because 'the lobby' wanted us to. Nor did we shy away from one because 'the lobby' opposed it." According to Ross, "Republican and Democratic presidents alike have consistently believed in a special relationship with Israel because values matter in foreign policy."[29] Jeffrey Goldberg similarly calls into question the single-factor thesis: "Forty years of polling has consistently shown that Americans support Israel in its conflict with the Arabs. Why? There are a multitude of plausible reasons. Both Israel and America were founded by refugees from European religious intolerance; both are rooted in a common religious tradition; Israel is a lively democracy in a part of the world that lacks democracy; Israelis seem self-reliant in the manner of American pioneers; and Israel's enemies, in many cases, seem to be America's enemies as well."[30] Given the pluralistic nature of American society, government decision making will inevitably reflect the conflicting claims of diverse groups and organizations. The claim that a single lobby dictates policy is simply unpersuasive.

Christian Zionists

A third explanation for the strong bond between Israel and the United States is the influence of Christian Zionism. Christian Zionists believe that the restoration of a Jewish homeland in the Holy Land is imperative for religious as well as prudential reasons. Religiously, they believe that the return to Judea is consistent with God's law. In addition, they believe that the restoration of a homeland is consistent with humanitarian norms, especially considering the suffering Jews have endured since they were expelled from Palestine, culminating in the Holocaust. Christian Zionists justify their strong support of Israel with several arguments, including the following: (1) supporting Israel is consistent with the divine will; (2) supporting Israel's security is consistent with the rule of law and the well-being of the nation of Israel; and (3) American society is rooted in Judeo-Christian values.

Although Christian Zionists tend to strongly support Israel and its policies, their support is rooted in religion. While acknowledging that Jews are God's chosen people with a divine title to the land of Canaan, Christian Zionists believe that the blessing and priority owed to the Jews do not automatically translate into support of the Israeli state. Christians are called to honor biblical covenants, but this does not mean that they are bound to support the Israeli government. Rather, they must honor and support the Jewish people. For example, Malcolm Hedding, the executive director of the International Christian Embassy in Jerusalem (ICEJ), stresses that the ICEJ's mission is solely religious in nature. "We are Biblical Zionists, not political Zionists," he declares.[31]

Despite the claim that its concerns are primarily spiritual, the ICEJ has contributed significantly to promoting close ties between Christians and Jews and in mobilizing public opinion on Israeli concerns.[32] Other religiously motivated organizations—such as Christian Friends of Israel (CFI), Christian Friends of Israeli Communities (CFIC), Olive Tree Ministries, Bridges for Peace, and Voices United for Israel—provide aid to Jews as well as support for Israel. Some of these organizations, like ICEJ and CFI,[33] focus chiefly on spiritual concerns, while others, like the International Fellowship of Christians and Jews (IFCJ)[34] and Ya Hovel,[35] emphasize financial and humanitarian aid. Finally, Christian organizations like Christians United for Israel (CUFI) stress political solidarity with Israel. The CUFI regularly sponsors "Standing with Israel" meetings throughout the United States to inform Christian laypersons and to encourage them to be politically active in Israel's cause. The CUFI also sponsors an annual conference in Washington, D.C., that brings together thousands of believers to hear leading religious and political leaders discuss Israel's security and welfare.

Some of the most influential Christian Zionists are Evangelical pastors. The late Reverend Jerry Falwell, a Baptist pastor and founder of the Moral Majority and Liberty University, used his position as a leading religious figure to influence public opinion in support of Israel. Similarly, Pat Robertson, head of the Christian Broadcasting Network and its "700 Club" television program, has used his position to mobilize support for Israel and for pro-Israel U.S. policies. Undoubtedly the most active Evangelical leader advancing the security and material interests of Israel is Reverend John Hagee, whose televised ministry reaches millions of viewers both in the United States and abroad. It is estimated that Hagee's ministry has channeled more than $60 million to Israel since 2006.

Like the lobby hypothesis, the view that Americans support Israel because of Zionist beliefs greatly oversimplifies reality and exaggerates the role of religion in foreign affairs.[36] To begin, Christian Zionists, like Evangelicals themselves, are not a cohesive movement but a disparate group of believers who share a commitment to historic Protestant beliefs, but interpret and apply them in a varied and multifaceted manner. Second, Christian Zionists do not maintain effective political institutions to effectively lobby Congress and the White House on an ongoing basis. From time to time, Christian Zionist groups and churches foster solidarity with Israel by holding conferences and meetings, such as Reverend Hagee's annual Christians United for Israel Summit in Washington, D.C., or by promoting short-term travel to the Holy Land. But these sporadic initiatives are not easily translated into effective political action on behalf of a "greater Israel." Third, Americans established a strong bond with Israel almost immediately following the creation of Israel in 1948, long before Evangelicals (including Christian Zionists) became politically active. Since Evangelicals did not take up international affairs advocacy until the end of the Cold War, their role in fostering close U.S.–Israeli ties is, at best, limited. Finally, the level of support for Israel by Christian Zionists is not significantly different from that of the American public. This high level of support by the American people for Israel and the Jewish people is only slightly lower than the support from religious Zionists.

Prophetic Christianity

A fourth, less persuasive explanation for American support of Israel is the dispensationalist thesis. As noted earlier, conventional wisdom holds that Evangelical support is rooted in biblical prophecy and more particularly a dispensationalist perspective, popularized by the widely read *Left Behind* series of novels about the end-times. To the secular media, such prophetic literature is further confirmation of Evangelicals' lack of a sophisticated understanding of the world and misuse of religion for political ends.

The noted author Joan Didion, for instance, in an article ostensibly reviewing Tim LaHaye and Jerry Jenkins's *Armageddon: The Cosmic Battle of the Ages*, wrote about the Bush administration as though it were led by a cabal of dispensationalists eager to impose a fundamentalist worldview on American society. The article—"Mr. Bush & the Divine"—implied that the president, influenced by a simplistic faith, made decisions based on fundamentalist religious grounds. Didion wrote:

> The perfect beauty of the fundamentalist story as applied to the public arena is that it transfers responsibility for any chosen mission from the believer in that mission to the nonbeliever..., [it] transforms even the most calculated political play into a reward for faith, [and] conveniently serves as the last word on any error that might surface.

Didion continued:

> There are obvious problems, made manifest over the past two years, in letting this kind of personality loose on the fragile web of unseen alliances and unspoken enmities that constitutes any powerful nation's map of the world. The fundamentalist approach to information, whether that approach is innate or learned, does not encourage nuanced judgments.[37]

Karen Armstrong, noted author of numerous books on Middle East religions, similarly attributed President Bush's decision making to his alleged fundamentalist Christian perspective. Although she provided no evidence to support her argument, she nevertheless linked Bush with the dispensational worldview, noting that whatever his religious beliefs, "the ideology of the Christian right is both familiar and congenial to him." She then wrote:

> This strange amalgam of ideas can perhaps throw light on the behavior of a president, who, it is said, believes that God chose him to lead the world to Rapture.... It explains his unconditional and uncritical support for Israel, his willingness to use "Jewish End-time warriors" to fulfill a vision of his own—arguably against Israel's best interests—and to see Syria and Iran ... as entirely responsible for the unfolding tragedy.[38]

Ironically, although Didion and Armstrong implied that President Bush was guided by Christian fundamentalist beliefs that impede nuanced political judgments, they themselves succumbed to a reductionist, simplistic, and untenable hypothesis—namely, that the president, as an Evangelical believer, was influenced by dispensationalist claims. A more careful investigation would have revealed what Stephen Spector discovered in his study of this topic: that Evangelical faith is personal and individualistic, and that "any examination of their beliefs requires a nuanced understanding of the way that their faith prescribes and accords with policy." Spector adds: "That applies to Bush as well, and to the influence that Christian Zionists, and his own convictions, had on his Middle East policy."[39]

Despite the popularity of prophetic literature, especially Jerry Jenkins's and Tim LaHaye's prophetic novels, the influence of dispensationalism has been greatly exaggerated. As I noted previously, only a small portion of all Evangelicals are dispensationalists. Moreover, while many Evangelicals take biblical prophecy seriously, their faith is not focused on prophetic concerns. Indeed, their primary religious concern is not with end-times scenarios, but with the present challenges of faithfully serving Christ in all aspects of life. While Evangelicals consider preparation for Christ's Second Coming important, most do not dwell on such eschatological events as the nature and timing of the last judgment or events preceding Christ's return. To be sure, some Evangelical leaders, like Reverend John Hagee, founder of Christians United for Israel, the largest Evangelical pro-Israel interest group, and pastor of the Cornerstone Church in San Antonio, Texas, emphasize biblical prophecy and the end-times. But most Evangelical pastors do not dwell on such issues.

Some survey data suggest that prophetic perspectives influence not just Christians but the general public as well. A 2003 public opinion poll, for example, found that while 63 percent of Evangelicals believed that Israel fulfilled biblical prophecy, at least 36 percent of all those surveyed agreed.[40]

Similarly, a subsequent (2006) Pew poll found that 69 percent of Evangelicals believed that God gave the Jews the land of Israel and that 42 percent of all those surveyed shared this belief.[41] What is surprising about these findings is that eschatology and divine promises are common beliefs among not only Evangelicals but also the general public.

In sum, the major reason for Americans' continued support of Israel is their identification with Israel's moral values, religious institutions, constitutional traditions, democratic practices, and humanitarian norms. There can be little doubt that pro-Israel lobbying influences U.S. foreign policy toward Israel. Moreover, Christian Zionism and Prophetic Christianity clearly play an important role in the U.S. government's strong commitment to Israel. But interest group politics and religion alone do not fully explain American support. The only adequate account is one that emphasizes the close moral bond that is rooted in shared values and institutions.

Evangelical Approaches to Israel

Because of the plurality of biblical interpretations and theological approaches prevalent among Evangelicals, developing consensus on Middle East policies is difficult, if not impossible. Thus, while some believers may use the Bible to justify support for Israel, most will refrain from offering specific advice on domestic Israeli policies or U.S. actions toward Israel and the Middle East peace process.

This reticence is evident in the few general pronouncements that Evangelical churches have offered over the years on the Middle East peace process. The NAE, for example, has issued countless resolutions on domestic and international affairs, but only two on the matter of Middle East peace, one in 1970 and the other in 1978. The 1970 declaration acknowledges that both Israelis and Arabs have a right to exist as sovereign nations, expresses concern for the care and rehabilitation of Jewish and Arab refugees, and calls on NAE-affiliated churches to pray for peace in the Middle East. The 1978 resolution, issued in anticipation of Middle East peace negotiations, similarly calls on churches to pray for peace and to support governmental action to promote the territorial integrity and political independence of states, support for refugees, and border modification that ensures peace and security. The NAE resolution also declares: "We affirm that the gifts and calling of God are irrevocable, that God has not rejected His people Israel nor forsaken the Arabs, but will yet fulfill His promise." The failure of the NAE to address more fully the challenges of Middle East peace are no doubt due to different perceptions of the problem and, more significantly, to a lack of agreement about the theological significance of Israel and the Jewish people.

The Southern Baptist Convention (SBC) has similarly refrained from issuing public policy declarations on the Middle East. Although SBC churches tend to be strongly supportive of the Jewish people and of the Israeli state, the SBC has been reluctant to issue denominational declarations on the politics of the Middle East. Perhaps its most significant statement on Israel was a two-page resolution adopted at the convention's 2002 annual meeting. That resolution is significant because it makes both theological and political affirmations and offers several general comments on the promotion of peace between Israel and its neighboring states. It calls on Christians to pray for the peace of Israel, acknowledges God's special purposes and providential care for the Jewish people, affirms the historic connection between the Jewish people and the land of Israel, and asserts Israel's right to exist as a sovereign state. The resolution also condemns terrorism, denounces revenge as a political strategy, affirms that Israel must be held accountable for its treatment of strangers and aliens, calls on Palestinians to reform their government and to repudiate terrorism, and urges the United States and other nations to assist in helping to secure peace in the region. In 2008, the SBC adopted another resolution to celebrate the sixtieth anniversary of the creation of Israel. After commemorating Israel's six decades of statehood, the brief statement calls on world leaders to renounce the growing threat of anti-Semitism and pledges prayer for Israel, "the birthplace of our Lord and a bastion of democracy in the Middle East."

The absence of clear biblical guidance on contemporary political affairs, however, has not impeded some Evangelical leaders and pastors from offering policy pronouncements or making public declarations about U.S. foreign policy toward Israel. Some leaders, for example, believe that God has given the Jewish people the entire Holy Land, and they strongly oppose Israeli withdrawal from the Occupied Territories. Thus, some Evangelical leaders believed that the Israeli government's withdrawal from Gaza in 2008 was contrary to God's will. Televangelist Pat Robertson went so far as to ascribe the paralyzing stroke of Israeli Prime Minister Ariel Sharon as a consequence of his decision to return Gaza to the Palestinian Authority.

Since the 1990s, a small but growing number of Evangelicals have tried a different approach. For them, the only way to reconcile the competing and conflicting land claims of Jews and Palestinians is through political accommodation based on justice. Furthermore, they claim that peace can only be advanced in the Holy Land when the legitimate interests of both peoples are affirmed and the government of Israel pursues just, nondiscriminatory policies toward Palestinians. Since most Evangelicals begin with a presumption favoring Israel and the Jewish people, these centrist and progressive Evangelicals counter the traditional claims of Christian Zionists by highlighting the just claims of Palestinians, especially Palestinian Christians. Theologically, they affirm the validity of God's covenants with the Jewish people, but also stress, contrary to Christian Zionists, that these covenants, while perpetual and irrevocable, are conditional on faithfulness to God.

Mark Harlan, a former professor at the Jordan Evangelical Theological Seminary in Amman, captures this dual commitment to covenant and faithfulness:

> The promise of land, seed, and blessing to Abraham's descendants is an irrevocable covenant from God. The experience of these blessings, however, was conditioned by the faithful obedience of each generation of Israel. The purpose of the Mosaic covenant (plainly conditional) was to make clear to Israel the faith-obedience necessary to participate in the blessings of the promises given to Abraham.[42]

Professor Gary Burge of Wheaton College similarly stresses the conditionality of God's covenant with Abraham's descendants, claiming that the ultimate owner of the land is God himself. He writes:

> [T]he nation of Israel is promised possession of the land as an everlasting gift, but this promise is conditional; it depends on Israel's fidelity to the covenant and its stipulations. The land has a relationship with God, too. This land is the land where he lives, and by association with him, it is holy. Thus Israel may possess this promise of residence in the land and still be expelled from it through unfaithfulness.[43]

In 1986, a number of scholars and church leaders established Evangelicals for Middle East Understanding (EMEU) in order to advance non-Zionist perspectives on the Middle East. A major aim of EMEU has been to underscore the needs and concerns of Arab Christians and to promote interaction between Christians living in America and those living in the Middle East. Thus, EMEU has sponsored numerous consultations and conferences and organized Middle East tours to promote a better understanding of non-Israeli perspectives on the Middle East peace process. There can be little doubt that a long-term resolution of the quest for political self-determination for Jews and Palestinians can only be reconciled through confidence-building measures and mutual accommodations that result in two states in the Holy Land. Given the overwhelming support of Evangelicals for Israel, EMEU performs an important function in highlighting the legitimate political claims of

Palestinians and the need for authorities to apply the rule of law equitably to Jews and gentiles, Israelis and non-Israelis.

To a significant degree, EMEU's perspective is similar to that of mainline Protestant churches. When Israel became independent in 1948, mainline Protestant churches were generally sympathetic to the new state. But within a short span of time, they began to shift their allegiance away from Israel and toward the Palestinians. By the time of the Six-Day War in 1967, mainline Protestants had become increasingly critical of Israel, while Evangelicals had become strongly aligned with Israel, viewing the Israeli army's takeover of Jerusalem as a watershed event. This alignment has continued almost unchanged for the past forty years. If anything, mainline denominations like the Presbyterian, Methodist, and Lutheran (the Evangelical Lutheran Church in American branch) churches have become even more anti-Zionist, while Evangelical support for Israel has increased even further.

The emergence of more centrist perspectives on the Middle East among Evangelicals is also evident in two public letters sent by Evangelical leaders to President George W. Bush. The first, sent in July 2002 and signed by more than sixty leaders, was written to counter the widespread perception that Evangelicals opposed a Palestinian state. After noting that "the American evangelical community is not a monolithic bloc in full and firm support of present Israeli policy," the letter declared that "significant numbers of American Evangelicals reject the way some have distorted biblical passages as their rationale for uncritical support for every policy and action of the Israeli government." The letter urged the president to provide evenhanded leadership that supports the legitimate interests of both Israelis and Palestinians. However, Richard Land, the head of SBC's Ethics and Religious Liberty Commission (essentially the SBC's government affairs office), expressed a number of concerns with the letter. He criticized the document for failing to condemn the anti-Semitism propagated by the Palestinian Authority. More significantly, Land suggested that the letter implied "an assumption of moral equivalence between Israel and the Palestinian Authority, and that is dangerous nonsense."[44]

The second letter, sent in July 2007 and signed by thirty-four Evangelical leaders, highlighted Evangelical support for a two-state solution. The letter declares:

> We...write to correct a serious misperception among some people including some U.S. policymakers that all American evangelicals are opposed to a two-state solution and creation of a new Palestinian state

that includes the vast majority of the West Bank. Nothing could be further from the truth. We, who sign this letter, represent large numbers of evangelicals throughout the U.S. who support justice for both Israelis and Palestinians. We hope this support will embolden you and your administration to proceed confidently and forthrightly in negotiations with both sides in the region.

Although Evangelicals have undertaken a number of initiatives to encourage a balanced and just U.S. policy toward the Arab-Israeli conflict, a large majority of Evangelicals remain strongly committed to Israel. And so long as Palestinians remain divided over the legitimacy of Israel and radical elements resort to terrorism, Evangelical support for Israel is unlikely to diminish.

Finally, even though religious beliefs play an important role in how Evangelicals think about Israel and the Jewish nation, it is important to emphasize that nonreligious factors are also important. Interestingly, even prophetic Zionists and ardent dispensationalists are moving beyond religious claims. For instance, prophetic Zionist Pat Robertson claims that "Evangelicals support Israel because it is a democratic state where individual freedom is honored and the rule of law is enforced."[45] Reverend John Hagee also justifies support of Israel on more than religious grounds. Indeed, he established CUFI because he perceived growing threats to Israel from Iran and its two chief proxies, Hezbollah in Lebanon and Hamas in Gaza and the West Bank. According to the CUFI website, "Israel is in peril. The President of Iran has threatened to wipe Israel off the map and he's rapidly acquiring the nuclear technology with which to make good on this threat. In the meantime, Iran's proxies in Hezbollah and Hamas are arming themselves at an alarming rate, and Hamas has been firing missiles into Southern Israel."

Reverend Ted Haggard, the former head of the NAE, similarly claimed that his support for Israel was based not on end-times beliefs but on geopolitical realities, especially the fact that Israel was a democratic state and a U.S. ally.[46] For Haggard, biblical Israel includes not only the people and territory of the current state but also all other Jews throughout the world. "Israel is Israel even if the state of Israel did not exist," declared Haggard.[47] He strongly supports the Jewish people and their state because he believes that Scripture calls on Christians to support God's chosen people. But the justification for such support is rooted in God's covenants, not in the prophetic call to restore Jews to the Promised Land prior to Christ's Second Coming.

A 2002 public opinion poll found that Evangelicals identified with Israel for a variety of reasons, reinforcing Robertson's, Hagee's, and

Haggard's multidimensional accounts. According to the survey, 35 percent of Evangelicals supported Israel for theological reasons, 24 percent because it was a democracy, and 19 percent because it was a U.S. ally in combating terrorism.[48]

In conclusion, Evangelicals' strong support of Israel is one of their most distinctive foreign policy views. Although conventional wisdom claims that Evangelicals support Israel because of dispensational theological claims, this is a canard. In addition, while biblical prophecy influences the views of many believers, it is not the only or even the primary source of Evangelical support for Israel. To be sure, religion plays a critical role in Evangelicals' support of Israel, but other factors—such as political ideals, humanitarian values, and security considerations—also contribute to this close bond.

7 THE RISE OF EVANGELICAL FOREIGN POLICY ADVOCACY

When the "new" Evangelicals (sometimes called neo-Evangelicals) emerged in the 1940s to challenge the separatism of the Fundamentalists, leaders like Carl F. H. Henry and Harold Ockenga began calling not only for greater cultural engagement but also for a more holistic expression of redemption—one that focused not only on the spiritual task of saving souls but also on the reformation of cultural values and social structures. Nonetheless, for much of the 1950s and 1960s, Evangelicals were reluctant to engage in collective political action.

The two issues that first galvanized Evangelical action were prayer in public schools and abortion. And only in the late 1980s, when international religious freedom emerged as a major political concern, did Evangelicals begin to address foreign affairs in a serious way.

This is not to suggest, however, that Evangelicals had been completely inward-facing. Indeed, from the early 1950s—especially after the Communist Party's takeover of China and the expulsion of Christian missionaries—Evangelicals had been ardent anti-communists. Because they believed that communism was antithetical to the Christian faith, they staunchly supported American containment doctrine. But despite their anti-communist crusades, the NAE—unlike the National Council of Churches—did not make foreign policy advocacy a priority. This all changed in the 1980s, as Evangelicals became better informed about the world, developed greater sophistication about political decision making, and gained a deeper appreciation for the important moral role of American foreign policy.

To a significant degree, the international political advocacy of Evangelicals has been shaped by their fundamental religious beliefs and ethical concerns. Because of their core moral values—such as the sanctity of human life, the priority of families and the well-being of children, religious liberty, and poverty reduction—they have challenged the U.S. government to be more concerned with such issues as human trafficking, religious persecution, and humanitarian relief. Some observers, however, attribute the rise of Evangelical foreign policy advocacy not to a concern with issues per se but, rather, to a belief in American exceptionalism. Political scientist James Skillen, for example, argues that the motivation for Evangelical political advocacy arises not from theological or biblical beliefs, but from a specific civil religion—one rooted in Puritanism that assumes that America is "a chosen nation, a city set on a hill to be a light to the world."[1] In his view, Evangelicals act to renew this civil religion rather than to pursue global public goods such as peace and international justice.

There can be little doubt that American exceptionalism has significantly influenced the history of America's foreign relations, especially under the Wilsonian banner of propagating human rights and democratic governance. But what does American exceptionalism mean? What are its foreign policy implications? And more specifically, what does this notion imply for Evangelicals? To begin with, a theologically grounded belief in American exceptionalism does not imply support for imperialism and self-righteousness or a belief in national superiority. Rather, this notion suggests that America bears a responsibility to countries that are unable to attain similar levels of economic and political prosperity. Reverend Richard Land, the head of the Ethics and Religious Liberty Commission of the Southern Baptist Convention (SBC), argues that the idea of American exceptionalism represents an obligation to serve others. He states: "Most Evangelicals...do not believe that America has a special claim on God, but they do believe that God has a special claim on them, that to whom much has been given much is required, and that we have an obligation and a responsibility to be the friend of freedom and to share freedom, to speak out in defense of freedom, and to help foster freedom."[2]

The issue that first began to capture Evangelical interest in the late 1980s was the problem of religious persecution, especially in the Soviet Union and other communist countries. But as the Cold War came to an end, the Evangelical global agenda expanded to such issues as international religious freedom, human trafficking, debt relief for low-income countries, and health care, especially the HIV/AIDS pandemic in Africa. Although each of these initiatives entailed cooperation with other political groups, policy reform would have been unlikely without the widespread grassroots support of Evangelicals. Moreover, given their opposition to ecumenism, Evangelicals demonstrated a surprising willingness to cooperate with Jews, secular public policy advocates, religious minorities, and others to advance human rights— collaboration that Allen Hertzke terms an "unlikely alliance."[3]

As noted earlier, Evangelicalism has been, and remains, a decentralized, grassroots movement. As a result, Evangelicals find it difficult to assess global problems from an informed, moral perspective and nearly impossible to devise a cohesive, coherent public policy strategy. Unlike the Roman Catholic Church, which has a centralized authority that speaks authoritatively, Evangelicals have an underdeveloped political theology and a weak organizational structure. On the other hand, Evangelicals' decentralized, grassroots character allows for greater flexibility and adaptability at the local level. As a result, when Evangelicals mobilize, their "entrepreneurial activism" can lead to significant political influence.

For example, in the early 1990s, the World Evangelical Fellowship, a leading international alliance of Evangelical denominations, began spearheading the cause of religious liberty by designating a day of prayer to raise awareness of religious persecution. Similarly, when Evangelical entrepreneurs like James Dobson, Pat Robertson, Charles Colson, Franklin Graham, and others have taken up issues like religious persecution, global hunger, or the mass killings in southern Sudan through their extensive constituent mailings, television programs, and radio broadcasts, they have been able to influence public opinion and to mobilize many believers to undertake some type of political action. Thus, to the extent that Evangelicals have influenced U.S. foreign policy, they have done so by mobilizing their members to action—providing, as Paul Marshall has noted, the "foot-soldiers" for moral reform.[4] Additionally, because Evangelicals have continued to emphasize foreign missionary activities, they have been able to develop and maintain extensive ties with believers in the global South—relationships that provide not only greater understanding of global human rights concerns but also contacts that advance such interests. Indeed, as Hertzke has noted, "the community most likely to identify with the New Christendom of the global [S]outh, with the suffering church, is the very one with social networks and motivation capable of mobilizing pressure on the political system."[5]

Some observers argue that Evangelicals' dominant foreign policy concern remains the welfare and security of Israel. But as I argued in the previous chapter, there is no widespread consensus on the religious or political justifications for such support. This lack of agreement is evident in the fact that the NAE has adopted only two short resolutions on the Middle East in its sixty-five-year history. The first one—a short statement issued in 1970, shortly after the Six-Day War—is a tepid declaration affirming "the rights of all nations in the Middle East, both Israeli and Arab, to exist as sovereign nations." The second declaration, issued in 1978, similarly calls for the self-determination for the Jewish and Palestinian peoples and for peaceful relations between them. To be sure, Evangelicals—like most North Americans—strongly support Israel. But this support is due to a number of factors, including shared Judeo-Christian values, the belief that Jews have a special role in salvation history, and Israel's democratic government. Israel, in short, does not provide a case study to illuminate Evangelical's rising influence in foreign policy advocacy. We must turn to other global issues.

International Religious Freedom

The right to believe and practice one's religion is among the most fundamental human rights. Although the NAE had repeatedly condemned communist ideology for its atheism and repression, it first championed the broader issue of religious freedom in a 1972 resolution. Three years later, the NAE again took up the cause of religious persecution, adopting a resolution that called on believers to pray for and financially support those suffering from religious oppression. In the 1980s, Evangelical groups, led by the NAE, began lobbying the U.S. government to grant asylum to Pentecostals and other religious minorities facing persecution and discrimination in the Soviet Union. As a result of American prodding, the Soviet government allowed a growing number of religious minorities to emigrate. Many who were Christian gained admission into the United States, where Evangelical churches and support groups played an indispensable role in facilitating their resettlement.[6]

Yet Evangelicals remained largely unaware of and unconcerned about the plight of persecuted Christians outside the Soviet Union. Mainline Protestant denominations were similarly oblivious, focusing instead on structural issues like global inequality, arms control, international peace, and racial justice. Secular human rights organizations like Amnesty International and Human Rights Watch did not even monitor religious persecution. Thus, even though some 200 million Christians lived in countries where they faced significant religious persecution, and another 400 million believers faced nontrivial restrictions on their religious freedom, the cause of religious liberty remained a neglected problem.

That began to change in the mid-1990s, when Michael Horowitz, a Jewish human rights lawyer, began urging Evangelical leaders to stop neglecting the suffering of their fellow believers. [7] In 1996, Horowitz and Nina Shea, director of religious freedom at Freedom House, a nongovernmental organization concerned with promoting political and civil liberties, hosted a conference for Evangelical leaders and other policy activists to highlight the global persecution of Christians. Later that year the NAE adopted a declaration—"A Statement of Conscience Concerning Worldwide Religious Persecution"— to highlight religious discrimination and oppression around the world.[8] The statement boldly declares: "Religious Liberty is not a privilege to be granted or denied by an all powerful State, but [is] a God-given human right. Indeed, religious liberty is the bedrock principle that animates our republic and defines us as a people." While acknowledging that the U.S. government could not "end all evil throughout the world," NAE leaders argued that the United States could nonetheless adopt policies to limit religious persecution. Accordingly, the statement called on the U.S. government to increase monitoring of and accountability for religious persecution. A third development that helped to galvanize Evangelical concern about religious persecution was the publication of Paul Marshall's *Their Blood Cries Out.*[9] By graphically describing the suffering of Christians in Islamic countries (like Iran, Pakistan, Saudi Arabia, and Sudan), communist regimes (like China and North Korea), and other countries, the book awakened the consciences of many Evangelicals. As Marshall observed, American religious and secular elites were completely apathetic about the ongoing persecution of Christians, and even after Evangelicals turned a spotlight on religious persecution, most mainline Protestant Churches (the Episcopal Church being an exception) and the National Council of Churches remained on the sidelines.

In 1997, a bill (sponsored by Rep. Frank Wolf and Sen. Arlen Specter) on religious persecution was introduced and overwhelmingly passed by the U.S. House of Representatives. But because this measure called for economic sanctions against regimes abusing the right of religious freedom, it was strongly opposed by the business community. A less demanding, more flexible bill (sponsored by Sen. Don Nickels and Sen. Joseph Lieberman) was then introduced in the Senate. On October 9, 1998, the Senate overwhelmingly approved this measure. Since there was no time left to resolve differences in the two bills, Representative Wolf, an Evangelical, signaled his support for the more moderate Nickels-Lieberman bill, and the following day the House approved it by acclamation. Although Clinton administration officials had opposed both measures, President Clinton signed the International Religious Freedom Act (IRFA) into law later in the month.[10]

The new law called for the establishment of two entities. First, the Office of International Religious Freedom (IRF) was created within the Department of State. The office, headed by an ambassador-at-large, was charged with promoting religious liberty worldwide by, among other things: (a) advising the Secretary of State on how best to advance this goal; (b) submitting to Congress an annual report on the status of religious freedom in all countries; (c) designating any country that commits "systematic, ongoing and egregious violations of religions freedom" as a "Country of Particular Concern" (CPC); (d) recommending that countries classified as CPC be subject to potential sanctions;[11] and (e) promoting religious freedom training for new diplomats. The IRFA also established an independent, bipartisan U.S. Commission on International Religious Freedom (USCIRF). Although the nine-member commission is an official organization staffed by full-time government employees, it is not a governmental body. Rather, it is an independent advisory agency that issues an annual report to the president, secretary of state, and Congress on the countries and issues that pose the greatest threat to religious freedom. Moreover, while the commission does not devise policies, it offers recommendations on how best to advance religious liberty.

Despite the important institutional developments initiated by the IRFA, the Department of State has made little progress in advancing international religious freedom.[12] Thomas Farr, the first director of the IRF Office, argues persuasively that religious freedom concerns have not been made a key component of U.S. foreign policy.[13] This is due partly to the secular worldview that predominates among American cultural elites, including the U.S. Foreign Service. Although government officials are undoubtedly concerned with egregious religious persecution, their limited understanding of religion tends to inhibit policy initiatives that advance religious freedom.

Second, promoting religious liberty abroad is difficult since the pursuit of this goal often conflicts with other U.S. foreign policy interests. For example, the United States is eager to foster cooperative economic and political ties with China while also seeking to advance religious freedom in that land. At times, these two interests have come in conflict, necessitating trade-offs. Similarly, the U.S. government has been deeply concerned with North Korea's nuclear proliferation while also seeking to encourage greater respect for human rights and religious freedom. Reconciling these two goals has not been easy.

Third, ties between the Department of State's IRF Office and the commission have at times been strained, thereby impeding a coherent foreign policy approach to international religious freedom. Whereas the IRF Office has sought to advance religious freedom through quiet diplomacy, the USCIRF has highlighted countries that pursue religious discrimination.[14]

While it is clear that much still needs to be done to make the pursuit of religious freedom a more salient dimension of U.S. foreign policy, we ought not underestimate the impact of IRFA. As Laura Bryant Hanford, a former congressional staffer who played a key role in the development of the law, has noted, the adoption of IRFA has brought about a "sea-change" in the U.S. government's approach to religious freedom. Her assessment ten years after the passage of the law is that "IRFA's mechanism and structure will continue to ensure the issue is addressed at a level unthinkable a decade ago, and countless religious believers today enjoy a greater measure of freedom as a result."[15]

Of course, the U.S. government is not the only entity working to advance religious freedom in the world. Religious networks and NGOs also continue to play an important role. Domestically, they promote religious liberty by disseminating information about religious persecution and by lobbying decision makers. For example, Evangelicals, led by the World Evangelical Alliance, continue to sponsor an International Day of Prayer for the Persecuted Church (IDOP). Since its beginning in 1996, the annual IDOP has become the largest worldwide prayer day of its kind, involving more than 100,000 U.S. churches. Internationally, religious actors also help advance the cause of religious freedom by providing information on religious persecution. Since missionaries and faith-based NGOs generally maintain close contact with indigenous people, they are often the best informed about human rights abuses, offering excellent data sources for embassy reports on religious persecution.

Notwithstanding these initiatives, anti-Christian persecution continues to thrive, especially in Muslim countries. For example, after the United States intervened in Iraq and toppled the regime of Saddam Hussein, persecution of Christians increased dramatically. Whereas the Christian population was estimated to be 1.2 million in 2003, by 2011 fewer than 500,000 Christians remained in Iraq, most believers having fled in the first three years after the invasion. Similarly, after the mass demonstrations in Egypt forced the fall of the Hosni Mubarak dictatorship, persecution of Coptic Christians increased noticeably. More recently, many Christians have been murdered in Nigeria, a country deeply divided between Christians and Muslims. According to Open Door, a nongovernmental organization that monitors Christian persecution, the countries that persecuted Christians the most in 2011 were North Korea, Afghanistan, Saudi Arabia, Somalia, Iran, Maldives, Uzbekistan, Yemen, Iraq, and Pakistan.[16] Although religious NGOs continue to play an important role in documenting ongoing religious persecution, Evangelicals' concern with issues of religious freedom has declined in recent years. The NAE, for example, has issued a number of major pronouncements on such issues as immigration and nuclear weapons, but has released no major declaration on the ongoing persecution of Christians.

Allen Hertzke argues that one important lesson of the campaign for international religious freedom is that legislation alone is not sufficient to produce "transformational change." "For that," he claims, "ongoing social movement mobilization may be required."[17] But since social movements, like the one that helped bring about IRFA, are hard to maintain, the passage of laws and the creation of institutions are essential if important goals are to be pursued over the long term. Laura Bryant Hanford writes:

> Public advocacy can heighten attention, show solidarity with the persecuted, create an incentive to avoid the shame of exposure, and establish a useful "good cop, bad cop" dynamic.... [R]elying on public advocacy alone presumes both sustained interest on the part of advocates and the public, and a strong impact on policy-makers' actual decisions. In too many cases, both assumptions have been unrealistic, which is why IRFA proponents fought so hard to create legal requirements for decision-making and action.[18]

In the end, the reduction of religious persecution in the world will not be realized through observance of legal statutes alone but also through the hard work of diplomatic negotiation. American diplomats, however, must be convinced of the priority of international religious freedom and seek to advance that goal. But as Farr and others have noted, the dominant worldview at the Department of State has not ranked religious freedom as one of the country's vital foreign policy interests.[19] Still, to the extent that significant religious freedom achievements have been realized in the first ten years of IRFA, they have been realized chiefly through diplomacy. According to Hanford, "The major successes of the last 10 years—CPC designations, policy changes, prisoner releases, constitutional clauses and many more—were won by the dogged work of diplomacy."[20]

The great achievement of IRFA was that it established institutions that increased governmental accountability over global religious issues, especially religious persecution. As a result of IRFA, a new foreign policy "architecture" was established that requires annual reporting on religious freedom, diplomatic training on religious concerns, and heightened awareness of the importance of religious freedom in the overall conduct of U.S. foreign policy.[21] Although the institutionalization of religious freedom concerns is an important achievement, ongoing political advocacy will be necessary to ensure that religious freedom remains a significant element of American foreign policy. But the Evangelical community can be proud of the fact that it played an important role in bringing us to this point.

Human Trafficking

Most people think that slavery ended in the nineteenth century. But every year more humans are trafficked across borders against their will than at any time in the past. Human trafficking is roughly tied with the illegal arms industry as the second-largest criminal industry in the world, behind the drug trade.[22] The Department of State estimates that there are roughly 12.3 million adults and children in modern-day slavery—that is, in some form of bondage, including forced labor, sex trafficking, bonded labor, and forced enlistment of child soldiers.[23]

Evangelicals have taken a particular interest in the fight against sex trafficking.[24] Reliable information on forced labor and especially child commercial sex is difficult to secure, but recent estimates by the International Labor Organization and the United Nations Children Fund (UNICEF) estimate that 1.2 million children are forced into the commercial sex trade annually.[25] The interest in curbing sex trafficking was not new for Evangelicals. In 1865, Catherine and William Booth founded the Salvation Army to care for the destitute and oppressed in London. Since one of the major social evils confronting the poor in London at the time was commercial sex trafficking, the Booths' new organization established a number of initiatives to help rescue children and women from such exploitation. One of these initiatives involved establishing homes to shelter and care for victims as they transitioned out of prostitution. In addition, the Salvation Army played an important role in helping to secure the passage of a law raising the age of minors from thirteen to sixteen.

The campaign to establish a more vigorous U.S. foreign policy toward sex trafficking was initiated in the late 1990s by several leaders of the religious liberty campaign. Michael Horowitz began prodding Evangelicals, human rights activists, and feminists to confront the staggering evils and horrific depravity of this global criminal industry. Other early leaders in this movement included John Busby (Salvation Army), Joe Mettimano (World Vision), Lisa Thompson (NAE, later Salvation Army), Marian Bell (Prison Fellowship), Laura Lederer (human rights activist), and Jessica Neuwirth (Equality Now). But these individuals would have been unable to transform

U.S. law and federal government policies without widespread grassroots support from Evangelicals. This support was brought to bear through the pivotal lobbying efforts of leaders like Kevin Mannoia and Richard Cizik of the NAE, Charles Colson of Prison Fellowship, and Richard Land of the Southern Baptist Convention (SBC). Additionally, a number of Evangelical organizations made human trafficking a policy concern, and some, like the SBC and the NAE, adopted resolutions in support of the campaign to combat human trafficking.[26]

It is important to stress that the human trafficking initiative was ultimately successful because Evangelical groups cooperated with other groups, including human rights and feminist organizations. As with the religious liberty campaign, the initiative to confront global sex trafficking required cooperation among "strange bedfellows"—to use Allen Hertzke's apt description.[27] And as Hertzke shows, the successful passage of human trafficking legislation was made possible by the "scaffolding"—that is, the organizational ties and human relationships—that had been forged in the earlier religious freedom initiative.[28]

What did the human trafficking campaign accomplish? A major goal had been to place this human rights issue at the forefront of U.S. foreign policy. Accordingly, the law passed by Congress in October 2000—the Trafficking Victims Protection Act (TVPA)—called on the U.S. government to make human trafficking a priority by focusing on prevention of such human rights abuses, the protection of victims, and the prosecution of offenders. More specifically, the TVPA created the Interagency Task Force to Monitor and Combat Trafficking, called for the establishment of a new office in the Department of State, mandated that the Department of State issue a report every year on the status of "severe forms" of trafficking in persons (TIP), and established guidelines for sanctions against countries that failed to meet minimum standards in combating this crime. More specifically, the law requires that the Department of State's annual report on human trafficking classify all countries according to their effectiveness in combating this crime.[29]

The TVPA law was subsequently strengthened with the passage of additional legal measures in 2003, 2005, and 2008. In particular, the human trafficking campaign received a significant boost when the Bush administration substantially increased funding both to combat trafficking and to assist victims. But identifying and prosecuting major human trafficking offenders is difficult because of the secret, elusive nature of this criminal activity. This is especially the case for the sex trade of children. According to a recent Department of State human trafficking report, in 2010 the total number of convictions for human trafficking crimes worldwide was only 3,619. Of this number, 1,850 convictions, or more than half of the total, were in Europe, whereas in East Asia and the Pacific, an area where significant human trafficking occurs, only 177 offenders were convicted.[30]

Although some Evangelical groups that were originally involved in the campaign have since shifted their attention to other concerns, the Salvation Army and the International Justice Mission (IJM) have continued to make human trafficking a top priority. Indeed, Lisa Thompson, who heads the Salvation Army's advocacy, also continues to oversee the Initiative Against Sexual Trafficking, an alliance of church and parachurch organizations supporting the anti-trafficking initiative.

Because Evangelicals believe that humans are made in God's image, advancing human dignity is an important Evangelical imperative. Applying this principle to the problem of modern-day slavery, however, remains a daunting challenge. Since human trafficking is carried out clandestinely, gathering data on victims and offenders is a difficult undertaking not only for churches and religious nongovernmental organizations but also for governmental agencies. Consequently, mobilizing political action to reduce and eliminate contemporary labor, financial, and sexual bondage is an elusive, challenging task.

North Korean Human Rights

North Korea is one of the most repressive, reclusive, and poor countries in the world, imposing enormous suffering on its people. Its totalitarian grip allows the country's communist government to deny not only civil and political liberties but also fundamental freedoms of conscience and religion. It is estimated that the regime holds between 100,000 and 200,000 political prisoners in concentration camps. Because of the regime's persistent abuse of human rights, many citizens have attempted to flee the country. Geography, however, limits the potential number of refugees, as the only option is to escape to China through its 1,300-kilometer border. But because of the significant growth in the number of North Korean refugees, China stopped accepting them in 1999, refusing to allow the UN High Commissioner for Refugees (UNHCR) to monitor and assess the movement of people across the border. Instead, China began forcibly returning North Koreans to their homeland and imposing harsh penalties on those who sheltered refugees. Moreover, since refugees faced imprisonment, isolation, torture, and even death upon repatriation, the number of North Koreans attempting the dangerous journey dwindled dramatically, with few ultimately succeeding in finding refuge elsewhere.[31]

Political repression and religious persecution in North Korea is not a recent development. Rather, human rights have been abused ever since communists took power in the late 1940s. Not only has the autocratic government maintained policies and regulations that have resulted in great hunger and suffering, but when the country faced a multi-year famine in the mid-1990s, the regime's policies resulted in the deaths of 1 to 2 million persons. Although the United States, along with other Western nations, has provided humanitarian assistance, this aid has not always gone to people with the greatest needs, since the authorities have diverted some of it to help sustain the regime.

After George W. Bush was elected president, human rights became a more prominent concern of the U.S. government. In the 1990s, the primary U.S. foreign policy goal for North Korea was curbing the country's quest for nuclear weapons. The concern with nonproliferation led to a 1994 bilateral framework agreement that called on North Korea to halt the operation and construction of nuclear reactors suspected of being part of a covert nuclear weapons program in exchange for two proliferation-resistant nuclear reactors. Additionally, the agreement called on the United States to supply North Korea with fuel oil. In 2002, the United States charged that North Korea was secretly enriching uranium, contrary to the 1994 accord, and suspended all fuel shipments. This development, along with President Bush's designation of North Korea as part of an "axis of evil," not only led to renewed animosity and distrust between the two nations but also contributed to a shift in focus from security concerns to humanitarian issues.

A number of developments contributed to the rise of Evangelical grassroots interest in North Korean human rights. The first was China's policy of forcibly repatriating refugees.[32] Second, in 2002 several North Korean youths entered the U.S. Consulate in Shenyang, China, and requested asylum. When the U.S. government refused their request, they went on a hunger strike that received global media coverage. Although the refugees were eventually resettled in South Korea, this event prompted debate in Congress over American refugee and asylum policies.[33] Third, the Department of State's 2001 Annual Report on International Religious Freedom designated North Korea a Country of Particular Concern (CPC) for the first time. This action, along with reports from the U.S. Commission on International Religious Freedom, further heightened public awareness of religious persecution in North Korea.

In response to these and other developments, Evangelical groups began to address the North Korean human rights problem, focusing in particular on religious persecution. As noted earlier, in April 2002, the NAE adopted a "Statement of Conscience Concerning Worldwide Religious Persecution" that emphasized persecution in Sudan and North Korea.[34] This coincided with a "persecution summit" that brought together Evangelical activists, human rights advocates, and political leaders. Subsequently, the Hudson Institute's Center for Religious Freedom, working with Evangelical leaders and human rights activists, developed a "Statement of Principles on North Korea" that sought to balance American security concerns with an emphasis on human rights.[35] Issued in January 2003, the statement was inspired by the Cold War "Helsinki process," which had helped strengthen human rights in Soviet-dominated Eastern Europe. This process was set in motion with the signing of the Helsinki Agreement of 1975, which acknowledged the permanence of the Soviet Union's Eastern European borders while also acknowledging the legitimacy of such human rights as open borders, family reunification, and free exchange. In time, the human rights claims permitted by the Helsinki accords would undermine the legitimacy of the communist empire. The animating insight of the statement was that security concerns needed to be coupled with accountability on human rights. The statement declared: "We believe that little is lost, and much gained, by immediately broadening negotiations with the Pyongyang regime to include the plight of those who live under its rule."

In response to growing political mobilization among members of the religious–human rights coalition that had previously backed the international religious freedom and human trafficking initiatives, Senator Sam Brownback introduced the North Korea Human Rights bill in the U.S. Senate in late 2003. A similar, though slightly less robust, bill was also introduced in the House of Representatives. After subsequent revisions, Congress unanimously passed the legislation, which President Bush signed in October 2004.[36]

Fundamentally, the chief aim of the North Korea Human Rights Act of 2004 was to elevate the status of human rights in North Korea and make it a fundamental element of American foreign policy. Some of its major provisions include: (1) appointment of a Department of State special envoy for North Korean human rights; (2) financial support for private, nonprofit organizations to promote human rights, democracy, the rule of law, and free enterprise in North Korea; (3) humanitarian aid to North Korea through U.S. NGOs, provided the aid can reach those who are most vulnerable; (4) an increase in the number of North Korean refugees that the United States will accept; and (5) increased humanitarian aid to victims of human trafficking from North Korea. According to Michael Horowitz, Evangelicals played "the key role" in bringing about the legislation. "It was the evangelical passion" notes Horowitz, "that was the powerful animating force, the energizing force around this issue."[37]

Of course, it is one thing to enact a law and another to succeed in pursuing desired objectives. Since advancing human rights in North Korea requires changes in their repressive policies, reducing human rights abuses has remained an elusive goal. Fundamentally, human rights and religious freedom will improve only when North Korean leaders decide to undertake domestic reforms. Since external pressures might help to advance domestic reforms, highlighting regime human rights abuses can potentially contribute to this goal. Nongovernmental groups' persistence in calling attention to North Korean oppression is therefore noteworthy, as is the neglect of such concerns by neighboring states, especially China and South Korea. In December 2005, a large number of religious leaders and human rights activists gathered in Seoul. The aim of the Seoul Summit was to foster global awareness of North Korea's human rights abuses and to mobilize international public support for domestic reforms, including stopping the punishment of citizens who attempt to flee the country, dismantling the country's concentration camps, and repatriating more than 80,000 South Korean citizens and soldiers captured or abducted during the Korean War.

Although the 2004 law required that the U.S. government emphasize human rights concerns in its international relations with North Korea, the country's ongoing quest for nuclear weapons has impeded the humanitarian agenda. Realizing that American diplomacy had remained focused on nuclear proliferation issues, Evangelicals and human rights activists continued to press government officials to make human rights a priority. In July 2005, they issued a "Statement of Principles" signed by many Evangelical leaders, calling for a "third way"—one that balanced humanitarian and security concerns more effectively. The statement declared: "We believe that the United States must do more to advance the cause of North Korean human rights and democratization."[38]

The challenge of reconciling human rights and security issues became more difficult in 2006, after North Korea conducted a number of ballistic missile tests in July and a nuclear weapons test in October. As a result, American diplomacy shifted almost exclusively to security concerns, making six-party multilateral negotiations (including Russia, Japan, South Korea, and China) a top priority. The difficulty in balancing security and human rights issues was starkly illustrated in 2008, when Jay Lefkowitz, the Bush administration Special Envoy for North Korea, gave a talk at the American Enterprise Institute in which he called for a new, more balanced approach.[39]

But Secretary of State Condoleezza Rice implicitly rebuked Lefkowitz, indicating that the United States would not link human rights to American non-proliferation strategy.[40]

Despite the efforts of religious and human rights leaders to promote religious freedom and improve human rights in North Korea, little progress has been made. Nevertheless, Evangelicals can take pride in their political engagement on a foundational moral issue. Barrett Duke, vice president of the SBC's Ethics and Religious Liberty Commission, has observed that Evangelicals have contributed to the analysis of North Korean human rights concerns because of the priority Christians give to human dignity. Duke writes: "The Bible teaches us that God holds human life to be invaluable, and it teaches us about the sanctity of life. So when we defend human life against oppression and aggression, we are acting in conformity with God's own heart."[41]

The Sudan Peace Process

Evangelical concern with Sudan's civil war began with religious persecution in southern Sudan. Although tribal conflict had long existed in Sudan, a bitter civil war between the Muslim north and the Christian/animist south began in 1983. The war started when the government in Khartoum began imposing Islamic law (Sharia) on non-Muslims in the southern, oil-rich region of the country. When the people in the south resisted this development, bitter fighting ensued. The Muslim regime resorted to scorched-earth practices: rampant killing of civilians, burning of villages, destruction of crops, and mass deportation. When relief organizations sought to provide humanitarian aid to the refugees, government forces would confiscate food and medical aid or impede their delivery. The genocidal campaign even involved slavery—a practice that Christian Solidarity International, a Swiss-based Christian NGO, confronted with a "slavery redemption" campaign.[42]

Despite the growing condemnation of human rights abuses by religious and human rights groups, the Muslim regime continued its war of attrition against the Sudan People's Liberation Movement (SPLM). Although some 2 million Africans died as a result of this genocidal war, what mobilized Evangelicals was not so much the mass killing as the realization that the war was being waged to persecute and kill persons who did not accept Islam. Thus, when leaders like Charles Colson of Prison Fellowship, Franklin Graham of Samaritan's Purse, and James Dobson of Focus on the Family began highlighting Sudan's religiously based genocidal campaign, a broad grassroots movement emerged and began calling on the U.S. government to respond to the humanitarian crisis. One small, informal association—the Midland Ministerial Alliance, a group of some two hundred churches from President Bush's hometown of Midland, Texas—was especially successful in publicizing the suffering of southern Sudanese.

As a result of the growing awareness of the mass suffering in Sudan, a loose coalition of Evangelicals, human rights groups, and religious NGOs began lobbying Congress and the president to take action. President Bush responded by appointing former Senator John Danforth as Special Envoy to Sudan, while the House and the Senate took up the issue in their respective chambers. After intense lobbying, in October 2002, Congress passed the Sudan Peace Act—a law that called for increased pressure on the Khartoum regime to end the fighting.[43] Fundamentally, the law gave the president tools to pressure the Khartoum regime to halt the genocidal campaign that had resulted in hundreds of thousands of deaths in the south. In particular, the law provided for financial aid to the southern area of Sudan not controlled by the government, required that the government and rebels negotiate in good faith, established a timetable by which to achieve a settlement, and authorized the president to prevent the Sudanese regime from using oil revenues for purchasing weapons or for failing to negotiate in good faith.

Partly because of American governmental pressure, a Comprehensive Peace Agreement (CPA) was signed at the end of 2004. The CPA called for a cease-fire between the ruling Muslims and the southern rebels (SPLM), the sharing of oil revenues, and the creation of a power-sharing government. Fundamentally, the CPA gave southern Sudan a six-year period of autonomy, during which time it would determine whether the country would remain unified or be partitioned between the north and the south. During this transitional period, the parties agreed that a census would be taken in 2007, followed by elections in 2009. A referendum in the south would then be undertaken in early 2011 to determine whether southern Sudan would become a separate state. To assist in keeping peace in Sudan, the United Nations established a 10,000-person peacekeeping force known as UNMIS—UN Mission in Sudan.

Implementation of the CPA proved to be especially difficult.[44] One contributing factor was the death in mid-2005 of John Garang, the head of the SPLM. A second impediment involved a bitter conflict in Darfur, a large, barren region in western Sudan.[45] Since the Darfur crisis led some religious and human rights groups to shift their attention to the immediate humanitarian needs in that region, maintaining pressure on the Khartoum regime to fulfill the terms of the CPA became more difficult. For example, while Evangelical groups continued to focus primarily on the peace process in southern Sudan, mainline Protestant and African-American churches remained more involved in halting the killing in Darfur. Although the Darfur conflict was the dominant media concern during the 2005–2008 period, by the time that President Barack Obama assumed office in early 2009, that dispute had become less prominent, allowing north-south concerns to regain center stage.[46] Even though a number of issues remained unresolved—most prominently the dispute over the oil-rich Abyei region along the north-south border[47]—the referendum on independence was held as scheduled in January 2011. The people voted overwhelmingly in support of secession, and leaders began preparing for independence.

On July 9, 2011, officials announced the birth of the new state of South Sudan. Although the country faces many daunting challenges because of its poverty and isolation, the greatest challenge remains the maintenance of peace between the north and the south and among the various tribal groups that constitute the south. Violence has flared not only between North and South Sudan but also between tribal groups in the new country. In January 2012, for example, some 2,000 people were killed in the eastern part of South Sudan when 6,000 fighters from one ethnic group attacked another group. It would be a pity if, after partitioning Sudan, the peoples of the new country failed to work peacefully and cooperatively to help build the institutions required to advance the well-being of its citizens.

The HIV/AIDS Pandemic

One of the most destructive diseases to emerge in modern times is HIV/AIDS.[48] Its impact has been devastating, especially in Africa. The disease is difficult to contain because the effects of the HIV virus are not apparent to those with the illness, who can therefore, in the absence of testing, unknowingly spread it to others. And since the disease is principally transmitted through sexual relations, an effective program to combat the disease would necessarily demand challenging prevalent cultural mores by encouraging greater moral self-restraint.[49] When the disease first became known in the United States, it was associated with sexual promiscuity, especially among homosexuals. Not surprisingly, many Evangelicals initially regarded the disease as a by-product of immorality and an expression of divine wrath for sinful behavior.[50] In 1988, the NAE adopted a resolution that, among other things, highlighted the moral dimensions of the problem and the need for compassion for those who had contracted the disease. The resolution declares:

> Although there is the urgent need for education regarding AIDS, education without reference to values ignores the moral dimensions of the

problem. Therefore, government or private sector programs that deny the moral element of the problem are inadequate remedies. While there are innocent sufferers of the disease, the fact remains that two primary groups of individuals with AIDS are practicing homosexual men and drug addicts who share needles. The nexus between immoral behavior and the spread of AIDS virus is self-evident.... But legislation and the best efforts of public health officials have their limits. Our Christian faith offers hope for the victims of AIDS. This faith offers also a realistic way of life that will curb the spread of this tragic disease in that our faith calls for chastity before marriage and fidelity in marriage. For this reason, the National Association of Evangelicals (NAE) calls upon the Christian Church to proclaim the hope that God has provided in Jesus Christ and to promote the practice of biblical sexual morality.[51]

In the 1990s, however, Evangelicals began to challenge the stigma against AIDS when it became evident that the disease was transmitted not simply among homosexuals and drug addicts but also through heterosexual sex or even innocent contact with tainted blood. To a significant degree, the change in attitudes was led by individuals who witnessed the human devastation resulting from the AIDS pandemic in Africa, where the explosive transmission of the HIV virus spread through promiscuous heterosexual relations. When missionaries and relief and development workers began to describe the magnitude of human suffering wrought by AIDS in sub-Saharan African countries, especially the hundreds of thousands of orphans who had lost parents to the disease, Evangelicals began to have a change of heart. Although the general religious public was slow to respond, Evangelical leaders like Franklin Graham, head of Samaritan's Purse; Reverend Rick Warren, the pastor of Saddleback Church; and Richard Stearns, the head of World Vision, played a crucial role in developing a compassionate response to the pandemic.

In 2002, Evangelical leaders began sponsoring a number of conferences and colloquia to increase awareness of the AIDS pandemic and, more important, to mobilize political support for humanitarian aid. In February 2002, for example, Graham convened an international conference in Washington, D.C., for some 800 Christian leaders to mobilize support for an anti-AIDS campaign. Prior to that event, Graham had been in touch with Senator Jesse Helms (R–NC) and challenged Helms to use his position to promote humanitarian assistance to AIDS victims. On one occasion, Senator Helms told Graham, "Well, Franklin, I'm going to have to change some of the positions

I've had in the past." Thus, when Helms addressed the 2002 conference, he declared his support for increased government aid to African victims, declaring: "I was wrong, and I'm going to take the latter days of my time in the Senate to do everything I can to help push this [comprehensive anti-AIDS initiative]."[52]

A year later, in June 2003, the NAE, World Relief, MAP (Medical Assistance Programs) International, and World Vision sponsored a two-day forum involving some 250 ministers, missionaries, and donors to confer with government officials and political leaders on global AIDS. As a result of the meeting, Evangelical leaders adopted a statement of conscience on the global AIDS crisis. The foreword of that statement aptly captures the shift among Evangelicals:

> AIDS is the greatest humanitarian crisis of our time; it may be the greatest humanitarian crisis of all time. The flames of this pandemic are leaping across continents, consuming all they touch with no regard for race, culture, religion or economic status.... Regrettably, the response to the cries of those infected with and affected by HIV/AIDS has been largely silence. The Church was not the first to the frontlines of this conflagration. However, we believe the Church is uniquely positioned to serve as the pivotal agent in turning the tide against AIDS through its message of reconciliation, faithfulness, hope, and compassionate care.[53]

The increasing concern among Evangelicals for the AIDS crisis was also evident in the coverage devoted to this issue by *Christianity Today*, the most influential Evangelical magazine. According to political scientist Chan Woong Shin, from 1994 to 1999, the magazine published three articles on AIDS as a domestic issue and three articles on AIDS as a global issue. From 2000 to 2008, however, the journal published six articles on AIDS in the United States and an astounding fifty-four articles on AIDS as a global pandemic, a total that reflects the dramatic rise in concern for the disease.[54] Soon after Bill Frist became Senate Majority Leader, he met with a group of religious leaders to discuss the AIDS crisis, declaring that Evangelicals had "now stepped up to the plate." He indicated that Evangelicals "represent a great hope" on the AIDS issue. "The ultimate cure," he told the group, "cannot be found without the church."[55]

By the time George W. Bush assumed office in January 2001, Evangelical awareness and concern for the AIDS pandemic had begun to rise. But it was the president's passionate concern to alleviate human suffering that transformed the moral concern for AIDS victims into one of the largest humanitarian initiatives in world history. When he took office, the U.S. government was spending about $500 million to halt the spread of AIDS. In his presidential memoir, *Turning Points*, Bush writes that while this financial support was far more than that of any other country, it was "paltry compared with the scope of the pandemic." "I decided," he writes, "to make confronting the scourge of AIDS in Africa a key element of my foreign policy."[56]

One of the president's first acts to address the pandemic was to support a United Nations initiative to deal with AIDS, tuberculosis, and malaria. When UN Secretary General Kofi Annan called for the creation of a Global Fund to fight these three diseases, Bush announced that the United States would make a founding contribution of $200 million and pledged to increase this amount if the program proved effective. A year later, in June 2002, he announced the creation of a program to reduce the mother-to-child transmission of HIV. Scientists had discovered a new drug (Nevirapine) that could dramatically reduce the odds that a pregnant woman with HIV would transmit the virus to her baby. Since tens of thousands of children were being born with the virus, leading to early death, the Bush administration called for an allocation of $500 million to make this new drug available throughout Africa.

But Bush knew that these efforts, while significant, were not sufficient to effectively confront the pandemic. In 2002, between 6,000 and 8,000 people in Africa were dying daily from AIDS, and the rate of infection was not abating, despite widespread initiatives to distribute condoms. Accordingly, on the day that he announced the mother-child initiative, Bush told Josh Bolten, his deputy chief of staff, "This is a good start, but it's not enough. Go back to the drawing board and think even bigger."[57] Senior White House officials worked secretly over the next several months on a comprehensive initiative that involved prevention, treatment, and humanitarian care. When senior officials met to discuss the proposed five-year, $15-billion-dollar initiative, some advisers expressed concern about the high cost of the program. President Bush, however, was convinced that the United States had a moral responsibility to help relieve the widespread suffering caused by this disease. In his memoir, he indicates that Michael Gerson, his chief speechwriter and senior adviser, captured the essence of his sentiments when he declared, "If we can do this and we don't, it will be a source of shame."[58]

In his State of the Union address in January 2003, President Bush announced a new AIDS initiative—the President's Emergency Plan for

AIDS Relief (PEPFAR). The goals of the program were to prevent 7 million new AIDS infections, treat at least 2 million people with life-extending drugs, and provide care to children orphaned by AIDS. Although some critics have suggested that the initiative was intended to distract attention from the president's "war on terror," it is clear that what inspired President Bush to undertake this extraordinary initiative was the belief that this was the right thing to do. In discussing this initiative soon after it was announced, President Bush described the moral basis of his program as follows:

> We have a chance to achieve a more compassionate world for every citizen. America believes deeply that everybody has worth, everybody matters, everybody was created by the Almighty, and we're going to act on that belief and we'll act on that passion.... As I said in my State of the Union, freedom is not America's gift to the world, freedom is God's gift to humanity.... [I]n the continent of Africa, freedom means freedom from fear of a deadly pandemic. That's what we think in America. And we're going to act on that belief. The founding belief in human dignity should be how we conduct ourselves around the world—and will be how we conduct ourselves around the world.[59]

At the time of the initiative, the primary approach to prevention involved the distribution of condoms. But since the rate of transmission continued to rise, leading to 13,700 new infections daily, this approach was clearly insufficient. By 2003, the total number of Africans with the HIV virus was close to 20 million, with more than 1 million dying annually from AIDS-related causes. Additionally, since only 50,000 Africans were receiving antiretroviral (ARV) drugs that could prolong life, the number of AIDS deaths continued to soar. By 2003, it was estimated that Africa had close to 14 million children orphaned by AIDS.

Thus, PEPFAR was a medical as well as a humanitarian initiative—aimed at halting the AIDS pandemic, caring for those with HIV, and meeting the humanitarian needs of children and adults who had suffered the loss of loved ones. To advance these objectives, PEPFAR called for $15 billion in medical and humanitarian aid, of which $9 billion would be for new programs focused on a select group of countries.[60] Some of the distinctive elements of PEPFAR included: (1) the establishment of specific numeric targets for prevention, treatment, and care; (2) the broadening of the scope of prevention programs to include an emphasis on abstinence and fidelity; and (3) a dramatic increase in funding for treating people with AIDS.[61]

The UN Global Fund and other similar AIDS initiatives addressed AIDS prevention by focusing almost exclusively on condom distribution. What made PEPFAR unique was its adoption of an initiative pioneered in Uganda—the so-called ABC program—which called for Abstinence, Being Faithful, and using Condoms. The inclusion of abstinence and fidelity were important, but considered unrealistic by some, and controversial by others, who preferred to approach the problem from a purely pragmatic perspective. But moral expectations were important not only for the long-term success of containing the HIV pandemic but also for garnering political support from religious conservatives. Clearly, Evangelicals would not have supported the program without inclusion of a call for abstinence and faithfulness as part of a comprehensive anti-AIDS initiative. PEPFAR's emphasis on treating AIDS patients was also noteworthy. In the early 1990s, the annual cost for treating AIDS patients with ARV drugs was about $12,000, but by the beginning of the new millennium, a generic version of these medicines had become available for as little as $295 per year. The proposed program called for allocating roughly half of its spending to supplying these new drugs.

Enacting legislation to fund PEPFAR required significant cooperation between liberals and conservatives in both the Senate and the House of Representatives. Congressmen Henry Hyde (R–IL) and Tom Lantos (D–CA) introduced the bill—the United States Leadership Against Global HIV/AIDS, Tuberculosis, and Malaria Act of 2003—into the House of Representatives. As the chairman and ranking minority member of the body's International Relations Committee, who were regarded as influential human rights legislators, they were able to successfully mobilize support for the initiative and bring the bill to the floor, where it passed by a vote of 375 to 41. In the Senate, Majority Leader Bill Frist, an Evangelical physician who took annual medical missionary trips to Africa, and Dick Lugar, the chairman of the Foreign Relations Committee, provided significant leadership in building support for the legislation. Other senior senators who played important roles in the bill's adoption were Jesse Helms of North Carolina, Joe Biden of Delaware, and John Kerry of Massachusetts. The president signed the bill into law on May 27.

Although Evangelicals did not spearhead this AIDS initiative, they were instrumental in supporting it. Holly Burkhalter, a health policy adviser, observes, "the real turning point in American AIDS policy came when conservative Christians made the cause their own."[62] When confronted with the widespread suffering of the pandemic, they responded with compassion, calling for significant action to stem the tide of this deadly disease. Believing that moral behavior was essential to halting the spread of the

HIV virus, they called for a comprehensive approach to the problem that included increased funding for treatment, a broader approach to prevention, and significant humanitarian aid for orphans and other AIDS victims.

Additionally, some Evangelical organizations have received PEPFAR funds, while some churches, like Rick Warren's Saddleback Church, have established their own AIDS initiatives and humanitarian projects for orphans and widows. Most important, however, has been the significant role of indigenous Evangelical churches in providing moral education as well as tangible care to victims. A 2006 *Christianity Today* editorial describes the vital role that indigenous churches can make in combating AIDS:

> Healthy churches are unrivaled in their comparative advantage of working at the grassroots. Africans have a saying, "Not all are infected, but all are affected." Specifically, grassroots work includes HIV testing, counseling, preventing mother-to-child transmission, paying school fees for orphans, providing food aid, treating opportunistic infections—and especially weeping with those who weep, and rejoicing with those who rejoice. In addition, church leaders can model a theology of sexuality that affirms abstinence before marriage and faithfulness after marriage. And our most important and unique contribution remains sharing the gospel that offers forgiveness and the power to change.[63]

In 2007, President Bush called on Congress to reauthorize PEPFAR for an additional five years, doubling its funding. Congress subsequently approved the initiative, authorizing an additional $39 billion to continue to address the AIDS pandemic as well as an additional $9 billion to cover tuberculosis and malaria.

By any measure, PEPFAR has been extraordinarily successful. As of the end of 2008, it had provided ARV drugs to 2 million persons; preventive support, including counseling and testing, to some 57 million; and humanitarian care to another 10 million. According to former Secretary of State Condoleezza Rice, PEPFAR will be remembered "as one of the greatest acts of compassion by any country in history."[64]

Preliminary Conclusions about Evangelical Political Advocacy

Why did Evangelicals become politically involved in these issues? Although each of these issues involves a threat to human dignity, promoting human rights alone does not fully explain Evangelicals' advocacy on these specific concerns. After all, there are many other global problems that threaten human dignity. Similarly, while each of these five issues involves core moral values, concern with political morality alone cannot account for Evangelicals' political activism. To be sure, Evangelicals would not have been involved if these issues had not threatened core biblical values. However, the catalyst for action on each of these issues was not theological reflection or denominational declarations but, rather, the initiative of individuals, religious groups, and church associations. While Evangelical political ethics provided the framework for social and political analysis, religious and political leaders provided the initiative in mobilizing advocacy support from church groups and human rights NGOs.

In advancing each of these five foreign policy initiatives, Evangelicals contributed substantively to the definition of the issues and to the mobilization of grassroots support to influence legislative action. Several factors contributed to the effectiveness of Evangelical political advocacy. First, Evangelicals supported issues that involved fundamental moral concerns, such as religious freedom, peace, caring for the sick, and providing humanitarian aid to children. While such values are not unique to Christianity, Evangelicals could bring a special urgency to these issues, believing that such concerns were consistent with God's providential order. To be sure, informed observers did not achieve complete consensus on how best to advance the moral goals of freedom, human rights, and peace. Still, what ensured legislative success was the broad and deep moral consensus about the foreign policy goals being pursued.

Second, Evangelicals were successful in advancing these foreign policy concerns because they did not attempt to justify their actions with explicit biblical references. Instead, inspired by broad moral concerns about human dignity and peace, Evangelicals grounded these initiatives in moral values and applied prudential judgments to political advocacy. This approach contrasts with those (some of whom we'll meet in the next chapter) who seek to rely more heavily on biblical principles to justify foreign policy initiatives. To be sure, biblical analysis is essential when church groups carry out political action. But since the Bible is not a manual on politics or international affairs, church leaders need to be cautious in using Scripture to justify policy recommendations. Indeed, the overuse or misuse of Scripture can result in great harm to the church.

Third, Evangelicals succeeded because they were willing to cooperate with disparate political groups who shared a commitment to core moral issues. All five foreign policy initiatives involved adopting laws to help structure foreign policy initiatives. Since successful congressional action necessarily depends upon broad electoral support, the passage of legislation could have been realized only through cooperation among a variety of religious and human rights groups. Typically, foreign policy is the realm of diplomats and national security officials. But legislation can also contribute to foreign policy by establishing priorities and mandates and creating institutions that structure the foreign policy enterprise. The five legislative acts that were adopted to address each foreign policy problem have helped to advance those concerns by structuring American foreign policy approaches to each problem. The laws have done this by creating domestic political demands and constraints as well as demands and constraints on foreign states.

Fourth, Evangelicals were prepared to compromise and accept a second- or third-best alternative. Politics is not the art of advancing ideals but, rather, the art of the possible. In politics—domestic and international—leaders must be prepared to live with less than ideal solutions. This can be very difficult, especially when people are inspired to eliminate perceived evil and injustice or to advance a moral goal. The importance of moral trade-offs is illustrated by the anti-slavery campaign waged by William Wilberforce in the early nineteenth century. Rather than hold out for the idealistic policy of eliminating slavery, Wilberforce settled for the realistic goal of ending the slave trade.[65] On each of the issues covered here, Evangelicals were willing to forge coalitions and to accept second-best alternatives in order to advance goals that they deemed morally desirable. Enacting PEPFAR legislation involved numerous conflicts that could only be resolved through compromise; for example, Evangelicals were forced accept the widespread use of condoms, while liberals had to accept the ABC educational program that emphasized abstinence and fidelity. Even more problematic for Evangelicals was the Bush administration's decision to exempt AIDS programs from the policy (the so-called Mexico City policy) that prohibited nongovernmental organizations from receiving federal funds if they performed or promoted abortion as a means of family planning.[66] In short, Evangelicals contributed to public policy reforms because of their willingness to accept outcomes that were less than the ideal.

Fifth, Evangelicals played an important role in these five initiatives by mobilizing grassroots political support. Although this pressure was most noteworthy on international religious freedom, religious leaders were also involved in mobilizing local support among church groups and religious associations on the other issues as well. Sustaining grassroots political action is especially difficult when addressing elusive foreign problems, such as North Korean human rights abuses or international sex trafficking. Not surprisingly, Evangelical political engagement has been difficult to sustain.

Finally, Evangelicals contributed to the urgency and priority of these five foreign policy initiatives because they regarded the needs of foreign peoples as worthy of moral support. As noted in chapter 4, one of the distinctive traits of Evangelical political ethics is its internationalist perspective. Since the whole world is part of God's creation, Evangelicals view the world as a coherent moral community—a global society where local affinities and national citizenship do not limit the boundaries of moral concern. Indeed, because the world is a unitary moral society, domestic needs and wants do not necessarily override responsibilities to foreign peoples. For example, the desire to address international religious freedom emerged from the desire to show solidarity with Christians who were being persecuted for their faith in foreign societies. Similarly, the mobilization of support for AIDS victims came about not simply as a response to a medical crisis but also as a way of showing compassion toward orphans and others who had been made destitute by AIDS. In sum, Evangelicals' global worldview contributed to the urgency and priority that they brought to foreign policy issues such as human rights abuses, war, religious persecution, and disease.

8 SHORTCOMINGS OF EVANGELICAL FOREIGN POLICY ADVOCACY

Scripture can help structure public policy debate, but it is impossible to devise a biblical blueprint for dealing with specific global problems such as immigration, job creation, Middle East peace, or climate change. Moreover, articulating goals and intentions is simply the first stage of a complex, multidimensional process of making and implementing foreign policy. The challenge is not simply to identify morally legitimate objectives but also to devise strategies that help to advance goals while avoiding, as much as possible, harmful side effects. Peter Berger has written: "It is the easiest thing in the world to proclaim a good. The hard part is to think through ways by which this good can be realized without exorbitant costs and without consequences that negate the good. That is why an ethic of responsibility must be cautious, calculating a perennially uncertain mass of means, costs and consequences."[1]

Developing an ethical foreign policy is challenging because international issues and global problems typically involve competing moral claims. The quest for a clean atmosphere and a prosperous economy are worthy goals, but they are not necessarily complementary. A just foreign policy needs to be judged not simply in terms of its intentions or outcomes but also through an ethical framework that focuses on goals, means, and results.[2] Foreign policy should pursue the right goals by the most efficient means in order to maximize desired outcomes. But since public policies are rarely moral at all three levels, decision making will inevitably involve trade-offs among goals, means, and ends. To be sure, outcomes are of utmost importance. A policy whose goals and means are moral, but whose results are harmful, is morally indefensible. However, a perspective that only judges policies by results is also unacceptable. Thus, all three dimensions must be taken into account. Finally, it is important to recognize that public policymaking is probabilistic—there is no certainty that the methods will result in the desired outcome.

Consequently, the development of public policies must be undertaken with an abundance of caution.

For example, condemning religious persecution in foreign lands is relatively easy, but devising foreign policies that effectively advance religious freedom is much more difficult. When religious freedom is the chief foreign policy goal, it can be easily encompassed within an overall strategy of the expansion of liberty. But when this objective must be reconciled with other legitimate objectives—such as the quest for harmonious relations or the pursuit of nonproliferation of weapons of mass destruction (WMD)—the pursuit of religious freedom becomes more difficult. Such was the challenge facing the George W. Bush administration as it pursued both human rights and nuclear nonproliferation with North Korea. It is also the challenge that the United States faces in fostering religious freedom in China while simultaneously seeking to advance international economic cooperation and stable political relations among the Pacific Basin countries.

If one adopts a moral absolutist ethic where violence is never condoned, even in confronting gross injustice, then the use of state coercive power is never warranted. Since killing is evil, war is always unacceptable. But as Saint Augustine noted long ago, the nature and character of the "City of God" and the "City of Man" are radically different. The former is concerned with spiritual life, where love and mercy are preeminent. But in the latter, the state is entrusted with power and authority to sustain communal order and pursue proximate justice in a world filled with passion, greed, and sin. Absolutist ethics may work in the heavenly kingdom, but they are inappropriate for statecraft.

In this chapter, I examine and critique several foreign policy initiatives advanced by Evangelical groups. Each involves fundamental moral values, but on each Evangelicals have fallen short.

Climate Change

Global warming is one of our most difficult and intractable contemporary problems. There is substantial scientific evidence that the earth is getting warmer. Whereas the earth's temperature increased one degree (Fahrenheit) over the course of the twentieth century, environmental scientists estimate that the earth's temperature could rise by three to eight degrees in the twenty-first century. To a significant degree, the earth's rising temperature is attributed to the increasing use of fossil fuels (petroleum, coal, and natural gas) in generating energy. The burning of coal and petroleum is problematic because the resulting air pollution (chiefly carbon dioxide) traps solar radiation, much like the glass of a plant breeder's greenhouse. The "greenhouse effect" occurs because gases allow more of the sun's heat to be absorbed by the earth than is released back into space. Although human-made gas emissions are responsible for only a part of the greenhouse effect, they nonetheless play an important role in determining the earth's climate. According to the 2007 report of the UN Intergovernmental Panel on Climate Change (IPCC), a group of about 2,500 distinguished scientists, human activity is the main cause of global warming, "very likely" causing most of the rise in the earth's temperature since 1950.[3]

How should the world respond to the threat of global warming? The international community began to note the challenges of promoting sustainable development in 1992, at the UN Conference on Environment and Development, known also as the Earth Summit. One outcome of that conference was the establishment of a treaty on climate change. But while the convention called for action to reduce the use of fossil fuels, it did not establish binding targets. As a result, signatory states implemented few reforms. This task was left to the 1997 UN climate conference in Kyoto, Japan. At that meeting, diplomats established a framework—the Kyoto Protocol, essentially an addendum to the 1992 Climate Treaty—that called on industrialized countries to reduce their greenhouse emissions by about 5 percent below their 1990 level by 2012. To achieve this goal, the convention established significant cuts in pollution—8 percent for the European Union, 7 percent for the United States, and 6 percent for Japan. Significantly, no binding targets were established for China, India, or other developing nations. The accord called for a reduction of roughly 30 percent in the projected carbon emissions of industrialized countries; it required significant cuts in the energy consumption of developed nations, especially the United States, which accounts for nearly one-fourth of the world's greenhouse emissions.

According to Kyoto guidelines, the protocol would become a binding convention only when fifty-five countries accounting for at least 55 percent of the world's 1990 greenhouse emissions had ratified it. Even though China, India, and the United States refused to adopt the Kyoto Protocol, the treaty took effect in 2005 after Russia ratified it.[4] Since then, however, it has become clear that the Kyoto framework is itself woefully inadequate to confront the challenge of climate change. Consequently, the United Nations sponsored a global climate summit in Copenhagen, in December 2009, to develop a successor to the Kyoto accord. The conference, however, not only failed to establish new binding reductions in greenhouse emissions but also two major signatory states—Japan and Russia—announced that they would not accept Kyoto's emissions ceilings beyond 2012, when the agreement expires.[5]

What explains the inability of the international community to adopt a treaty that significantly curbs greenhouse emissions? Fundamentally, confronting climate change is difficult because curbing fossil fuel use is regarded as an impediment to economic growth. Since job creation requires ample, low-cost energy, and since coal, petroleum, and natural gas are the primary sources for industrial energy, a fundamental trade-off exists between reducing greenhouse gases and expanding economic production. Additionally, climate change raises questions about how to allocate responsibility for past and current greenhouse gases. In dealing with this issue, the Kyoto Protocol assigned responsibility chiefly to the developed nations and exempted emerging economies, including China and India. The moral logic for this approach is that the developed nations should bear the major responsibility for curbing greenhouse gases since they are overwhelmingly responsible for the bulk of current emissions.[6] Developing nations argue that until they have achieved adequate living standards they should be exempted from any binding limitations on the use of fossil fuels. Although this approach has merit, if the emerging economies, especially China and India, are not included in a global accord, reductions in global emissions will be impossible, since the rapid expansion of coal-based energy currently under way in China and India would negate any gains from pollution reduction elsewhere. The problem with Kyoto, therefore, is that it fails to confront the rising use of coal and petroleum by emerging economies. One scholar has written that Kyoto is problematic precisely because it fosters the illusion that serious progress is being made to confront climate change.[7]

How should Christians approach the challenges of sustainable development? More specifically, how should they respond to global warming? Throughout the 1990s, Evangelicals began to address this issue, emphasizing both the importance of stewardship of resources and the pursuit of sustainable development. The first principle, sometimes called "creation care," focuses on the responsible use of the earth's resources in order to sustain them across generations. Evangelicals emphasize the scriptural mandate to care for and protect the earth, based on the divine claim that "The earth is the Lord's" (Ps. 24:1). The second principle calls attention to the need to subdue and develop the natural order. In Genesis 1:28, God tells Adam to "be fruitful, and multiply, and replenish the earth, and subdue it." Psalm 115:16 states: "The heaven, even the heavens, are the Lord's: but the earth hath he given to the children of men," implying that persons, as subowners, have a responsibility to use the earth's resources in meeting human needs. A third principle that has emerged in the climate debate is concern for the poor, since the detrimental effects of climate change are likely to fall disproportionately on them, especially those living in lowlands vulnerable to rising sea levels.

In view of the difficult trade-offs between growth and reduced carbon use, it is not surprising that the American electorate is deeply divided about how (or whether) to confront climate change. According to a 2008 survey by the Pew Research Center, a substantial majority (70 percent) of those polled thought that there was substantial evidence for global warming, but only 47 percent thought that people were chiefly responsible for this phenomenon. Significantly, only 35 percent of those polled thought it should be a "top priority" of the U.S. government.[8] A 2008 survey by the Barna Group found that American Christians tend to reflect the distribution of the public at large. The survey found that 63 percent of Christians believed that climate change was occurring, while 40 percent were "very certain" of this development. Evangelicals, however, tended to be skeptical about climate change, with only 27 percent agreeing that it was happening. According to the survey, 62 percent of Evangelicals did not think that humans were a major cause of climate change, while 60 percent believed that proposed solutions would hurt the poor, especially in developing countries (60 percent).[9]

The first prominent Evangelical initiative on climate change was a declaration titled "Climate Change: An Evangelical Call to Action," issued in February 2006 and signed by eighty-six leading pastors, college presidents, leaders of religious NGOs, and heads of parachurch organizations.[10] The document was first drafted in 2005 by the Evangelical Environmental Network (EEN), a movement of Evangelicals concerned with environmental protection, and then submitted to the NAE leadership for formal endorsement. The NAE, however, refused to endorse the statement. As a result, leading proponents started the Evangelical Climate Initiative (ECI), which released the statement to the public in February 2006.[11] The document's preamble states: "As American evangelical Christian leaders, we recognize both our opportunity and our responsibility to offer a biblically based moral witness that can help shape public policy in the most powerful nation on the earth, and therefore contribute to the well-being of the entire world." The statement makes four claims: (1) human-induced climate change is real, (2) the consequences of climate change will be significant and will hit the poor the hardest, (3) Christian moral convictions demand a response to this environmental issue, and (4) the need to act is urgent.[12] Since only one part of this short declaration is concerned with biblical perspectives, it is unclear how this call to action can offer, as the statement asserts, "a biblically based moral witness." Moreover, while the declaration suggests that governments, businesses, churches, and individuals should pursue actions that would help reduce carbon dioxide emissions, no specific recommendations are presented. Recognizing that the declaration had little impact on the public policy debate, a year later the ECI developed a framework of ten principles to guide government policymaking on climate change.[13]

The principal Evangelical opposition to the ECI has come from the Cornwall Alliance, a group of scholars and religious leaders concerned with environmental stewardship. Previously called the Interfaith Stewardship Alliance, this group emerged in 2000 when it issued a declaration that challenged some of the prevailing assumptions of environmentalism. The declaration, which has been signed by more than 1,500 clergy, theologians, and policy experts, was inspired by three key concerns. First, the declaration challenged the prevailing view of humans as "principally consumers and polluters rather than producers and stewards." Second, it challenged the romantic view that "the earth, untouched by human hands, is the ideal." And third, noting that it was important to distinguish legitimate from illegitimate environmental concerns, it argued that the prevailing beliefs about "man-made global warming, overpopulation, and rampant species loss" were unfounded. Thus, when the ECI issued its "call to action," the alliance responded with a detailed rebuttal study titled "A Call to Truth, Prudence, and Protection of the Poor: An Evangelical Response to Global Warming." More recently, the alliance has revised and greatly expanded the original study, shifting the focus from a response to the original ECI statement to a more comprehensive examination of the theology, science, and economics of global warming.[14]

Interestingly, although the NAE adopted two short resolutions on environmental protection in the early 1970s, it has not taken a position on the role of greenhouse emissions and global warming.[15] However, some leading pastors, along with Richard Cizik, the NAE's vice president for governmental affairs, tried to mobilize support on this issue. In early 2007, fifteen influential Evangelicals, including James Dobson, chairman of Focus on the Family; Don Wildmon, head of American Family Association; and Tony Perkins, president of the Family Research Council, called on NAE leadership to either discipline or terminate Cizik because of his aggressive stance on global warming.[16] Critics claimed that Cizik failed to represent Evangelical public opinion in seeking to shift public concern toward the environment and away from issues like the sanctity of life and the integrity of marriage. Although the NAE took no action on Cizik (he was subsequently forced out for comments regarding same-sex civil unions), the public challenge illuminated the deep fissures among Evangelicals. In short, the NAE has not addressed climate change because Evangelicals are divided not only on the nature, scope, and impact of the problem but also on the types of public policies that could generate cost-effective, clean energy.

Southern Baptists have similarly refused to take a position on climate change. While the SBC has repeatedly encouraged its members to pursue actions that are consistent with sustainable development, it has refused to support dramatic curbs on the use of fossil fuels. Indeed, in a 2006 resolution, the SBC expressed concern that environmentalism was threatening to divide the Evangelical community and to distract its members from more fundamental concerns. It called on its members to "resist alliances with extreme environmental groups whose positions contradict biblical principles," while at the same time encouraging them to pursue their God-given responsibilities to care for creation.[17] A 2007 resolution addressed climate change more directly, claiming that since "the scientific community is divided regarding the extent to which humans are responsible for recent global warming," its members should "proceed cautiously in the human-induced global warming debate in light of conflicting scientific research."[18] And Reverend Jerry Falwell, the Fundamentalist televangelist, went so far as to preach a sermon at his Lynchburg, Virginia, church titled "The Myth of Global Warming." In his sermon, he declared that he was raising "a flag of opposition to th[e] alarmism about global warming and urging all believers to refuse to be duped by these 'earthism' worshippers."[19]

Given the complexity of global warming, it is not surprising that Evangelicals have been uncertain how to address this issue.[20] As a result, unlike the initiatives examined in the previous chapter, Evangelicals have contributed little to climate change initiatives. Arguably their most important contribution has been on the theological front. Although Evangelicals disagree on the science of global warming, they share a core theological basis for addressing environmental degradation. In his analysis of the Evangelical debate over climate change, Benjamin Phillips captures some of the principal areas of theological consensus among Evangelicals. He writes:

Most [E]vangelical statements appeal to the fact that God is the creator of the world as a basis for understanding the value of nonhuman creation, and many note that God is its owner. Virtually every [E]vangelical statement on the environment and climate change acknowledges that God has commissioned humanity with the responsibility of stewardship/dominion over the earth and that the execution of this responsibility has been perverted by sin, with negative impact on the environment. Evangelicals have also, almost without exception, affirmed the responsibility of Christians to care for the poor as an important factor in considering environmental policy.[21]

In short, even though Evangelical environmentalism has contributed little to the public policy debate on global warming, Evangelicals have ironically contributed to increased concern with the prudent care of the earth. In particular, the increased focus on biblical thought on the environment has encouraged greater concern among believers with creation care and stewardship of the earth's resources.

U.S. Immigration Reform

Although immigration is a domestic political concern, it is also an international affairs problem. The issue of illegal aliens raises concerns not only about mercy and compassion for persons seeking a better life but also about the legitimacy of regulating cross-border migration. While the former may appear to be more directly associated with morality, international legal and political rules governing admission into a state are also a matter of justice. Indeed, international political morality concerns not simply the rights of persons but also the moral legitimacy of the institutions that sustain society.

As I noted earlier, the structure of the international community is based upon the political independence and territorial sovereignty of states—a development that emerged with the Treaty of Westphalia of 1648. Under the current international political system, each state is responsible for the affairs within its territorial boundaries. Since states regulate membership, they determine the policies governing the admission of aliens. Of course, people have a right to leave their homeland (emigration), but they do not possess a right to enter another country (immigration). That decision lies with the host state.[22]

How one conceives of the international community will significantly determine how one assesses transnational migration issues. Some scholars, like Hedley Bull and Michael Walzer, argue that the world should be regarded as a society of states.[23] According to them, international peace and justice can be realized only through peaceful, law-abiding states that honor obligations toward other states and toward their own citizens. Similarly, philosopher John Rawls argues that global justice is best advanced through well-ordered societies.[24] Although Bull, Walzer, and Rawls approach the problem of international peace and justice from different perspectives, they concur that the division of the world into distinct political communities is not only morally legitimate but also the foundation of a humane, peaceful global order. For them, borders matter.

Other theorists, however, maintain a cosmopolitan perspective, viewing the world as an integrated transnational community. Philosopher Peter Singer, for example, thinks that state boundaries are morally insignificant—a view shared by other cosmopolitan thinkers like Charles Beitz and Allen Buchanan.[25] According to this perspective, since human rights are basic entitlements, state sovereignty is subsidiary to the protection and promotion of human welfare. Since territorial boundaries are morally insignificant, the rules governing transnational migration should be relaxed, if not eliminated. Additionally, since national bonds are a source of division and partiality, citizenship is an impediment to global harmony.

The UN Charter—the constitution of the world—runs contrary to this cosmopolitan worldview. The cosmopolitan quest for more open borders is unlikely to gain much support since it challenges the legal and political foundations of the contemporary international political system. Moreover, disregard for existing state-mandated migration rules is likely to rouse opposition from citizens and exacerbate political conflicts within and among states. Migration politics, in short, is not simply about compassion for aliens desiring to settle in a different country. Rather, such politics inevitably must confront the legal and political realities of the existing global political order.

In the United States, federal law governs the admission of aliens. The U.S. government first began regulating immigration in 1924 with a statute that set annual quotas based on nationality. In 1965, however, Congress adopted legislation—the Immigration and Nationality Act—that altered the basis of immigration quotas from nationality to immigrants' skills and family unification. One of the unanticipated outcomes of the new law was a significant increase in total migration—with the number of immigrants doubling between 1965 and 1970, and doubling again between 1970 and 1990. Moreover, the new system radically transformed the ethnic character of migration, shifting admissions from people from Europe to those from Asia and Latin America.

Each year the president determines the number of immigrants and refugees to be admitted in accordance with existing statutes. In recent years, the total number of aliens admitted annually has been about 1 million. But since a far greater number of people would like to settle in the United States, the demand for visas far exceeds the supply. Consequently, tens of thousands of foreigners enter the United States secretly every year or decide to remain in the country, beyond the terms specified in the visa.

To confront the issue of illegal immigration, Congress passed the Immigration Reform and Control Act of 1986 (IRCA), granting amnesty to millions of undocumented aliens on the condition that employers hire only legal workers in the future. The federal government, however, never established an effective identification, monitoring, and enforcement system. Subsequently Congress passed two additional measures to address immigration issues—the 1990 Immigration Act, and the 1996 Illegal Immigration Reform and Immigrant Responsibility Act. The first statute increased the immigration ceiling and created new preferences for families and foreigners with special skills. The second eased deportation of illegal aliens. Despite these laws, more than twenty-five years after the adoption of IRCA—hailed at the time as the solution to illegal immigration—a large number of undocumented aliens continue to live in the United States. It is estimated that in 2011, some 10 to 12 million people were living in the United States without documentation. Many of these persons entered the country legally but remained beyond the terms specified in their visas; others entered the country illegally, most likely by crossing the southwestern U.S. border with Mexico. In short, the U.S. immigration system has not successfully reconciled domestic demand for alien laborers and secure borders with the desire of many foreign peoples to live and work in the United States.

Although illegal aliens provide a source of low-wage labor to businesses, the growth of undocumented aliens poses several significant problems. These include: (a) limited enforcement of existing laws, thereby undermining the rule of law; (b) the creation of a dual social order—one legal and one illegal—that impairs communal cohesion; (c) the imposition of rising financial obligations on local communities that provide educational, social, and medical services to undocumented aliens; and (d) a weakened legal immigration system caused by the expectation that illegal migration is a viable alternative to the slow, cumbersome process of legal migration. In 2006, President Bush decided to address some of these issues by offering a comprehensive immigration reform (CIR) initiative. Some of the elements of the CIR plan were greater border control, stricter enforcement of existing labor laws, and the creation of a path to legalize ("regularize") undocumented aliens.[26]

How should Christians view the problem of illegal immigration? Should undocumented aliens be welcomed, deported, or simply neglected? Should believers emphasize compassion or focus on the enforcement of existing laws?

What contribution can Evangelicals make to this public policy concern? In 2006, the NAE decided to address such questions by adopting a resolution that called for both border control and empathy toward undocumented immigrants. The resolution states: "It is appropriate for the borders of the United States to be secured in order for immigration to conform to the laws of the United States. As people of faith we support immigration reform that reflects human dignity, compassion, and justice integral to a nation under God."[27] The resolution also expressed concern about the growing "spirit of hostility" toward immigrants and refugees, calling on believers to show compassion toward their neighbors.

After Congress began considering CIR in 2007, religious groups—including Evangelicals, the Roman Catholic Church, and mainline Protestant denominations—began to reassess this issue. As a result, in 2009 the NAE adopted a resolution that shifted the focus from border security and legal enforcement to the well-being of aliens.[28] The two-page resolution is divided into three sections: Biblical Foundations, National Realities, and Call to Action. The first section acknowledges that all persons are made in the image of God and that Christians are called to show respect toward all human beings. In the second section, the document suggests that the significant increase in migration has led to numerous problems. "The challenge today," the resolution declares, "is to determine how to maintain the integrity of national borders, address the situation with millions of undocumented immigrants, devise a realistic program to respond to labor needs, and manifest the humanitarian spirit that has characterized this country since its founding." The resolution declares that the fundamental "national reality" is that the United States is not admitting an adequate number of aliens to meet the country's economic needs. As a result, many aliens have entered the country illegally—not only to advance their own economic interests but also to provide cheap labor to U.S. businesses. The resolution states: "[d]ue to the limited number of visas, millions have entered the United States without proper documentation or have overstayed temporary visas."

In our assessment of the NAE statement, Peter Meilaender and I question the religious leaders' competence to assess the adequacy of the government's visa policy. We write:

> But how many visas would be "enough," and how would one decide that question? By considering U.S. demand for foreign workers? Or the number of foreign workers seeking to come here? Does it make a difference whether we are considering skilled or unskilled labor?

How do we weigh the benefits to American consumers, in the form of cheaper goods and services, against the costs to American labor, in the form of wage competition? Or how should we allocate visas among workers, family members, and refugees? All of these difficult but critical questions are simply buried beneath the bland assumption that we are not admitting "enough" immigrants.[29]

The third section—Call to Action—offers several policy recommendations. These include ensuring that border patrols emphasize "respect for human dignity"; facilitating the entry of a "reasonable number of immigrant workers"; reconsidering (and, by implication, increasing) the number of visas available for family reunification; reevaluating the impact of deportation on families; providing a qualified amnesty for illegal aliens; protecting the civil rights, especially with respect to fair labor practices, of all those present in the United States; and enforcing immigration laws "in ways that recognize the importance of due process of law, the sanctity of the human person, and the incomparable value of family." When these suggestions are taken together, it is clear that the authors of the NAE statement believe that a more expansive and flexible immigration system is needed—one that will facilitate "earned legal status for undocumented aliens" and give greater priority to family reunification.

Interestingly, the document is silent about how the widespread presence of illegal aliens in the country undermines the rule of law, and little is said about the financial burdens that they impose on the citizenry for social, medical, and educational services. Even the two recommendations that concede the need to monitor the border and enforce the laws emphasize the need to protect human rights of those seeking entry rather than maintenance of border security.

Does this resolution illuminate important biblical norms that can assist Evangelical parishioners in assessing the issue of illegal migration? Does it show how biblical and moral principles can help structure a just governmental response to this complex issue? In effect, does the declaration contribute to a more informed public policy debate? Regrettably, the NAE resolution fails in its educational task because it oversimplifies issues, offers simplistic moral judgments, and fails to illuminate moral trade-offs among competing goals. Most important, the document fails to discuss the context in which migration flows occur. In reading this document, one would never know that the problem of regulating international migration is an important issue in world politics.

A fundamental weakness of the NAE's document, like that of other short denominational statements on complex issues, is its excessive generality. The resolution declares that persons are made in the image of God and should be treated with compassion. But the references to the Good Samaritan and to Old Testament migrations of peoples are too general to provide meaningful policy guidance. Although showing compassion toward persons is important, moral values like human dignity and generosity are in themselves inadequate to guide immigration reform because government is called to establish priorities among competing worthy goals—such as balancing the claims of refugees against those of guest workers, or the claims of illegal aliens against those of legal aliens who seek family unification. Clearly, compassion is a necessary but insufficient ethic to address the difficult demands of an overburdened immigration bureaucracy.

The NAE resolution calls for a variety of measures, some of them general and some of them specific. For example, the resolution attributes the rise in illegal immigration to the limited number of visas issued by the U.S. government. It then goes on to recommend that the U.S. government establish a more flexible mechanism to facilitate entry into the United States for "a reasonable number of immigrant workers and families." The resolution also calls for increased visas to encourage family unification and to establish ways by which undocumented aliens can gain legal status. These may be wise, prudential suggestions, but they are not justified by the document's brief biblical and moral analysis.

As I noted earlier, the Bible is not a manual on international politics. Scripture provides important values and perspectives, but it does not offer directives on public policy issues. Nevertheless, Evangelicals have a deep yearning to justify their political choices and policy predilections with Scripture. In the CIR debate, some Evangelical leaders and teachers have succumbed to this practice, using Scripture to either support or oppose amnesty.[30] Others have simply emphasized biblical principles relevant to the policy debate. For example, M. Daniel Carroll R., a seminary professor, highlights several biblical themes that relate to aliens, such as the inherent worth of persons, the priority of hospitality, and the reminder that Christians are aliens in this world.[31] Similarly, Matthew Soerens and Jenny Hwang, two staff members of World Relief, call for CIR, buttressing their claims by appeals to Scripture.[32] Like the NAE resolution, they suggest that the Bible teaches that strangers should be welcomed with generosity and kindness.

James K. Hoffmeier, an Old Testament scholar, offers a more nuanced application of Scripture to the immigration debate. Rather than simply highlighting biblical principles, he shows how such norms related to ancient Israel and how they might relate to contemporary geopolitics. Hoffmeier writes:

> People who take the teachings of Scripture seriously and want to treat people graciously will no doubt struggle to find an ethical and legal balance between helping those who are needy on the one hand yet are residing in the nation illegally on the other. Then too one must accept the fact that the Old Testament law draws a distinction between the legal alien and the foreigner. Consequently the Christian will continue to wrestle with being compassionate and yet recognizing that illegal immigrants, like themselves, need to submit to the laws of the land.[33]

Regardless of how one interprets Scripture, it is clear that the Bible is an insufficient policy guide on CIR. Scripture is, of course, essential in establishing the building blocks for structuring the moral analysis of public policy. But great care needs to be taken when applying Scripture to public policy issues, lest it be misused for political ends and thereby damage the church's credibility.[34]

If Evangelicals wish to contribute to a more informed debate on CIR, then they will have to give greater attention to the political ethics of immigration. And to do this, they will have to address several mid-level political questions, such as:

- What is the nature and purpose of the state? Is the state morally legitimate, and if so, does the government have a responsibility to make and enforce laws within its territorial boundaries?
- What is the moral relationship between citizens and foreigners? Should obligations to fellow citizens be stronger than to foreigners? If so, how much assistance should be extended to citizens from other states? Finally, what principles should guide the admission of aliens?
- What is the moral status of the decentralized, state-based global order? Is the division of the world into independent sovereign states morally just? If so, are the state-imposed restrictions on migration also morally legitimate? If not, should Christians oppose citizenship and encourage a cosmopolitan world with open borders?

Although articulating ideals like compassion for and hospitality to strangers is important, ideals are insufficient in devising prudent foreign policies.

Churches seeking to advance justice must do more than proclaim biblical ideals. They must do the hard work of integrating biblical analysis with a comprehensive analysis of the competing and conflicting interests among citizens and aliens. Finally, if churches are to maintain their spiritual independence and moral credibility, they should refrain from issuing simplistic policy pronouncements without carrying out the hard work of political ethics. The danger here is more than simply offering poor advice; the real threat to the church lies in the misuse of biblical authority for political ends.

Coercive Interrogation and the War on Terror

In the aftermath of the terrorist attacks of September 11, 2001, that resulted in the death of close to 3,000 innocent civilians in New York City and Washington, D.C., the Bush administration embarked on a war against Al Qaeda, the Taliban, and other radical Islamic groups. President Bush declared that in prosecuting the war against terrorists, the United States would make no distinction between the terrorists themselves and those who harbor and support them. Unlike interstate wars, a military campaign against nonstate actors is an irregular or unconventional war. Since terrorists carry out their operations covertly and seek to inflict fear in society by targeting innocent civilians, the effort to defeat such enemies is especially difficult. In conventional wars, the aim is to defeat the enemy's armed forces. In unconventional or asymmetric conflicts, however, the primary goal is not simply to punish terrorists but also to prevent them from carrying out destruction. Since preventing attacks is only possible with timely, accurate information, intelligence is essential in prosecuting an irregular war. In such a military conflict, the challenge is how to elicit information from captured unlawful combatants without violating fundamental moral and legal norms.

In prosecuting the War on Terror, the Bush administration decided early on that terrorists were to be regarded as unlawful combatants—to be treated humanely but not entitled to the protections afforded under international law. Intelligence agents were authorized to use coercive interrogation techniques selectively in securing information from captured Al Qaeda combatants. The U.S. government also increased the use of "extraordinary rendition"—that is, sending prisoners to foreign countries where they could be interrogated with fewer legal constraints. As a result of the relaxation of norms against coercive interrogation, numerous abuses occurred in detention centers and prisons. These abuses precipitated, in turn, an intense public debate about the manner in which the military and intelligence agencies were pursuing the War on Terror.

In an effort to raise public awareness about coercive interrogation, in 2006 religious leaders established the National Religious Campaign Against Torture (NRCAT). Their aim was to build a coalition among people of faith to pressure the U.S. government to halt inhumane treatment of detainees.[35] Subsequently, major church denominations, including the Presbyterian Church USA, the Christian Church (Disciples of Christ), and the U.S. Conference of Catholic Bishops, issued declarations and study documents condemning torture.

The first evidence of Evangelical concern with coercive interrogation appeared in February 2006, when *Christianity Today*, the leading Evangelical monthly, published an article condemning the practice. A year later, Evangelicals entered the debate when a small group of theologians and activists, led by David Gushee, issued "An Evangelical Declaration Against Torture: Protecting Human Rights in an Age of Terror."[36] This eighteen-page document was placed on the agenda of the NAE and adopted on March 11, 2007, with little discussion by its board of directors. Although the declaration did not emerge from the NAE, its endorsement, coupled with subsequent signatures from numerous other Evangelical leaders, reinforced the perception that the document was an expression of Evangelical thought on the War on Terror.

Although the declaration is titled "An Evangelical Declaration Against Torture," this title does not accurately describe its content. For one thing, the claims and analysis, outside of biblical references, are not rooted in distinctive Evangelical precepts. To the extent that its ideas on human rights are based on theological and biblical principles, those norms are Christian, not uniquely Evangelical. To be sure, the fact that the NAE leadership and numerous other Evangelical leaders signed the document provides legitimacy and reinforces the notion that the statement represents the views of a significant segment of the Evangelical electorate. Public opinion surveys, however, do not support this view. Indeed, a 2009 survey suggests that Evangelicals are more supportive of coercive interrogation in confronting terrorism than other Christian groups. According to the poll, 62 percent of white Evangelicals said that torture could be used often or sometimes against suspected terrorists in order to gain important information—a percentage that was higher than that of other religious or secular groups.[37]

The title is also problematic because the declaration is fundamentally about the sanctity of human rights, not the protection of civilians from terrorist aggression. The declaration's fundamental message is that life is sacred and that all human beings, whether citizens or terrorists, are entitled to human dignity. Paragraph 3.3 states: "Human rights apply to all humans. The rights people have are theirs by virtue of being human, made in God's image. Persons can never be stripped of their humanity, regardless of their actions or of others' actions toward them." Although one of the state's principal tasks is to ensure the safety of its people, the declaration seems to be far more concerned with the rights and well-being of detainees than with the security and welfare of potential victims.

Moreover, while the statement condemns torture, it does not define this practice. To be sure, intentional cruelty involving extreme pain is generally accepted as torture. But are threats and psychological pain equivalent to severe physical harm? Are deception and isolation torture? What about sleep deprivation and loud music? In view of the lack of conceptual agreement, Judge Richard Posner has observed that torture "lacks a stable definition."[38] Given the definitional challenges posed by the idea of torture, political ethicist Jean Bethke Elshtain has observed that "[i]f we include all forms of coercion or manipulation within 'torture,' we move in the direction of indiscriminate moralism and legalism."[39]

Does this document help inform the citizenry about the challenges of protecting society from terrorism? Does it illuminate fundamental biblical and moral norms that contribute to the development of ethical policies regarding the use of force in the War on Terror? Does the declaration offer principles that can contribute to a more secure and humane society? According to Daniel Heimbach, an Evangelical ethicist and seminary professor, the statement offers an extended condemnation of torture without ever defining what it vehemently rejects. Instead of condemning coercive interrogation, Heimbach argues that the drafters could have contributed to the public debate if they had examined the role of force in the current War on Terror and explored "at what point coercion crosses from moral to immoral."[40]

Keith Pavlischek, a national security ethicist, is similarly critical of the declaration's posturing and its failure to confront the moral obligations of the state in protecting citizens from terrorism. He writes: "The rights and obligations of legitimate political authority to protect and defend the commonweal are seriously underdeveloped. This is an odd omission for a document staking out a position on issues related to detainee policy in 'an age of terror.'"[41] Pavlischek is also troubled by the document's pacifist orientation. For him, as for most Christians, the church has historically supported the just-war tradition, which allows the state to use coercive force in the service of public justice. But since the declaration's basic premise is that life is sacred, the document fails to examine the boundaries of the state's responsibility to protect human rights and to differentiate between just force and unjust violence, between lawful combatants and unlawful terrorists. Pavlischek writes:

> International terrorists deserve to be treated justly. They do not deserve to be treated either as lawful combatants with the full rights due to honorable prisoners of war, or as ordinary criminals, with all the attendant due process rights. They are not ordinary criminals; rather, they are part of a global political-religious-ideological insurgency that employs terror as one means toward a well-articulated political end. However much we may quibble over the precise distinctions between what we do owe unlawful combatants by way of treatment or due process after capture, in distinction from that which we owe lawful combatants after capture, justice requires us to treat them precisely as the [Bush] administration treats them, as unlawful enemy combatants.[42]

Intelligence is critical in preventing terrorist actions. Given the secret, decentralized nature of terrorist organizations, electronic and photographic surveillance is unlikely to provide adequate information to prevent future terrorist acts. What is necessary is human intelligence, gathered either by spies or by interrogating detainees. Given the immorality and illegality of torture, does this mean that all manipulative techniques of interrogation are prohibited? How must detainees be interrogated? When a community faces extreme emergencies—that is, a community's safety and well-being are threatened—is limited coercive interrogation (what some observers call "torture light") morally permissible?

Stephen Carter, a professor of legal ethics, describes that challenge of interrogation as follows: "If those who possess the information would rather not part with it, the government will always be tempted...to require it out of them. The greater the sense of threat, the greater the temptation."[43] Legal philosopher Paul Kahn has observed that it is impossible to conceive of anti-terrorism without torture. Terror and torture, he writes, are "reciprocal rituals of pain" where sovereignty is beyond the law.[44] Thus, when the state cannot protect society from terrorism, it will be tempted to go beyond the law in protecting itself. Zachary Calo, a law professor, argues that in conditions of "supreme emergency"—when the fundamental values and security of a political community are threatened—some forms of torture may be morally warranted. He justifies his argument by attempting to find an intermediary position between the absolutist prohibition against torture and the conditional perspective based on necessity. Following the thought of political theorist Michael Walzer, Calo writes:

The only adequate response to necessity involves wrestling with the complexities that define the relationship between tragedy and democratic liberalism. It is into that dark space, neither transcendent nor pedestrian, to which the debate must move, so that we might more ably confront what Reinhold Niebuhr describes as the confusion which always exists in the area of life where politics and ethics meet.[45]

There is little doubt that torture—defined as inflicting severe physical harm on prisoners—is immoral and illegal. And as James Turner Johnson has noted, torture is inconsistent with the just-war tradition: first, because harm may not be inflicted on those not directly involved in using force; and second, because intentional harm or abuse is contrary "to what it means to be a good human person."[46] Perhaps Evangelicals need to be reminded that this practice is evil. But the challenge for Christians in the post-9/11 era is not simply to condemn the physical abuse of detainees but also to illuminate how a just government should respond to the threat of terrorism. In effect, the moral task is to reconcile the governmental responsibility to protect the innocent with actions that are consistent with biblical morality.

In Nazi Germany, Dietrich Bonhoeffer, a leading pastor of the Confessing Church, had to confront the challenging ethical task of reconciling his temporal duties to obey the German state with his spiritual obligations to follow God. In the end, Bonhoeffer became not only a staunch dissident but also an active participant in operations to kill Hitler. In addressing the complex challenges of a disobedient and unfaithful Lutheran Church and an evil political regime, Bonhoeffer found that moral principles were inadequate to deal with the challenges that he faced. Eric Metaxas writes of Bonhoeffer's struggle as follows: "Principles could carry one only so far. At some point every person must hear from God, must know what God was calling him to do, apart from others."[47] After he was imprisoned for undermining the Nazi regime, Bonhoeffer wrote about the moral challenges posed by the existential conditions that he confronted:

In the course of historical life there comes a point where the exact observance of the formal law of a state...suddenly finds itself in violent conflict with the ineluctable necessities of the lives of men; at this point responsible and pertinent action leaves behind it the domain of principle and convention, the domain of normal and regular, and is confronted by the extraordinary situation of ultimate necessities, a situation which no law can control.[48]

In sum, the NAE declaration provides a compelling case that human rights are important and that life is a basic entitlement. But proclaiming that human life is sacred does not ensure the protection of society from terrorist attacks. Christians—and decision makers responsible for human rights and the safety of citizens—need more than the enunciation of fundamental moral and legal claims. They need guidance in how to reconcile competing moral goods—namely, the humane treatment of enemies with the protection of citizens from terrorism. The NAE statement contributes little to this fundamental moral task.

Reducing Nuclear Weapons

Historically, military force has been viewed as a morally legitimate means to protect and defend the interests of states. Theologians and political theorists developed an elaborate theory of military force, known as "just-war theory," that specifies when a state may resort to war and how such a war should be conducted. The invention of nuclear weapons in 1945, however, profoundly challenged this moral tradition since nuclear weapons had such immense destructive power that they could no longer be regarded as instruments of warfare. Given their enormous power, nuclear weapons posed three fundamental moral issues. First, was the development and possession of such weapons moral? Second, could a state threaten their use when facing major aggression? And third, if deterrence failed, could a state use nuclear arms? In view of the moral challenges posed, a military theorist defined the emerging role of nuclear weapons in 1946 as follows: "Thus far the chief purpose of our military establishment has been to win wars. From now on its chief purpose must be to avert them."[49]

As a result, the major aim of U.S. Cold War nuclear strategy was to deter major aggression from the Soviet Union. Since it was impossible to defend society from an attack by nuclear ballistic missiles, the only feasible way to prevent nuclear war was through nuclear deterrence—that is, the promise of unacceptable retaliation. To this end, both superpowers developed and deployed tens of thousands of nuclear weapons during the Cold War to contend with any potential threat. According to strategic doctrine, so long as the United States could carry out unacceptable retaliation, global order would prevail.

Despite Cold War military competition between the United States and the USSR, the two superpowers were able to complete a number of major arms-control agreements that limited the number and type of strategic weapons.[50] When the Cold War ended in 1991, and the Soviet Union disintegrated into separate countries, the danger of superpower military conflict vanished, opening the opportunity for radical reductions in the strategic arsenals of both countries. To reflect this dramatic transformation in superpower global politics, both Russia and the United States carried out dramatic cuts in the number of their nuclear weapons. These reductions were codified in three accords—the START Treaty of 1991, the Moscow Treaty of 2002, and the New START Treaty of 2010.[51] At the same time, the international community became more concerned with the possibility of additional countries acquiring nuclear capabilities. In 1968, the world's major powers signed the Nuclear Non-Proliferation Treaty (NPT), which went into effect two years later. The NPT seeks to prevent the spread of nuclear weapons while simultaneously facilitating the peaceful use of nuclear technology.[52]

To ensure that military doctrine reflects the ongoing political changes in the international system, the U.S. Department of Defense periodically reassesses its strategic doctrine. Since the end of the Cold War, the United States has carried out three such reappraisals—known as Nuclear Posture Reviews (NPR)—one in 1994, another in 2001, and the most recent in 2010. The 2010 NPR identifies five major areas of concern: (1) preventing nuclear proliferation and nuclear terrorism, (2) reducing the role of nuclear weapons in U.S. security, (3) maintaining credible deterrence at a reduced level of nuclear force, (4) strengthening regional stability, and (5) maintaining a secure and effective nuclear arsenal.[53] It then recommends a variety of initiatives to implement these broad aims.

For example, to further reinforce the goal of nonproliferation and the maintenance of a secure deterrent, the report recommends that the United States forgo nuclear testing, encourage the ratification of the Comprehensive Nuclear Test Ban Treaty, and abstain from developing new nuclear warheads. Additionally, to reduce reliance on nuclear weapons, the NPR recommends that the United States refrain from using or threatening to use nuclear weapons against nonnuclear states that are party to the NPT and are in compliance with its provisions. Most significantly, the report calls for the long-term elimination of nuclear weapons. The report states:

> The long-term goal of U.S. policy is the complete elimination of nuclear weapons. At this point it is not clear when this goal can be achieved.... The conditions that would ultimately permit the United States and others to give up their nuclear weapons without risking

greater international instability and insecurity are very demanding. Among those are the resolution of regional disputes that can motivate rival states to acquire and maintain nuclear weapons, success in halting the proliferation of nuclear weapons, much greater transparency into the programs and capabilities of key countries of concern, verification methods and technologies capable of detecting violations of disarmament obligations, and enforcement measures strong and credible enough to deter such violations. Clearly, such conditions do not exist today. But we can—and must—work actively to create those conditions.[54]

Although nuclear pacifists like George F. Kennan and Jonathan Schell had sought to encourage a denuclearized world during the Cold War, the movement for a nuclear-free world developed significant momentum in 2007, when four former senior government officials—George P. Shultz, William J. Perry, Henry A. Kissinger, and Sam Nunn—published a widely read article calling for the elimination of nuclear weapons.[55] To further advance this aim, they wrote three additional articles and established the Nuclear Security Project.[56] In recent years, other groups have continued to advance the cause of a denuclearized world.[57] Thus, when the NPR declared that the long-term objective of the U.S. government was a nuclear weapons–free world, this was not a new idea but, rather, a vision that already had gained support among a growing number of government officials and scholars alike. The challenge that remains, however, is not simply to articulate the goal of a denuclearized world but also to create the political preconditions by which such a vision can be realized.

Since the end of the Cold War, nuclear weapons among developed, democratic states have become much less significant in global affairs. Indeed, in view of the large cuts in nuclear arsenals by both Russia and the United States, as well as the ongoing adjustments in nuclear strategy, both countries have achieved remarkable progress in reducing the danger of nuclear conflict. It is estimated that, at the height of the Cold War, the two superpowers had about 70,000 nuclear weapons, whereas by 2011 the total number of deployed nuclear warheads for both countries was less than 6,000.[58] Therefore, the most pressing nuclear problem in 2012 was not the status of the strategic arsenals among the major powers but the threat of nuclear proliferation, especially to rogue states or terrorist groups.

As noted in chapter 4, in 1986 the NAE issued "guidelines" to help structure moral reflection about nuclear deterrence in the context of pursuing peace, freedom, and security. At that time, there was a significant ongoing public debate about the role of nuclear weapons in American national security, and the guidelines were intended to assist Evangelicals in their analysis of the role of strategic weapons in pursuing a free, peaceful international system. Since the subject of nuclear strategy is of comparatively limited importance in the post–Cold War era, it is therefore surprising that the NAE decided to enter the policy debate on nuclear arms by adopting a statement titled "Nuclear Weapons 2011."[59]

The short declaration is divided into three parts: biblical foundations, pastoral concerns, and policy implications. The biblical section highlights four principles: the sanctity of life, the restraint of evil, the promotion of peace, and respect for "creaturely and generational limits." The pastoral section emphasizes the priority to love God, the need to love enemies, and the provision of moral guidance to those working in the nuclear weapons industry.[60] In cultivating the love of enemies, the statement declares that reliance on nuclear weapons has the potential to dehumanize citizens because of the threat of nuclear destruction.[61] In addressing the moral concerns surrounding employment in the nuclear weapons industry, the statement suggests that since some people may be "troubled by the ethical ambiguities" involved in making and maintaining weapons of mass destruction, they should seek assistance from pastors and chaplains who can guide them in "prayerful reflection." In the policy section, the declaration suggests that a thoughtful application of "evangelical principles" supports the following initiatives: (1) maintaining the taboo against using nuclear weapons, (2) pursuing mutual reductions in nuclear armaments, (3) increasing safeguards against the accidental use of nuclear arms, and (4) preventing the unauthorized spread of fissile material.

What motivated the NAE's Board of Directors to adopt this resolution? Did they regard current American arms-control initiatives, such as the New START Treaty or the 2010 NPR report, as inadequate? Did they want to encourage the four elder statesmen's call for a nuclear-free world? Or did they desire to strengthen the moral analysis of ongoing strategic initiatives? Whatever the reasons, given the document's simplistic and pacifistic nature, it is unlikely to foster either greater awareness of strategic concerns among Evangelical leaders and parishioners or a more discriminating moral analysis of nuclear strategy by national security professionals. Moreover, defense officials are unlikely to refer to the document since it neglects the most pressing nuclear-weapons issues, including the rise of new nuclear powers, the threat of nuclear terrorism, and the dangers of nuclear proliferation. Unlike the U.S. Catholic Bishops' pastoral letter of 1983,[62] which provided a compelling biblical, moral, and policy analysis of the problem of nuclear deterrence, or even the 1986 "guidelines" of the NAE's peace, freedom, and security program, this statement provides little moral analysis of the dilemma posed by the quest for a nuclear-free world.

Since the comparative advantage of church groups is in biblical and moral analysis, not global politics, policy initiatives undertaken by Evangelicals should ideally emphasize moral education rather than policy advocacy. The NAE statement seems to acknowledge this when it declares: "We write as church leaders, not military strategists. We speak because nuclear weapons...raise profound spiritual, moral and ethical concerns." But instead of explaining the nature of those concerns and showing how they relate to national security, the declaration proceeds to offer policy advice. For example, it suggests that deployment of tactical nuclear weapons should be prohibited. Additionally, it notes that "many knowledgeable observers argue that the mere possession of nuclear weapons decreases rather than increases national security," thereby implying the desirability of a nuclear-free world. Although these and other suggestions may have merit, they are rooted in the prudential judgments of other like-minded observers, not in the dispassionate moral analysis that church leaders can and should be offering to parishioners as well as the general public.

Since the end of the Cold War, the role of nuclear arms in international security has declined dramatically and will continue to do so, provided that political conditions permit further mutual, verifiable reductions. The NAE's claim that "the nuclear peace that has prevailed since 1945 has been based on the threat of imminent and mutual destruction" was of course the situation during the Cold War, but it is most assuredly not the case now. Nuclear arms continue to play a limited role in deterring aggression, but they are increasingly less important in the international relations of major powers.

Since international conflict is rooted in politics, not armaments, the quest to reduce the role of nuclear armaments in the modern world will depend upon the quality of global politics. Indeed, the possession of nuclear weapons by developed, democratic states poses little danger to world order. The chief threat to peace arises from territorial disputes such as over Kashmir, Israel/Palestine, and the Korean peninsula and from fragile states like Iran, North Korea, and Pakistan. Additionally, the quest for WMD by Al Qaeda and other terrorist groups poses a significant threat to global order. The quest for a nuclear-free world is a worthy goal, but so long as political rivalries continue, the United States will have to proceed cautiously in further reducing its reliance on nuclear deterrence. This is the conclusion of the 2010 NPR, and the NAE would have been wise to pay far more attention to this document in preparing its own analysis of nuclear weapons.

In its eagerness to participate in the policy debate, the NAE issued an advocacy document that offers few moral insights into the security challenges that major and minor states continue to face in the contemporary global system. Given the expertise of religious leaders, the drafters of the NAE document would have been wise to concentrate on biblical and moral analysis and leave the prudential judgments on national security policy to professionals with expertise in military and political affairs.

Conclusion

The policy shortcomings identified in this chapter are not due to the failure to adopt legislation and bring about desired policy reforms. Rather, the limitations of the Evangelical foreign policy initiatives are rooted in the inadequate application of biblical ethics and moral reasoning to the issues examined in this chapter. Since these issues are complex, it is not surprising that religious leaders and political activists define each of them in a variety of ways and offer strategies that vary significantly. Moreover, these issues are challenging because they involve fundamental ethical dilemmas, requiring trade-offs among competing moral goods. Since no simple solutions exist, categorical moral judgments are unwarranted.

As noted at the beginning of this chapter, the challenge in moral analysis is to devise strategies that advance worthy goals and produce the least harmful by-products. For example, addressing climate change is an elusive global issue, not simply because scholars hold different conceptions of the nature of the problem, but also because reductions in greenhouse emissions can impede the pursuit of economic growth. What makes this problem intractable is that it involves competing moral goals—namely, promoting jobs versus reducing the use of fossil fuels. Since economic growth will demand greater energy, the quest for economic expansion is inconsistent with demands to curb fossil-fuel use. Perhaps the best strategy in the meantime is to articulate broad biblical norms relevant to the issue and be more cautious in advocating specific public policies. Indeed, this issue illustrates an important principle of moral politics: Christians should remain staunchly committed to the defense of biblical and moral principles but offer prudential recommendations with humility.

International migration is also an important issue in global ethics. Since the international community comprises distinct sovereign states, governments are responsible for protecting the human rights of all persons within the sovereign territory of the state, regardless of people's legal status. Additionally, governments need to maintain humane immigration policies that allow legal entry (visas) to a reasonable number of migrants, including refugees. Since the demand for visas far exceeds the number authorized by the government, devising humane migration policies, including a response to those aliens who have arrived or remained without legal authorization, presents a morally challenging dilemma. While compassion is an important value in addressing the plight of the undocumented aliens, honoring the rule of law is equally necessary. Given the competing and conflicting claims on the status of the millions of undocumented aliens, it is not surprising that the government has failed to resolve the immigration dilemma. The critique of Evangelical engagement on this issue is not that the NAE failed to advance CIR but, rather, that the declaration failed to provide a competent, biblically based analysis of the problem. As a result, Evangelicals have contributed little to a more informed moral debate.

The Evangelical initiative on torture has similarly contributed little to a moral understanding of government's responsibility to protect the innocent from the threat of terror. As suggested earlier, declaring that the Christian faith affirms human rights and that all persons, victims and terrorists alike, must be treated with dignity contributes little to the cause of global justice. The challenge lies not in proclaiming the basic norm of human dignity but in illuminating how to protect civilians from terrorism. One strategy for countering terrorism is to detain and interrogate alleged militants. This was the policy followed by the George W. Bush administration. It is the policy that precipitated the NAE resolution. When President Barack Obama assumed office, he halted coercive interrogation of detainees and replaced detention and interrogation of militants with a more lethal strategy—killing terrorists with unmanned aerial vehicles (UAVs), like the Predator drone. By one estimate, from 2009 to 2011 the United States carried out 234 UAV attacks in the autonomous tribal areas of western Pakistan alone, killing close to 2,000 militants.[63] The NAE has not issued a resolution on drone warfare, but the new strategy poses significant moral challenges not unlike those involved with coercive interrogation. In sum, in confronting difficult issues like the protection of innocent civilians from terrorism, it is not enough to proclaim the sanctity of human life. The challenge is to prevent unjust aggression, and this requires much more careful analysis than what the NAE statement offers.

The problem of eliminating nuclear weapons is similarly challenging. Since the end of the Cold War, both Russia and the United States have dramatically reduced the size of their nuclear arsenals. But since nuclear technology exists, promoting a nuclear-free world will depend not only on technical and material developments but also on political reforms that reduce animosity and conflict among states and nongovernmental groups. The quest for a world with few or no nuclear arms is a worthy ideal, but religious groups will contribute most to this end if they help foster international trust and political harmony—the preconditions for a world with few or no nuclear weapons.

Evangelicals have contributed little to a competent understanding of these important public policy concerns and the moral dimensions of each of the issues. To a significant degree, they have failed to illuminate the complex, multidimensional nature of the issues and provided limited biblical and theological analysis to structure moral reflection on complex global concerns. The danger of simplistic denominational statements is not only that they fail to foster moral understanding of important public policy issues, but also that they can undermine the moral authority of the church.

TOWARD A MORE EFFECTIVE EVANGELICAL
GLOBAL ENGAGEMENT

How might Evangelical global engagement be further strengthened? The increasing concern of American Evangelicals with
domestic and international political affairs has been a salutary
development. The isolation and withdrawal of historic Protestants
from public life in the early twentieth century not only compromised the church's redemptive witness but also resulted in an overly
pietistic expression of spirituality. As a result, the emergence of a
more socially and politically engaged Evangelicalism in the mid-
1940s helped to restore traditional Protestant religion in America.
The rise of Evangelical political engagement, however, has presented a number of problems. In particular, how can Evangelicals
pursue political engagement without compromising the church's
fundamental spiritual task? Additionally, how can Evangelicals
contribute most effectively to the development of a humane and
just global order?

The Church and Political Engagement

Politics is divisive. It involves power, not love. And since political
action can dilute and even undermine the transcendent mission
of the church, political initiatives must be carried out with care
and caution. Alexis de Tocqueville long ago noted the danger of
political action by religious groups. In *Democracy in America*, his
profound reflection on the cultural, social, and political life of the
United States, he wrote: "[t]he church cannot share the temporal
power of the state without being the object of a portion of that
animosity which the latter excites."[1] Similarly, Herbert Butterfield,
the noted mid-twentieth-century British historian of international affairs, once observed, "It isn't the function of churches to
solve problems of diplomacy."[2] Thus, the goal in Evangelical global

engagement should be to influence moral analysis and reflection on foreign policy problems and global issues without getting directly involved in political decision making—to influence moral reasoning about issues without becoming a political pressure group.

Church groups can minimize the risk of losing moral authority if they pursue their task of global engagement by giving priority to their teaching mission and by emphasizing biblical norms rather than focusing on specific policy initiatives. This was the approach advocated by Carl F. H. Henry, a theologian who profoundly influenced the emergence and development of Evangelicalism in the 1950s and 1960s. While serving as the first editor of *Christianity Today*, he developed a set of principles on how Evangelicals should view the relationship of the church to politics:

1. The Bible is critically relevant to the whole of modern life and culture—including the social-political arena.
2. The institutional church has no mandate, jurisdiction, or competence to endorse political legislation, military tactics, or economic specifics in the name of Christ.
3. The institutional church is divinely obliged to proclaim God's entire revelation, including the standards or commandments by which men and nations are to be finally judged and by which they ought now to live and maintain social stability.
4. The political achievement of a better society is the task of all citizens, and individual Christians ought to be politically engaged to the limit of their competence and opportunity.
5. The Bible limits the proper activity of both government and church for divinely stipulated objectives—the former, for the preservation of justice and order, and the latter, for the moral-spiritual task of evangelizing the earth.[3]

It would be incorrect to view Henry's framework as a call for political inaction. On the contrary, Henry insisted that the Bible provided important principles of divine justice and righteousness. An important task of the church was to proclaim these biblical-theological norms, since God would judge individuals and nations in accordance with His precepts. The challenge for Evangelical leaders, therefore, was to engage in public affairs—helping to structure moral reflection on domestic and international political affairs—without compromising the spiritual, transcendent mission of the church. Reverend Richard John Neuhaus, in an important statement drafted for the

Institute on Religion and Democracy in 1981, offers a clear and compelling declaration of the church's central mission:

> The first political task of the Church is to be the Church. That is, Christians must proclaim and demonstrate the Gospel to all people, embracing them in a sustaining community of faith and discipline under the Lordship of Christ.... Communal allegiance to Christ and his Kingdom is the indispensable check upon the pretensions of the modern state. Because Christ is Lord, Caesar is not Lord. By humbling all secular claims to sovereignty, the Church makes its most important political contribution by being, fully and unapologetically, the Church.[4]

Nine years later, when launching his journal *First Things*, Neuhaus argued in a similar manner that transcendent moral values needed to have priority over the specific demands of public affairs. "First Things means," he wrote, "first, that the first thing to be said about public life is that public life is not the first thing. First Things means, second, that there are first things, in the sense of first principles, for the right ordering of public life."[5] How can churches and religious groups carry out this task? One important element is to identify and define fundamental international political issues that threaten fundamental biblical concerns. Problems like genocide, religious persecution, famine, or human rights abuse, for example, are far more important morally and biblically than specific issues like territorial disputes, international trade conflicts, and the reformation of global governance. A second dimension is the application of biblical morality to global issues. Once fundamental concerns have been identified, religious groups can illuminate and apply relevant biblical-moral norms to such problems. In dealing with religious persecution, climate change, or torture, for example, the church's chief contribution is to help structure moral analysis of such problems by illuminating and applying fundamental moral values. At the same time, biblical ideas should not be applied carelessly. For example, the principles of forgiveness and compassion should not be used to justify a default on a foreign debt or the forgiveness of egregious war crimes against military and political leaders. Similarly, the Old Testament notion of "welcoming the stranger" should not be used to justify unlimited admission of foreigners, thereby compromising the integrity of existing political communities.

The church's authority in public affairs is directly proportional to the quality of its understanding of global issues and the skill with which it identifies and applies relevant biblical-moral principles. Specific policy recommendations are the least significant contribution that religious groups can make. Since the church's competence is in moral affairs, not public policy analysis, Evangelical political engagement should give priority to the analysis of important moral global concerns, not policy advocacy. Indeed, the task of the church, or of religious associations like the NAE, is not to tell government officials what to do, but to help structure the analysis of important moral issues facing both individual nations and the international community. During the Cold War years, Christian ethicist Paul Ramsey critiqued the World Council of Churches for its excessive political activism, claiming that such engagement compromised its Christian witness. If the church was to pursue a more compelling witness, it was important to reduce its global political advocacy. Ramsey wrote:

> Christian political ethics cannot say what should or must be done but only what may be done. In politics the church is only a theoretician. The religious communities as such should be concerned with perspectives upon politics, with political doctrines, with the direction and structures of common life, not with specific directives. They should seek to clarify and keep wide open the legitimate options for choice, and thus nurture the moral and political ethics of the nation. Their task is not the determination of policy.[6]

Mainline Protestant churches did not follow Ramsey's advice. Instead, throughout the Cold War they issued countless declarations and resolutions on all sorts of foreign policy concerns, including arms control, the Middle East, U.S.–USSR relations, economic aid, and Third World development. The proliferation of such church recommendations, however, contributed little to the moral debate on complex global issues facing the U.S. government or international institutions like the United Nations, the World Bank, or NATO. Instead, they called into question the moral authority of the church itself because these political initiatives were often regarded as simplistic, divisive, and unrepresentative of their members' views. Indeed, as mainline churches and the National Council of Churches expanded their global political advocacy, their focus shifted from spiritual to temporal affairs, calling their spiritual influence into question. Additionally, as leaders became more active in political concerns, a significant gap emerged between the political ideals and beliefs of church leaders and those of parishioners. This gap, in turn, compromised the churches' ability to influence public policy debates.

In light of the dangers involved in religious political engagement, Evangelicals should proceed with caution in carrying out political action, especially when such initiatives involve policy advocacy. It is one thing for a church or religious organization to condemn policies and practices that it considers unbiblical or immoral. It is quite another for the church to tell government what its strategy should be in addressing such problems as human rights abuses in Zimbabwe, the quest for nuclear arms by Iran, or the legitimacy of economic sanctions in calling for regime change in Syria. It is therefore important to restate Ramsey's advice: church leaders should nurture moral reflection, not devise policy recommendations; and when a government strays from its legitimate tasks to pursue policies contrary to biblical morality, the church should condemn such action. For example, when the Nazi government expanded its sphere of influence to encroach on religious affairs in the 1930s, some Christian ministers responded by establishing an alternative church. This movement, known as the Confessing Church, believed that the church could only carry out its spiritual mission if it remained free and independent of governmental influence.

How, then, should Evangelicals approach the task of global political engagement? In chapter 4, I identified five principles of contemporary Evangelical political ethics: the primacy of the spiritual realm, the dual nature of Christian citizenship, the imperative of human dignity, the priority of individual responsibility, and the need for a limited state. Although these norms do not constitute a developed political theology, they nonetheless highlight distinctive features of an Evangelical worldview toward public affairs. Clearly, such principles can, and should, continue to structure Evangelical political thought and action. But these ideas alone are insufficient to advance an effective global engagement.

Evangelicals could rely, for example, on the social and political teaching of the Roman Catholic Church. As noted earlier, the tradition of Catholic Social Thought (CST) provides a body of moral principles that could help to promote a more just and peaceful global order. Because this tradition emphasizes reason and law in advancing justice and the common good, CST offers an optimistic framework for addressing global challenges such as war, human rights, and environmental protection. This tradition, however, is inconsistent with Protestantism's more pessimistic assumptions about human nature. Unlike CST's underlying faith in reason, Evangelicalism's conception of human nature questions the reliability of human reason as a basis for pursuing justice and the common good.

Evangelicals might therefore turn to a political theology that is more consistent with Protestantism's fundamental assumptions about sin and grace, such as the tradition of Christian realism. First introduced by Saint Augustine in his teachings about the radical distinction between the heavenly and earthly kingdoms, this approach was subsequently developed by other theologians and political thinkers. In the mid–twentieth century, noted Protestant ethicist Reinhold Niebuhr played a key role in further developing and popularizing this tradition.[7]

Niebuhr's political ethics were based on three core principles of Augustinian political theology: (1) the radical dichotomy between the "City of God" and the "City of Man," between the claims of the heavenly kingdom and the realities and responsibilities of temporal life; (2) the universality and ubiquity of human sin; and (3) the paradoxical character of human nature, expressed by both love and selfishness, altruism and egotism.[8]

First, Niebuhr believed that the heavenly and temporal kingdoms called for radically different approaches to life. Although love was the ultimate norm for citizens of the heavenly kingdom, it was a mistake to think that the temporal order could be governed based on this ethic. Love is not a reliable foundation for political society. Only government had the capacity and legitimacy to ensure order and advance justice.

Since humans are incapable of fulfilling the "law of love," social and political life must be judged instead by more limited measures. The challenge in moral politics is to foster initiatives that encourage and facilitate self-giving love. Religious moralists were not very helpful in this task, Niebuhr claimed, because they proclaimed the ideal of love as if it were self-enforcing. In his essay "Why the Christian Church Is Not Pacifist," Niebuhr wrote: "The gospel is something more than the law of love. The gospel deals with the fact that men violate the law of love. The gospel presents Christ as the pledge and revelation of God's mercy which finds man in his rebellion and overcomes his sin."[9] The gospel is thus a means by which limitations and imperfections are transcended—imperfectly and conditionally, to be sure, but transcended nonetheless.

Niebuhr argued that justice—defined as the acceptable resolution of conflicting interests and the fair distribution of resources—is the means by which conditional love is pursued within communities. Although both love and justice are closely interrelated, they are qualitatively different.[10] While love is self-giving concern for others, justice involves calculation, measurement, judgment, and the pursuit of fairness. Since justice, like love, is an ideal, it can never be fully fulfilled. The most that can be realized is partial or relative justice—an imperfect justice that balances competing interests. Communal harmony achieved through government and legal institutions is at best an approximation of brotherhood, or mutual love. It is an imperfect expression of mutuality because individuals and groups are never free of the power of egoism, which leads them to pursue their own interests as well as conceptions of justice in disregard of, or at the expense of, the values of others.

Second, Niebuhr's political ethics are based on belief in the universality and totality of human sin. Following Saint Augustine, Niebuhr regarded sin as universal and comprehensive, affecting all persons and every aspect of human life. No person is exempt from sin and no human action could successfully overcome self-love. Since reason itself is tainted by sin, reliance on moral principles can provide only a proximate guide to ethical action. Given the proclivity to self-interest and self-righteousness, the most effective way to advance the common good is not by identifying justice per se but by restraining self-interest.

Finally, Niebuhr assumed that human nature was dualistic—created by God but tainted by sin. Since people were created in the image of God, Niebuhr believed that persons had the capacity to love others, pursue the common good, and use freedom responsibly to promote justice, provided they acknowledged their finiteness, self-love, and pride. Because of the ubiquity and persistence of sin, however, humans could never love God and their neighbor fully. Self-love was always lurking in the background. Niebuhr's idea of human nature thus consisted of two dimensions, one leading to self-giving love and the other leading to self-interest. The first dimension equipped humans to promote the common good and foster just public policies; the second, by contrast, impaired justice by enthroning self-interest. Self-love and self-giving love were two sides of the same coin.

Since self-interest is especially pronounced in political communities, pursuing a just international order presents special challenges. Niebuhr was especially scathing toward idealists who regarded international cooperation as a simple task. "What is lacking among all...moralists, whether religious or rational," wrote Niebuhr, "is an understanding of the brutal character of the behavior of all human collectives, and the power of self-interest and collective egoism in all intergroup relations. Failure to recognize the stubborn resistance of group egoism to all moral and inclusive social objectives inevitably involves them in unrealistic and confused political thought."[11] According to Niebuhr, the only effective way to mitigate excessive national pride was through countervailing power—or what he termed "competing assertions of interest." More specifically, he argued that when major powers committed aggression, the only way to halt and rectify the evil was through war. This is why Niebuhr was a staunch defender of the Allied campaign to defeat Hitler and of the Cold War containment doctrine, designed to challenge Soviet communist aggression. He believed power was an essential instrument for pursuing an ethical foreign policy.

Given these foundational assumptions, Niebuhr devised a sophisticated system of political ethics to address global political problems. His Christian realist framework is characterized by four elements: the priority of power, the moral limits of political action, the need for humility, and the requirement for responsible political action.

According to Christian realism, power is the only way to sustain communal order and pursue proximate justice in political communities. Although love is an absolute ethic for believers, Niebuhr did not think that Jesus's morality was applicable to the task of creating and sustaining a humane political order, because voluntary human cooperation on a large scale is impossible. Therefore, political society needs government to ensure compliance and to confront the brutal realities of self-interest. The problem of communal order at the international level is even more difficult because no central authority exists to resolve conflicts among sovereign states. As a result, Niebuhr argued that the only way to pursue international order was by maintaining a fundamental balance of power among states.

As a result, Niebuhr was a staunch opponent of pacifism. He was supportive of believers who sought to model an alternative lifestyle based on Jesus's ethic, provided they did not use this approach as a political tactic. However, he opposed pacifists who considered their nonviolent approach not only morally superior but also more efficacious in confronting the problems of aggression and tyranny. According to Niebuhr, Christian idealists who were so concerned with avoiding violence were likely to end up supporting "the peace of tyranny as if it were nearer to the peace of the Kingdom of God than war."[12]

Second, Niebuhr's ethical framework assumes that because all political initiatives are tainted by partiality and self-interest, human actions are always imperfect, less than just. While the quest for the common good is often impaired by insufficient knowledge, the primary reason for the inadequacy of collective moral action, according to Niebuhr, is the inability to identify moral ideals dispassionately and then to faithfully implement them. Partiality and pride cloud perception and impair implementation. Since sin distorts all human initiatives, controlling the future is impossible. Niebuhr wrote: "The illusions about the possibility of managing historical destiny from any particular standpoint in history always involve ... miscalculations about both the power and the wisdom of the managers and of the weakness and the manageability of the historical 'stuff' which is to be managed."[13]

Even though all human political initiatives are imperfect, Christians should still pursue foreign policy initiatives that they regard as conducive to a just peace. Niebuhr thought that humane, morally worthy goals should be advanced while recognizing the inherent limitations of any effort to achieve them. Niebuhr captured the dialectical tension between the need for morally based public policy initiatives and the inherent shortcomings of all such initiatives in his defense and justification for democracy. "Man's capacity for justice," he observed, "makes democracy possible, but man's inclination towards injustice makes democracy necessary."[14]

Given such limitations, political action needs to be modest in scope. Modesty is important because human action, even when inspired by the loftiest ideals, is always compromised by human sin. Indeed, injustices are likely to increase when decisions are justified in moral terms without acknowledging the limits of reason and the partiality of behavior. According to Niebuhr, evil is likely to increase the most when leaders forget that they are "creatures" and pretend that they have virtue, wisdom, and power that is beyond their competence.[15] Pretension, not wrong action or improper judgment, was therefore the chief source of injustice.[16]

A third feature of Niebuhrian ethics is its call for humility in political affairs. Since understanding is always partial and human action is always tainted by sin, government leaders must avoid triumphalism in their political initiatives and programs. Such awareness, however, does not mean that moral judgments are impossible. On the contrary, people must use their knowledge and moral faculties to assess alternatives and then implement actions that are most consistent with available information. Although the Pauline assertion that "all have sinned and come short of the glory of God" can be interpreted to inhibit all moral judgment, Niebuhr argued that partial judgments are not only possible but also necessary. He wrote that while conflicts between enemies should disappear at the "ultimate religious level of judgment," it was quite appropriate to advocate distinct policy preferences on a provisional basis when confronting important political challenges.[17]

Niebuhr also advocated modesty because he opposed reducing political ethics to a single moral value. Since most issues and problems in international politics involve multiple moral norms, some of them in conflict with each other, simple moral verdicts are impossible. The ethical task is therefore to identify relevant moral norms, critically assess them in light of an issue or problem, and then identify the course of action that is likely to advance the common good most effectively. For Niebuhr, there was no single, overarching value to guide political thought. Rather, he used the Christian faith as a foundation to derive multiple values that he sought to integrate, in tentative and proximate ways, in order to meet specific challenges. Kenneth Thompson writes that Niebuhr was conspicuous among theologians for his insistence that there is no single, overarching norm for judging international affairs. He refused to see freedom, security, or justice as the controlling objective of American foreign policy. He agreed with Justice Holmes's claim: "People are always extolling the man of principle; but I think the superior man is one who knows he must find his way in a maze of principles."[18]

One of the major dangers in pursuing moral action internationally is that it can lead to self-righteousness and pride. Moralistic language, and in particular Manichean dualism, should be avoided. "The Christian faith ought to persuade us," wrote Niebuhr, "that political controversies are always conflicts between sinners and not between righteous men and sinners."[19] As a result, the task of moral politics is not to set up Christ's kingdom on earth but to pursue proximate justice by promoting peaceful coexistence, public order, and human liberty, while mitigating the effects of excessive self-interest. In this task, the Christian faith can provide important resources—such as truth telling, contrition, repentance, and forgiveness—that play an important role in inhibiting the spirit of vengeance and in promoting communal justice. In particular, the Christian faith can provide resources to foster humility and tolerance, thereby contributing to the development of a free society.

Finally, Niebuhr's Christian realism emphasizes the need for responsible, accountable action. In view of his emphasis on humility, the call for political engagement may appear contradictory. While Niebuhr cautioned against overambitious, self-righteous political initiatives, he was equally concerned with the dangers of inaction that might result from an ethic of perfectionism. Some moralists were so concerned with their own moral purity that they refused to confront injustice and tyranny because such action would compromise their ethic of love. But Niebuhr argued that the only way to sustain a stable and humane world was to harness power in the service of public justice. For Christian realists, therefore, the quest for a just international peace necessitates morally inspired, courageous political action. For Niebuhr, the great danger was not erroneous action but simply inaction. This is why he observed at the outset of World War II that the fundamental source of immorality was "the evasion or denial of moral responsibility."[20]

I have sketched elements of Niebuhr's Christian realism because it offers a framework that can help Evangelicals connect biblical and theological resources with the difficult and often intractable political challenges of the international community. In particular, Niebuhrian realism reminds

Christians that the quest for a just and a humane order in the world is a task achieved not through love but through the coercive power of government. Niebuhrian principles can remind Evangelicals that the demands of temporal affairs will necessarily involve power. In short, faith alone will not provide the requisite resources to carry out successful statecraft.

Principles for a More Effective Evangelical Political Engagement

If Evangelicals are to contribute to a moral political engagement in the world, they will need to understand the structure of global politics, including the role of the state in the global order, the nature of the international community, and the function of institutions in structuring the international relations of states and nonstate organizations. In addition, since churches have a comparative advantage in religious and moral teachings, Evangelicals should focus less on policy advocacy and more on the illumination of relevant moral and theological principles.

How, then, should Evangelicals engage in international affairs? How can they apply a Christian perspective to international political concerns without over-spiritualizing problems or plunging into overly specific policy advocacy? Here are some guidelines that can contribute to a more effective political witness.

1. *Develop a thorough understanding of the problem or issue*: If Evangelicals are to contribute to the moral analysis of American foreign policy, then they must be knowledgeable about the concerns they wish to address. Developing a competent understanding of a major global issue or problem is never easy. Policy issues such as climate change, international financial reform, and nation-building are not only complex and multidimensional, they are also morally ambiguous, requiring trade-offs among competing moral goods. As noted by sociologist Peter Berger, it is easy to proclaim a desired goal. What is difficult is to define the means by which that goal is to be attained, without incurring excessive costs or results that negate the good.[21] Even when political actors possess significant knowledge about a problem, they emphasize different perspectives and values, making consensus unlikely. In the American debate over how to respond to the large number of undocumented aliens, for example, some officials or advocates focus on border security, others on the number of visas, and

still others on due process for workers or the legalization of aliens who have lived in the country for a specified period of time. There is no simple way to reconcile these divergent perspectives and concerns, but if leaders wish to approach the problem authoritatively they must, at a minimum, acknowledge the legitimacy of competing values and the policy implications of divergent worldviews.

Such knowledge is acquired not by studying biblical and theological texts but also by developing social-scientific knowledge of the issues themselves. Typically, however, religious groups tend to oversimplify problems and underestimate their complexity. Such oversimplification is often evident among political advocacy groups, which tend to give precedence to those interests and values that accord with their policy preferences.

Religious advocacy groups, including Evangelical organizations, follow this pattern as well. The propensity to simplify issues was vividly illustrated in recent NAE declarations on immigration and nuclear arms. In its 2009 statement on immigration, the NAE approached the problem of international migration as if state border regulations were an impediment to a just, humane world. The fundamental message of the NAE declaration was that the U.S. government needed to establish more flexible and open borders, thereby "welcoming the stranger." But this conception of the world is at odds with the world's constitutional order as reflected in the United Nations system, where each member state is ultimately responsible for the security, welfare, and human rights of all persons within its territorial boundaries. The NAE statement, by giving precedence to migrants over border security and the rule of law, effectively promotes an alternative (cosmopolitan) global order. But it does so without providing a biblical or moral rationale for this view. Most important, however, that NAE declaration fails to illuminate the complex, multidimensional nature of the problem posed by undocumented aliens.

Oversimplification of issues was also evident in the NAE's 2011 declaration on nuclear weapons. The NAE issued this declaration with the ostensible aim of encouraging the United States to reduce its reliance on strategic nuclear weapons.[22] This is surely a worthy goal, given the destructive power of such weapons. Indeed, many strategic thinkers have argued that such powerful armaments are not useful as weapons of war but simply as instruments of deterrence. The problem posed by nuclear arms, however, is not simply or even primarily a military problem. As Carl von Clausewitz noted in his classic *On War*, the acquisition and use of military weapons is not an end in itself but, rather, a means to advance political objectives. In other words, armaments are simply tools that governments use to resolve interstate political disputes.

The challenge in building a just, peaceful world is, therefore, not simply the eradication of armaments but also the establishment of institutions that foster greater international cooperation and global peace. A more satisfactory approach to the problem posed by the world's nuclear arsenal must necessarily address the existing competition and conflict arising from distinct states, each of which seeks to maximize its own interests and cherished values. The development of nuclear capabilities, after all, did not arise because states were eager simply to wage war. Rather, the development of nuclear arsenals was a by-product of political competition and insecurity arising from the existing Westphalian global order. Global politics, not simply the reduction of military armaments, must therefore inform any effort to create a more peaceful and stable order in which nuclear weapons play a decreasing role. In the absence of a more comprehensive account of the interplay of politics and weapons, it is difficult to see how a statement by clergy can advance the goal of fostering a nuclear weapons–free world.

In short, Evangelical groups need to emphasize a thorough understanding of global issues before embarking on advocacy campaigns. To be sure, moral principles and theological perspectives can offer important insights into public policy debates, but morality alone is not sufficient to structure analysis. Political morality must be skillfully integrated into the issues and problems themselves.

2. *Identify and explain biblical principles*: The NAE and member denominations should emphasize that which they do best—namely, illuminating biblical norms that can inspire and guide individual behavior and collective action. Since the Bible is not a manual on politics, however, identifying and applying Scripture to social and political problems is a challenging task. Scripture must be interpreted and applied judiciously to public policy concerns, avoiding simplistic judgments and refraining from over-spiritualizing worldly problems.

As one might expect, Evangelicals, who believe that the Bible provides a full and sufficient revelation of God's will for humanity, rely heavily on Scripture not only for personal spiritual concerns but also for social and political guidance. Thus, it is not surprising that Evangelicals seek to guide their analysis of public affairs with references to the Bible. For example, the Evangelical declaration on climate change bases its call to action on Scriptural texts.[23] The declaration asserts that Christians must care about climate change for at least three reasons: love of God (Gen. 1; Ps. 24; Col. 1:16), love of neighbor (Matt. 22:34–40 and 25:31–46), and the demands of stewardship (Gen. 1: 26–28). While the Bible is clear about such norms, the policy conclusions drawn from them are not self-evident.

The identification and application of biblical norms needs to be undertaken with great care lest the definition of such principles be used to advance a particular policy agenda.[24] Not surprisingly, Evangelicals have been prone to overuse and misuse Scripture in public policy debates. For example, in the mid-1980s, a pastor of a large Evangelical church in Florida preached a sermon, using a text (Neh. 2:17) that called for the building of the wall of Jerusalem, as evidence to support President Ronald Reagan's strategic defense initiative—a space-based program to destroy incoming ballistic missiles.[25] Similarly, in 2006, the Evangelical Covenant Church (ECC) addressed the problem of undocumented aliens by spiritualizing the issue of migration in the following terms: "We walk with Jesus who was a wandering Galilean and resident alien often without shelter or place to rest his head. As faithful Christians, we are to welcome the stranger amongst us (Matt. 25:35), and to extend hospitality (Rom. 12:13), for we as the church are also a pilgrim people—aliens and exiles in the world (1 Peter 2:11). In so doing, we serve Christ himself."[26]

3. *Distinguish between the two kingdoms*: The church, as earthly representative of the universal kingdom of Christ, can provide a distinct perspective on global issues, such as arms control, foreign aid, or immigration. But the two realms of church and state are not similar. Since spirituality and statecraft are distinct, when religious leaders address temporal affairs, they need to resist the temptation to apply spiritual guidelines directly to public affairs. The propensity to "spiritualize" temporal affairs was illustrated by Reverend John Buchanan, editor and publisher of *The Christian Century*, in his reflections on how to address the problem of undocumented aliens in the United States. Buchanan described the church's perspective on migration as follows: "Our loyalty is to a kingdom that knows no borders or boundaries. We proclaim a God who welcomes us as strangers, which impels us to welcome the aliens and strangers in our midst. And we have a biblical teaching that says the law and the prophets are summed up in the command to love our neighbors as ourselves."[27] But what is the implication of this religious claim for the regulation of migration? How does this spiritual perspective apply to the governmental control of borders? If public officials followed Buchanan's interpretation, the existing Westphalian global order would be undermined and, in time,

cease to exist. Consequently, government officials charged with maintaining and enforcing the sovereign laws of countries will approach migration not from a religious perspective but as a temporal political problem in the "City of Man."

One consequence of the "two kingdoms" distinction is that biblical norms do not translate neatly into specific public policies. All persons, for example, bear the image of God and therefore possess equal and innate human dignity. But this equal dignity does not automatically create membership entitlements. The college where I teach admits only some students out of a large pool of applicants. A person may wish to work for a particular company, but the decision of whether to offer him a job rests with the employer, not the applicant. Membership in states is carefully regulated, requiring passports, visas, and other documentation before an alien may cross national borders. Individuals are free to leave their own country, but do not necessarily have a right to enter another.

Another important implication of the "two kingdoms" doctrine is that Christians, while sojourning in the "City of Man," are not freed from sin. One of the most important insights from Neibuhrian political theology is that all human initiatives are tainted by sin. Humans must avoid believing that their own policies and programs are devoid of self-interest. In politics, the moral struggle is not between the godly and the ungodly, the righteous and the sinful but, rather, among and within sinful individuals and groups. According to theologian Richard Mouw,

> The line between good and evil cannot be easily drawn between groups of people. The real conflict is between differing sets of basic life-guiding principles. Believers may have the right principles, but they continue to be plagued by their innate sinfulness. The antithesis reaches into each of us. And because of the working of common grace, unbelievers often perform better than we might expect, even when they serve perverse principles.[28]

4. *Illuminate and apply political theology*: While biblical norms are necessary in structuring moral reasoning on public affairs, they are not sufficient to address complex problems like nuclear arms, climate change, or immigration. Additional theological and political resources are necessary to help bridge the world of faith and the temporal realities of global politics. As a result, if Evangelicals are to address global issues effectively, they will need to devise a biblical and theological framework—a political

theology—that illuminates the relationship of faith to the temporal order. Such a political theology can help define, among other things, the nature of dual citizenship, the respective roles for the church and the state, and the nature and role of government in the state and global society. Whereas Scripture offers general guidance on spiritual and temporal life, political theology helps to mediate between the biblical norms and the specific problems of domestic and international political life.

Two factors have contributed to Evangelicals' neglect of political theology. First, the eagerness to act has undoubtedly impeded the development of a coherent system of theological and political ethics. Second—and more important—Evangelicals have typically addressed political issues by appealing directly to Scripture. But "Bible-only-ism" is not only ineffective in public life but also a potential threat to the integrity of religion. As D. G. Hart has noted,

> an appeal to the Bible on political matters, whether from Sarah Palin or Jim Wallis, is not essentially different from the attitude of fundamentalism. Appealing to an authority that has no standing within the legal and political institutions of society is likely going to be as unpersuasive as the fundamentalist pastor's sermon on behalf of prayer and Bible reading in public schools.[29]

In his classic *Christ and Culture*, H. Richard Niebuhr argued that Christians had devised five major theological approaches to the problem of how to relate faith to the demands of cultural and political life. It is therefore unlikely that Evangelicals could identify or develop one perspective for all believers. But theologies are human constructions, so theological pluralism need not be an impediment to biblical thought and action. Indeed, Niebuhr argued that God's plan for the world was in the mind of the Creator himself, not in the minds of his followers.[30] Humility is therefore essential in carrying out the task of cultural and political engagement.

Individual Christians come from different theological traditions and endorse a range of political theories. In thinking about international relations, they may prefer a realist or a cosmopolitan perspective. But while biblical norms are binding, particular theologies or political theories are not. The Bible does not dictate a particular strategy on how to deter terrorism or how to address issues of illegal immigration. Thus, when churches make official pronouncements on public policy, they need to make explicit their own theological and political presuppositions and distinguish between biblical principles and their own prudential policy recommendations. Their goal should not be to "win" any particular policy victory, but to help church members think more clearly about the possible political applications of biblical norms.

5. *Emphasize teaching over advocacy*: The church is the community of believers seeking to worship God, live according to the demands of the gospel, and share the good news of the grace of Christ. Since the church is not an interest group, lobbying government officials is not an important responsibility. Rather, its primary task is to preach and teach, calling church members to live as faithful followers of Christ and to proclaim the good news of redemption in Jesus Christ. When churches and denominational associations behave like political interest groups, they run the risk of losing their moral authority and spiritual credibility.

In dealing with the affairs of society, the church has a limited responsibility—namely, to illuminate biblical principles relevant to public affairs and to explain how such norms should influence human thought and action. In short, the church's teaching role is to help frame issues and problems from a biblical perspective. If evangelical leaders wish to advance public justice, they can do so by crafting documents that contribute to a fuller biblical understanding of major public concerns. Such documents can not only assist public officials responsible for making and implementing policies but also help parishioners develop perspectives that are rooted in biblical and theological analysis.

The 1983 U.S. Catholic bishops' pastoral letter on nuclear strategy, titled "The Challenge of Peace," stands as a model of how a church should pursue its teaching function.[31] Regardless of how one assesses the letter's recommendations, the document is significant because it provides an authoritative account of the problem—the dilemma posed by strategic nuclear arms in defense of legitimate national security objectives—along with a sophisticated analysis of how biblical and theological thought can be applied to the issue. The letter was influential because it addressed an intractable public policy issue at a time of growing public concern over the wisdom and morality of relying on strategic nuclear weapons that, if used, would have resulted in worldwide destruction. The drafting of the letter was carried out over three years by a group of specialists, involving multiple hearings with noted theologians, ethicists, military experts, and national security strategists. To ensure broad public engagement, the bishops issued two preliminary drafts, in 1981 and 1982, which were circulated widely and publicized by the media.

Although the pastoral letter was designed to educate American Catholics, the document was viewed as a resource for the general public as well, helping to illuminate the moral dimensions of a difficult public policy issue. The letter, in other words, was prepared to inform and influence citizens, political leaders, and government officials. The main contribution of the pastoral letter, however, was not its specific recommendations but, rather, its sophisticated moral assessment of U.S. nuclear strategy. Notably, the bishops emphasized that their authority was in biblical and moral analysis, not in the realm of prudential policymaking. They stressed that moral principles were to be viewed as binding, while the application of those principles to specific cases was not. The bishops wrote:

> When making applications of these principles we realize—and we wish readers to recognize—that prudential judgments are involved based on specific circumstances which can change or which can be interpreted differently by people of good will.... [T]he moral judgments that we make in specific cases, while not binding in conscience, are to be given serious attention and consideration by Catholics as they determine whether their moral judgments are consistent with the Gospel.[32]

The bishops admonish Christians "to enlighten one another through honest discussion, preserving mutual charity and caring above all for the common good." The pastoral letter declares: "Not only conviction and commitment are needed in the church, but also civility and charity."[33]

In sum, the pastoral letter is noteworthy because it illuminates how a religious group or church association can contribute to public policy debate through competent teaching. The church would have failed had it simply addressed the problem as a technical, military, or political problem. Instead, by bringing biblical, theological, and moral principles to bear on a difficult public policy concern, the Roman Catholic Church contributed to a deeper, wiser assessment of nuclear deterrence.

6. *Pursue public policy initiatives with humility*: In his short book *Politics for Evangelicals*, Paul Henry, who served in the U.S. House of Representatives until his untimely death in 1993, argued: "What is desperately needed is the moral humility to accept the fact that while God's standards are absolute and unchanging, we as individuals are never able to know or apply them with perfection."[34] As noted earlier, Reinhold Niebuhr also championed the need for humility. For him, the task of moral politics was

not to establish the kingdom of Christ on earth, but to pursue proximate justice. In this task, Christians could play an important role by modeling virtues such as truth-telling, contrition, compassion, and forgiveness. More particularly, Christians could contribute to the development of free societies by reinforcing humility, without which political tolerance is impossible.

A second reason why caution and humility are necessary in public affairs is the indeterminate and probabilistic nature of public policy. Political goals and intentions may be morally unassailable, but public policy is ultimately judged by its outcomes. And since few government policies are able to advance justice at the levels of goals, means, and results, trade-offs among these three dimensions are inevitable. Indeed, a well-known irony of policymaking is that initiatives often result not only in unintended outcomes but also in counterproductive results. The Immigration Reform and Control Act of 1986 (IRCA), for instance, granted amnesty to millions of undocumented aliens on the condition that employers hire only legal workers in the future. But the federal government never established an effective system requiring employers to comply with the law's hiring regulations. The heavy reliance of many business interests on undocumented workers also undermined enforcement of the employer sanctions. As a result, in the twenty-five years following the adoption of IRCA, the number of illegal aliens in the United States has grown nearly fourfold. Similarly, the strategic defense initiative (SDI), pursued by the Reagan administration in the mid-1980s as a way to provide some protection from enemy ballistic missiles, was regarded by some observers as immoral and unwise: immoral because it weakened the existing nuclear deterrent and potentially increased the possibility of war, and unwise because it involved massive expenditures on a dubious military initiative.[35] Yet, while SDI failed to provide an effective defensive shield, it nonetheless contributed in an unintended way to ending the Cold War by undermining the confidence of the Soviet Union in its capacity to sustain a continuing arms race with the United States.

Some of the policy initiatives examined earlier suggest that Evangelicals do not always pursue advocacy with tentativeness and humility. The NAE's statement on immigration, for example, expresses its views with high confidence, declaring:

The significant increase in immigration and the growing stridency of the national debate on immigration compel the National Association of Evangelicals to speak boldly and biblically to this challenging topic....Out of commitment to Scripture and knowledge of national immigration realities come a distinct call to action.[36]

The statement then goes on to make a number of specific recommendations, few of which fell within the competence of church leaders. This contrasts markedly with the more cautious approach taken by the Lutheran Church–Missouri Synod. In its 2006 "Joint Statement Regarding Immigration Concerns," Gerald Kieschnick, president of the Synod, and Matthew Harrison, executive director of the church's global relief program, state: "The challenges of illegal immigration are real and solutions must be found. While we accept our Christian responsibility to care for those in need, it is not the role of the church to specify particular civil legislation, either to its own constituency or to the government."[37] To be sure, Evangelical churches may—and occasionally must—voice concerns about public policy issues when they involve a threat to fundamental moral values. But if they offer opinions and judgments about how to address public concerns, they should do so with caution and care, highlighting the basis on which such recommendations are offered. Indeed, unless there is clear biblical basis for action, churches should avoid becoming centers of political advocacy, lest society begin to regard churches as interest groups. Paul Raabe, a Lutheran seminary professor, illustrates the desirability of individual engagement over denominational action in the immigration debate. He writes:

> The Lutheran church encourages her members to be responsible, active citizens. However, on the question of immigration laws, the Lutheran church does not have any special wisdom from the Word of God to determine which laws should be changed, if any, or how to change them. We leave that up to the consciences of individual citizens. But until the laws are changed, all Christians, including immigrants, should obey the laws of the land.[38]

In short, churches should participate in public policy debates when the issues involve fundamental moral values. But such involvement should emphasize structuring the moral debate, while deemphasizing policy advocacy.

7. *Finally, remember that Christians are pilgrims*: When conflict arises between the spiritual and temporal realms, the Bible teaches that

obedience to God must take precedence. When Peter and other apostles are brought before the Jewish Council (Sanhedrin) for teaching allegedly false doctrines, they declare that their first responsibility is to God, not the state. Peter boldly declares: "we ought to obey God rather than men" (Acts 5:29). Jesus himself says that his disciples should first pursue the "kingdom of God" and then fulfill other desires and obligations (Matt. 6:33).

Historically, Evangelicals have approached public affairs from two different perspectives—as crusaders or as pietists. Whereas *crusaders* seek to gain power in order to develop institutions and policies that are consistent with their moral values and religious preferences, *pietists* seek withdrawal in order to develop alternative moral communities based on their religious convictions and moral beliefs. The first approach emphasizes the development of governmental policies conducive to Christian morality; the second emphasizes the modeling of Christian virtues by churches, schools, and other mediating institutions. According to D. G. Hart, Evangelicals have frequently relied on the crusader model: "Evangelicals, often with benevolent intentions, have long been busybodies. Going back to the Second Great Awakening, they have organized any number of social or moral crusades. They did this, of course, thinking that the fortunes of the kingdom of God were at stake in the kind of society the United States would be."[39] Evangelicals have also been tempted by pietism, resulting in either over-spiritualizing worldly affairs or the more radical model of withdrawing altogether. But neither alternative is satisfactory.

One way of pursuing dual responsibilities to the church and to the state is through the model of pilgrim. Since Jesus commands his followers to be in the world but not of it (John 17:15–16), Christians are to work and serve Christ in the temporal city while maintaining their ultimate allegiance to God. A pilgrim is thus a believer who takes his temporal duties seriously but whose life is not ultimately determined by temporal demands. For the pilgrim, temporal responsibilities are important, but ultimate allegiance is to God. One of the most perceptive descriptions of the pilgrim model is an anonymous letter written to Diognetus in the third century, when Roman authorities were persecuting Christians. The letter states in part:

> Christians are indistinguishable from other men either by nationality, language or customs. They do not inhabit separate cities of their own, or speak a strange dialect, or follow some outlandish way of life.... With regard to dress, food and manner of life in general, they follow the customs of whatever city they happen to be living in,

whether it is Greek or foreign. And yet there is something extraordinary about their lives. They live in their own countries as though they were only passing through. They play their full role as citizens, but labor under all the disabilities of aliens. Any country can be their homeland, but for them their homeland, wherever it may be, is a foreign country. Like others, they marry and have children, but they do not expose them. They share their meals, but not their wives. They live in the flesh, but they are not governed by the desires of the flesh. They pass their days upon earth, but they are citizens of heaven.

If Evangelicals are to be authentic pilgrims, they must be *in* the world but not *of* the world. In *Bad Religion,* the *New York Times* columnist Ross Douthat argues that, contrary to conventional wisdom, the United States is not too religious but, rather, insufficiently religious. The problem is the rise of bad religion and the collapse of historic Christianity. According to Douthat, "today's United States needs to be recognized for what it really is: not a Christian country, but a nation of heretics."[40] American Christians, in his view, have ceased to be pilgrims, replacing core beliefs with "destructive pseudo-Christianities," such as the religion of prosperity or the narcissistic religion of self-esteem and self-discovery.

The challenge for contemporary Evangelicalism is to build on its important legacy of social and political engagement by remaining committed to public affairs while giving precedence to spiritual matters. The difficulty, of course, is in finding the proper balance between faith and the demands of temporal affairs. As I noted in chapter 2, a group of influential Evangelicals issued a "manifesto" in 2008 that called for the restoration of a less politicized faith. In order to renew a more authentic Evangelical faith, the manifesto declares:

Called to an allegiance higher than party, ideology, and nationality, we Evangelicals see it our duty to engage with politics, but our equal duty never to be completely equated with any party, partisan ideology, economic system, or nationality.... The politicization of faith is never a sign of strength but of weakness. The saying is wise: "The first thing to say about politics is that politics is not the first thing."[41]

Douthat echoes the manifesto, arguing that if an authentic Christianity is to be renewed in America, it will have to emphasize transcendence over partisanship, moral principles over ideology. Faith, he writes, should be "political without being partisan."[42]

Following these seven principles is likely to foster a more limited and circumspect political engagement by the church. This, however, does not mean that Evangelical influence will be reduced. On the contrary, by following these guidelines, Evangelical churches can avoid excessive and unwise political action and thereby strengthen their influence on American society. Nearly two centuries ago, Alexis de Tocqueville observed that religion in America was vibrant and influential precisely because it had no official, political role. In the late twentieth century, mainline denominations saw their membership and influence plummet as many historic Protestants came to view them as less concerned with preaching the word of God than with taking fashionable public stances on high-profile issues. Their decline opened the door for Evangelical churches, more intent on their ecclesiastical mission, to significantly increase their membership. It would be regrettable indeed if those same denominations, having helped to revitalize American religion, now found themselves tempted by the allure of political influence to follow the mainline churches back into irrelevance.

NOTES

INTRODUCTION

1. Walter Russell Mead, "God's Country?: Evangelicals and U.S. Foreign Policy," *Foreign Affairs*, 85 (September/October 2006), 24.
2. Mead, "God's Country?," 36.
3. ISAE, "How Many Evangelicals Are There?" Available at: http://isae.wheaton.edu/defining-evangelicalism/how-many-evangelicals-are-there/
4. In the 1960s, the National Association of Evangelicals (NAE) adopted seven resolutions condemning communism.
5. NAE, "Communism 1961." This resolution is available at: www.nae.net/fullresolutionlist
6. The NAE adopted five resolutions on religious persecution, three during the Cold War and two in the post–Cold War era. See resolutions at: www.nae.net/fullresolutionlist
7. Nicholas Kristof, "Following God Abroad," *New York Times*, May 21, 2002, A21.
8. Frances Fitzgerald, "The New Evangelicals," *The New Yorker*, June 30, 2008, 28–34.
9. "An Evangelical Manifesto: A Declaration of Evangelical Identity and Public Commitment," May 7, 2008, Washington, D.C., 20. Available at: www.evangelicalmanifesto.com

CHAPTER 1

1. Both Niccolò Machiavelli and Thomas Hobbes, considered the founders of modern political realism, questioned the existence of international moral norms, while modern diplomats, such as Harold Nicolson, a noted early twentieth-century British diplomat, claimed that international morality did not exist. See Harold Nicolson, *Diplomacy*, 3rd ed. (New York: Oxford University Press, 1973), 147.
2. A. J. M. Milne, "Human Rights and the Diversity of Morals: A Philosophical Analysis of Rights and Obligations in the Global System," in *Rights and Obligations in North-South Relations: Ethical Dimensions of Global Problems*, ed. Moorehead Wright (New York: St. Martin's, 1986), 21.

3. Michael Walzer, *Thick and Thin: Moral Argument at Home and Abroad* (Notre Dame, IN: University of Notre Dame Press, 1994), 1–19.

4. Michael Walzer, *Just and Unjust Wars: A Moral Argument with Historical Illustrations*, 4th ed. (New York: Basic Books, 2006), 19.

5. James Q. Wilson, *The Moral Sense* (New York: Free Press, 1995), 251.

6. Alberto R. Coll, "The Relevance of Christian Realism to the Twenty-First Century," in *Christianity and Power Politics: Christian Realism and Contemporary Political Dilemmas*, ed. Eric Patterson (New York: Palgrave Macmillan, 2008), 41.

7. Arthur Schlesinger, Jr., "The Necessary Amorality of Foreign Affairs," *Harper's Magazine*, August 1971, 72.

8. David Halloran Lumsdaine, *Moral Vision in International Politics: The Foreign Aid Regime, 1949–1989* (Princeton, NJ: Princeton University Press, 1993), 283.

9. George Kennan, *Realities of American Foreign Policy* (New York: Norton, 1966), 48.

10. George Kennan, "Morality and Foreign Policy," *Foreign Affairs* 64 (Winter 1985–86), 205–218.

11. Dean Acheson, "Ethics in International Relations Today," *Vital Speeches of the Day*, February 1, 1965, 227.

12. Arnold Wolfers, *Discord and Collaboration: Essays on International Politics* (Baltimore: Johns Hopkins University Press, 1962), 58.

13. Robert Kennedy, *Thirteen Days* (New York: Norton, 1968), 27.

14. Walter Russell Mead, *Special Providence: American Foreign Policy and How It Changed the World* (New York: Routledge, 2001), 35.

15. For an overview of how a religious-sensitive perspective can strengthen foreign policy analysis, see Jonathan Chaplin, ed., *God and Global Order: The Power of Religion in American Foreign Policy* (Waco, TX: Baylor University Press, 2010).

16. Walter Russell Mead, "God's Country: Evangelicals and U.S. Foreign Policy," *Foreign Affairs* 85 (September/October 2006), 24.

17. Quoted in Robert N. Bellah, *The Broken Covenant: American Civil Religion in Time of Trial* (New York: Seabury Press, 1975), 15.

18. James W. Skillen, *With or Against the World?: America's Role Among the Nations* (Lanham, MD: Rowman & Littlefield, 2005), 78.

19. Walter A. McDougall, *Promised Land, Crusader State: The American Encounter with the World Since 1776* (New York: Mariner Books, 1997), 18.

20. J. F. Kennedy, "Inaugural Address," January 20, 1961. Available at: http://www.jfklibrary.org

21. Ronald Reagan, "Remarks at the Annual Convention of the National Religious Broadcasters," January 31, 1983. Available at: http://www.reagan.utexas.edu/archives/speeches/1983/13183b.htm

22. Robert N. Bellah, *The Broken Covenant: American Civil Religion in Time of Trial* (New York: Seabury Press, 1975), 3.

23. Robert N. Bellah, "Civil Religion in America," *Daedalus, Journal of the American Academy of Arts and Sciences* 96 (Winter 1967), 1–21.

24. James W. Skillen, "Evangelicals and American Exceptionalism," *The Review of Faith & International Affairs* 4 (Winter 2006), 45.

25. Skillen, "Evangelicals and American Exceptionalism," 46.

26. USA Today/Gallup, December 10–12, 2010.

27. Pew Research Center, "American Exceptionalism Subsides: The American-Western European Values Gap," November 11, 2011. Available at: http://www.pewglobal.org/2011/11/17/the-american-western-european-values-gap/

28. Robert N. Bellah, *Beyond Belief: Essays on Religion in a Post-Traditionalist World* (Berkeley: University of California Press, 1991), 168.

29. McDougall, *Promised Land, Crusader State*, 37.

30. Madeleine Albright, *The Mighty & The Almighty: Reflections on America, God, and World Affairs* (New York: HarperCollins, 2006), 32.

31. John C. Bennett, *Foreign Policy in Christian Perspective* (New York: Charles Scribner's Sons, 1966), 36.

32. In that study, Jones sets forth the fundamental principles of international society based upon accepted treaties, conventions, declarations, and other international agreements. The code involves nine basic tenets, including: the sovereign equality of states, the territorial integrity and political independence of states, peaceful settlement of disputes between states, abstention from the threat or use of force, and respect for human rights. See Dorothy Jones, *Code of Peace: Ethics and Security in the World of Warlord States* (Chicago: University of Chicago Press, 1992).

33. Nicholas Wolterstorff, "Theological Foundations for an Evangelical Political Philosophy," in *Toward an Evangelical Public Policy*, eds. Ronald J. Sider and Diane Knippers (Grand Rapids, MI: Baker Books, 2005), 160.

34. Bennett, *Foreign Policy in Christian Perspective*, 37.

35. Charles Villa-Vicencio, *A Theology of Reconstruction: Nation-Building and Human Rights* (Cambridge: Cambridge University Press, 1992), 126.

36. Vaclav Havel, "Kosovo and the End of the Nation-State," *New York Review of Books*, July 10, 1999, 6.

37. Michael Novak, "Needing Niebuhr Again," *Commentary*, September 1972, 52.

38. Reinhold Niebuhr, *The Irony of American History* (New York: Charles Scribner's Sons, 1952), 72.

39. H. Richard Niebuhr, *Christ and Culture* (New York: Harper Torchbooks, 1951), 2.

40. Reinhold Niebuhr, "Why the Christian Church Is Not Pacifist," in *The Essential Reinhold Niebuhr: Selected Essays and Addresses*, ed. Robert McAfee Brown (New York: Yale University Press, 1986), 111.

41. Nicholas Wolterstorff, *Until Justice and Peace Embrace* (Grand Rapids, MI: Eerdmans, 1983), 70.

42. Emil Brunner once observed that love was always just, but that justice was not necessarily love. See Emil Brunner, *Justice and the Social Order* (New York: Harper and Brothers, 1945), 261.

43. Brunner, *Justice and the Social Order*, 261.

44. Wolterstorff, *Until Justice and Peace Embrace*, 72.

45. Desmond Tutu, *No Future Without Forgiveness* (New York: Doubleday, 1999).
46. Hannah Arendt, *The Human Condition* (Chicago: University of Chicago Press, 1958), 241.
47. Donald W. Shriver, Jr., *An Ethic for Enemies: Forgiveness in Politics* (New York: Oxford University Press, 1995).
48. Mark R. Amstutz, *The Healing of Nations: The Promise and Limits of Political Forgiveness* (Boulder: Rowman & Littlefield, 2005).
49. Jean Bethke Elshtain, "Identity, Sovereignty, and Self-Determination," in *Sovereignty at the Crossroads? Morality and International Politics in the Post–Cold War Era*, ed. Luis E. Lugo (Boulder: Rowman & Littlefield, 1996), 116.
50. For a discussion of the role of religious values and beliefs and public policy decision making, see Paul Charles Merkley, *American Presidents, Religion, and Israel* (Westport, CT: Praeger, 2004).
51. George W. Bush, "Immigration Reform: Address in California," April 24, 2006. Available at: http://www.presidentialrhetoric.com/speeches/04.24.06.html
52. "President Bush Delivers Graduation Speech at West Point," U.S. Military Academy, June 1, 2002. Available at: http://georgewbush-whitehouse.archives.gov/news/releases/2002/06/20020601-3.html
53. Peter Singer, *The President of Good & Evil: The Ethics of George W. Bush* (New York: Dutton, 2004), 2.
54. Merkley, *American Presidents, Religion, and Israel*, x.
55. For example, see Ole Holsti, *Public Opinion and American Foreign Policy*, rev. ed. (Ann Arbor: University of Michigan Press, 2004).

CHAPTER 2

1. Alister E. McGrath, *Christianity: an Introduction* (Oxford: Blackwell, 1997), 332.
2. Mark A. Noll, *America's God: From Jonathan Edwards to Abraham Lincoln* (New York: Oxford University Press, 2002), 42–50.
3. Noll, *America's God*, 166.
4. Robert D. Putnam and David E. Campbell, *American Grace: How Religion Divides and Unites Us* (New York: Simon & Schuster, 2010), 12.
5. James Reed, *The Missionary Mind and American East Asia Policy, 1911–1915* (Cambridge, MA: Harvard University Press, 1983), 18.
6. McGrath, *Christianity*, 327.
7. Mark A. Noll, "The Scandal of Evangelical Political Reflection," in *Being Christian Today: An American Conversation*, eds. Richard John Neuhaus and George Weigel (Washington, DC: Ethics and Public Policy Center, 1992), 78.
8. Quoted in John R. Stone, *On the Boundaries of American Evangelicalism: The Postwar Evangelical Coalition* (New York: St. Martin's, 1997), 144–145.
9. Gerald R. McDermott, "Evangelicals and Israel," in *Uneasy Allies?; Evangelical and Jewish Relations*, eds. Alan Mittleman, Byron Johnson, and Nancy Isserman (New York: Lexington Books, 2007), 131–133.

10. Christian Smith, *Christian America? What Evangelicals Really Want* (Berkeley: University of California Press, 2000), 16.

11. The Barna standard requires that respondents must be "born again" Christians—which means that they must have made a personal commitment to Jesus Christ and must believe that they are going to heaven as a result of their acceptance of Christ as personal savior. Additionally, respondents must indicate agreement with seven other beliefs. These additional criteria are: (1) saying that faith is important in their life, (2) sharing their Christian beliefs with non-Christians, (3) believing in the existence of Satan, (4) believing salvation is the result of grace, not works, (5) believing that Jesus lived a sinless life, (6) believing in the trustworthiness of Scripture, and (7) believing that God is the perfect, all-powerful deity who created the world and continues to rule it now. For a further discussion of the definition of Evangelicals, see Corwin Smidt, "The Measurement of Evangelicals, 'The Immanent Frame,'" Social Science Research Council Blog. Available at: http://blogs.ssrc.org/tif/2008/08/29/the-measurement-of-evangelicals/

12. McGrath, *Christianity*, 331.

13. David W. Bebbington, *Evangelicalism in Modern Britain: A History from the 1730s to the 1980s* (London: Unwin Hyman, 1989), 2–17.

14. Timothy Shah, "Some Evangelical Views of the State," in *Church, State and Citizen: Christian Approaches to Political Engagement*, ed. Sandra Joireman (New York: Oxford University Press, 2009), 115.

15. Andrew F. Walls, *The Missionary Movement in Christian History: Studies in the Transmission of Faith* (Maryknoll, NY: Orbis Books, 2005), 81.

16. See Walls, *The Missionary Movement in Christian History*, 82–83.

17. Rufus Anderson, "The Time for the World's Conversion Come," in *To Advance the Gospel: Selections from the Writings of Rufus Anderson*, ed. R. Pierce Beaver (Grand Rapids, MI: Eerdmans, 1967), 65.

18. Walls, *The Missionary Movement in Christian History*, 225.

19. "Response to Carl F. H. Henry," in *Evangelical Affirmations*, eds. K. S. Kantzer and C. F. H. Henry (Grand Rapids, MI: Zondervan, 1990), 97.

20. Jon R. Stone, *On the Boundaries of American Evangelicalism: The Postwar Evangelical Coalition* (New York: St. Martin's, 1997), 2.

21. David P. Gushee and Dennis P. Hollinger, "Toward an Evangelical Ethical Methodology," in *Toward an Evangelical Public Policy: Political Strategies for the Health of the Nation*, eds. Ronald J. Sider and Diane Knippers (Grand Rapids, MI: Baker Books, 2005), 120.

22. Institute for the Study of American Evangelicals, "How Many Evangelicals Are There?" Available at: http://isae.wheaton.edu/defining-evangelicalism/how-many-evangelicals-are-there/

23. Robert D. Putnam and David E. Campbell, *American Grace: How Religion Divides and Unites Us* (New York: Simon & Schuster, 2010), 16.

24. Smith, *Christian America?*, 16.

25. Carl F. H. Henry, *The Uneasy Conscience of Modern Fundamentalism* (Grand Rapids, MI: Eerdmans, 1947).
26. The sociologist D. Michael Lindsay has captured the growing influence and sophistication of Evangelicals in his book *Faith in the Halls of Power: How Evangelicals Joined the American Elite* (New York: Oxford University Press, 2008).
27. This decline is evident in the large and rapid fall in church membership in the principal Protestant denominations, including Methodist, Episcopalian, Presbyterian, and Lutheran churches. While the National Council of Churches (NCC)—with 36 denominations—continues to claim some 100,000 congregations with about 45 million members, this membership estimate grossly overstates the size of the mainline. To begin with, many churches overstate their membership because they include persons who were legitimately added to the membership list but who have stopped attending or have moved away. (The counting of church members is difficult since there are no widely accepted standards for membership. It is easy to add the names of family members who join a local church. But what happens when they move away, or stop attending, or the children move on?) Additionally, participation in worship and church activities is less frequent in mainline denominations than in Evangelical churches. The latter tend to define religious commitment in terms of the level of institutional engagement and financial support. Finally, as noted earlier, a large part of mainline churches are Evangelical and not aligned with the liberal religious and progressive political orientation of its leaders.
28. Walter Russell Mead, "God Country?: Evangelicals and U.S. Foreign Policy," *Foreign Affairs* 85 (September/October 2006), 36.
29. Kenneth L. Woodward, "Dead End for the Mainline? The Mightiest Protestants Are Running Out of Money, Members and Meaning," *Newsweek*, August 9, 1993, 46–48.
30. Joseph Bottum, "The Death of Protestant America: A Political Theory of the Protestant Mainline, *First Things,* August/September, 2008, 24.
31. According to one study on why the mainline was declining, three pollsters concluded that the reason was a loss of religious faith. They found that "the single best predictor of church participation turned out to be belief—orthodox Christian belief, and especially the teaching that a person can be saved only through Jesus Christ." See Benton Johnson, Dean R. Hoge, and Donald A. Luidens, "Mainline Churches: The Real Reason for Decline," *First Things,* March 1993. Available at: http://www.firstthings.com/article/2008/05/001-mainline-churches-the-real-reason-for-decline-8
32. Bottum, "The Death of Protestant America," 24.
33. "Understanding American Evangelicals: A Conversation with Mark Noll and Jay Tolson," Center Conversations, June 2004 (Washington, DC: Ethics and Public Policy Center), 2.
34. For a description and critique of this form of Christianity, see David Wells, *The Courage to Be Protestant: Truth-lovers, Marketers, and Emergents in the Postmodern World* (Grand Rapids, MI: Eerdmans, 2008).

35. David D. Kirkpatrick, "The Evangelical Crackup," *New York Times Magazine*, October 28, 2007, 38–68. See also Frances Fitzgerald, "Annals of Religion: The New Evangelicals," *The New Yorker*, June 30, 2008, 28–34.

36. David P. Gushee, *The Future of Faith in American Politics: The Public Witness of the Evangelical Center* (Waco, TX; Baylor University Press, 2008).

37. "An Evangelical Manifesto: A Declaration of Evangelical Identity and Public Commitment," May 7, 2008, 14. Available at: http://www.anevangelicalmanifesto.com/

38. "An Evangelical Manifesto," 15.

39. Putnam and Campbell, *American Grace*, 424.

40. Putnam and Campbell, *American Grace*, 421.

41. Lamin Sanneh, *Disciples of All Nations: Pillars of World Christianity* (New York: Oxford University Press, 2008), 275.

42. Sanneh, *Disciples of All Nations*, 276.

43. Pentecostalism is a renewal movement that began in the United States in the early twentieth century and takes its name from Pentecost, when the Holy Spirit descended upon the early followers of Jesus Christ (Acts 2). Although there are many Pentecostal church groups, they all share a belief in the importance of being "filled" or "baptized" in the Holy Spirit as a second experience after one's personal salvation. This subsequent filling of the Holy Spirit is manifested by the expression of spiritual gifts. Pentecostalism has spread to mainline Protestant churches as well as Roman Catholicism. Scholars call such believers "Charismatic Christians."

44. Sanneh, *Disciples of All Nations*, 275.

CHAPTER 3

1. Arthur Schlesinger, Jr., "The Missionary Enterprise and Theories of Imperialism," in *The Missionary Enterprise in China and America*, ed. John K. Fairbank (Cambridge, MA: Harvard University Press, 1974), 350.

2. Daniel J. Boorstin, *The Americans: The Democratic Experience* (New York: Random House, 1973), 562.

3. James Reed, *The Missionary Mind and American East Asia Policy, 1911–1915* (Cambridge, MA: Harvard University Press, 1983), 13.

4. See William Hutchison, *Errand to the World: American Protestant Thought and Foreign Missions* (Chicago: University of Chicago Press, 1987), 1.

5. Interdenominational Foreign Mission Association, *Missions Annual—1958* (New York: IFMA, 1958), 40.

6. A. Scott Moreau, "Putting the Survey in Perspective," in *Mission Handbook: U.S. and Canadian Protestant Ministries Overseas, 2004–2006*, eds. Dotsey Welliver and Minnette Northcutt (Wheaton, IL.: Billy Graham Center, Wheaton College, 2004), 18.

7. Moreau, "Putting the Survey in Perspective," 35.

8. The three largest Evangelical missions organizations were the Southern Baptist Convention, the Assemblies of God, and New Tribes Mission, accounting for

5,437, 1,708, and 1,496 missionaries, respectively. See Moreau, "Putting the Survey in Perspective," 13 and 35.

9. Boorstin, *The Americans*, 562–563.
10. Stephen Neill, *Colonialism and Christian Missions* (New York: McGraw-Hill, 1966), 11–12.
11. Jean Comaroff and John Comaroff, *Of Revelation and Revolution: Christianity, Colonialism, and Consciousness in South Africa* (Chicago: University of Chicago Press, 1991), 309–310.
12. Lamin Sanneh, *Disciples of All Nations: Pillars of World Christianity* (New York: Oxford University Press, 2008), 134. See especially chapter 4, which examines the interrelationship of missions and colonialism.
13. Andrew Preston, *Sword of the Spirit, Shield of Faith: Religion in American War and Diplomacy* (New York: Alfred A. Knopf, 2012), 183.
14. Neill, *Colonialism and Christian Missions*, 413.
15. Neill, *Colonialism and Christian Missions*, 413.
16. John K. Fairbank, "Introduction: The Many Faces of Protestant Missions in China and the United States," in *The Missionary Enterprise in China and America*, ed. John K. Fairbank (Cambridge, MA: Harvard University Press, 1974), 20.
17. Schlesinger, Jr., "The Missionary Enterprise," 371.
18. When missionaries confronted customs they regarded as repugnant and inconsistent with human dignity—such as child slavery, the victimization of widows in India (Sati), and foot-binding in China—they publicly condemned such practices and sought to prohibit them.
19. Walter Russell Mead, *Special Providence: American Foreign Policy and How It Changed the World* (New York: Routledge, 2002), 143.
20. Schlesinger, Jr., "The Missionary Enterprise," 336–373.
21. Hutchinson, *Errand to the World*, 76.
22. Fairbank, "Introduction," 7.
23. Since he was deeply committed to the religious neutrality of the state, he showed that Sati was not a religiously sanctioned tradition but, rather, a practice that had become widely accepted in Hindu culture. Accordingly, in condemning Sati, Carey argued that the Hindu scriptures did not support this tradition and that its abolition would not infringe on the religious freedoms of Hindu believers. Even though Carey first condemned Sati in 1804, the practice was not abolished for another twenty-five years— in great part because of the deep reluctance of Indian society to give up a widely accepted practice. See Vishal and Ruth Mangalwadi, *The Legacy of William Carey: A Model for the Transformation of a Culture* (Wheaton, IL: Crossway Books, 1999), 83–90.
24. Robert D. Kaplan, *The Arabists: The Romance of an American Elite* (New York: Free Press, 1995), 33 and 39.
25. Joseph L. Grabill, *Protestant Diplomacy and the Near East: Missionary Influence, 1810–1927* (Minneapolis: University of Minnesota Press, 1971), 27.
26. Fairbank, "Introduction: The Many Faces of Protestant Missions," 13.

27. Hutchison, *Errand to the World*, 100.
28. Quoted in Kaplan, *The Arabists*, 36.
29. Kaplan, *The Arabists*, 34.
30. Kaplan, *The Arabists*, 37.
31. In 1971 the men's and the women's colleges were integrated in order to offer a quality, co-educational high school.
32. Grabill, *Protestant Diplomacy and the Near East*, 300.
33. Robert D. Woodberry and Timothy S. Shah, "Christianity and Democracy: The Pioneering Protestants," *Journal of Democracy* 13 (April 2004), 50.
34. Alfred Stepan, "Religion, Democracy, and the 'Twin Tolerations,'" *Journal of Democracy* 11 (October 2000), 37–57.
35. This is a central claim in Woodberry and Shah's "Christianity and Democracy," 47–60.
36. Woodberry and Shah, "Christianity and Democracy," 53.
37. Hutchison, *Errand to the World*, 100.
38. Woodberry and Shah, "Christianity and Democracy," 52.
39. Grabill, *Protestant Diplomacy and the Near East*. See especially chaps. 8 and 10–12.
40. Grabill, *Protestant Diplomacy and the Near East*, 309.
41. William Inboden, *Religion and American Foreign Policy, 1945–1960: The Soul of Containment* (Cambridge: Cambridge University Press, 2008).
42. Inboden, *Religion and American Foreign Policy*, 160.
43. Inboden, *Religion and American Foreign Policy*, 177.
44. Edward E. Plowman, "Conversing with the CIA," *Christianity Today*, October 10, 1975, 62.
45. Mead, *Special Providence*, 150.
46. Mead, *Special Providence*, 154.
47. Hutchison, *Errand to the World*, 2.
48. Preston, *Sword of the Spirit, Shield of Faith*, 180.
49. For a penetrating account of the rise of imperialism in the United States at the end of the nineteenth century, see Warren K. Zimmerman, *First Great Triumph: How Five Americans Made Their Country a World Power* (New York: Farrar, Straus and Giroux, 2002).
50. Schlesinger, Jr., "The Missionary Enterprise," 372–373.
51. Boorstin, *The Americans*, 560.
52. Dana L. Robert, "The First Globalization? The Internationalization of the Protestant Missionary Movement Between the World Wars," in *Interpreting Contemporary Christianity: Global Processes and Local Identities*, eds. Ogbu U. Kalu and Alaine M. Low (Grand Rapids, MI: Eerdmans, 2008), 93.
53. Quoted in Schlesinger, Jr., "The Missionary Enterprise," 345.
54. Markku Ruotsila, *The Origins of Christian Anti-Internationalism: Conservative Evangelicals and the League of Nations* (Washington, DC: Georgetown University Press, 2008), 188.

55. Robert D. Woodberry, "The Missionary Roots of Liberal Democracy," *American Political Science Review* 106 (May 2012), 244.
56. To be sure, European Evangelical missionaries—that is, missionaries from non-state Protestant denominations—also played an important role in nurturing religious liberty, spearheading social reforms and in publicizing abuses by colonial powers. See Woodberry, "The Missionary Roots," 253–255.
57. Fairbank, "Introduction: The Many Faces of Protestant Missions," 8.
58. Mead, *Special Providence,* 146.
59. For SBC missions data, see: www.imb.org/main/page.asp?StoryID=4452&LanguageID=1709
60. Robert Wuthnow, *Boundless Faith: The Global Reach of American Churches* (Berkeley: University of California Press, 2009), 170. Robert Priest, a professor of mission and intercultural studies, thinks that Wuthnow underestimates the number of adults on STM trips. In his view the number is likely to be between 2 and 3 million adults. See Robert Priest, "Short-Term Missions as a New Paradigm," in *Mission After Christendom*, eds. Ogbu U. Kalu, Peter Vethanayagamony, and Edmund Kee-Fook Chia (Louisville, KY: Westminster John Knox Press, 2010), 86.
61. Robert Priest argues that at least 2 million young people (ages 13–17) participate every year in an STM trip, either domestically or internationally. See *Christianity Today*, July 2005, available at: www.christianitytoday.com/ct/2005/julyweb-only/22.0.html

CHAPTER 4

1. Carl F. H. Henry, *The Uneasy Conscience of Fundamentalism* (Grand Rapids, MI: Eerdmans, 1947), 34.
2. C. Henry, *The Uneasy Conscience*, 53.
3. J. Budziszewski, *Evangelicals in the Public Square: Four Formative Voices on Political Thought and Action* (Grand Rapids, MI: Baker Academic, 2006), 44.
4. For an overview of this statement, see *The Chicago Declaration*, ed. Ronald J. Sider (Carol Stream, IL: Creation House, 1974). The Chicago meeting included key figures like Carl F. H. Henry, Vernon Grounds, and Frank Gaebelein, along with progressive voices like Ron Sider, Jim Wallis, and Donald Dayton.
5. NAE, "Peace, Freedom and Security Studies—A Program of the National Association of Evangelicals," 1986. Available at: http://www.nae.net/fullresolutionlist.
6. Regardless of how one assesses the pastoral letter, this church document is a noteworthy achievement in both its sophisticated description of the nuclear dilemma and its application of biblical thought and moral reasoning to the problem. Indeed, the letter provides a model of how churches and religious organizations can bring moral analysis to bear on complex public policy concerns.
7. The PFSS program guidelines included the following important elements: (a) a definition of the nature of the problem of reconciling peacekeeping with the quest for human rights and political freedom; (b) a brief survey of some of the biblical and theological principles relevant to the problem; (c) an overview of some of the

major misconceptions that impeded effective political engagement on the issues of peace, freedom and security; and (d) an overview of some of the major concerns and principles inspiring the program.

8. NAE, "Peace, Freedom and Security Studies," 3.

9. NAE, "Peace, Freedom and Security Studies," 11.

10. Two major Evangelical critics of the NAE statement included social ethicist Ronald Sider and philosopher Nicholas Wolterstorff, while a number of scholars and mainline and Catholic leaders viewed the document as an important contribution to the nuclear debate. See Bruce Nichols, "Forestalling Armageddon: Evangelicals Join the Nuclear Debate," *Newsletter on Church & State Abroad,* Carnegie Council on Ethics & International Affairs, Number 9 (July 1987), 1.

11. NAE, "For the Health of the Nation: An Evangelical Call to Civic Responsibility," in *Toward an Evangelical Public Policy*, eds. Ronald J. Sider and Diane Knippers (Grand Rapids, MI: Baker, 2005), 363–375. The document is also available at the NAE website: www.nae.org. The excellent edited volume, which was issued at the time the NAE released the document, includes informative chapters on past Evangelical social and political action, a history of NAE public policy resolutions, Evangelical political ethics, and an analysis of specialized topics like human rights and peacekeeping.

12. NAE, "For the Health of the Nation," 363.

13. Richard Mouw, *Political Evangelism* (Grand Rapids, MI: Eerdmans, 1973).

14. NAE, "For the Health of the Nation," 366.

15. NAE, "For the Health of the Nation," 366.

16. This list of seven concerns is similar to the seven core principles set forth in the 2003 Roman Catholic statement on social and political life, titled *Faithful Citizenship*. The document, issued by the U.S. Conference on Catholic Bishops (USCCB), was developed to assist Catholics to better fulfill their responsibilities as citizens. Although the NAE statement does not reference the Catholic document, it is clear that a significant level of parallelism exists between the NAE document and the earlier Catholic document. The USCCB document is available at: www.usccb.org.

17. David Neff, "Love Language," *Christianity Today,* December 2010, 36.

18. As a result, out of a total of 4,000 delegates, the United States was assigned 400, the United Kingdom 80, Canada 50, and China 230. Additionally, at least 60 percent of the delegates had to be less than 50 years of age, while women were to have at least 35 percent of the seats. Tim Stafford, "Teeming Diversity," *Christianity Today,* December 2010.

19. According to Jenkins, while the Christian population in North America was about 260 million, the Christian population in the global South was more than four times that, with Latin America's Christian population estimated at 480 million, Africa's at 360 million, and Asia's at 313 million. More significantly, given the rapidly expanding number of believers in the global South, Jenkins estimates that by 2025, 50 percent of the world's Christian population will be in Africa and Latin America and another 17 percent in Asia. See Philip Jenkins, *The Next Christendom: The Coming of Global Christianity* (New York: Oxford University Press, 2002). The

main claims of this book were set forth in a widely read cover article in the October 2002 issue of *The Atlantic Monthly*.

20. The Pew Forum on Religion and Public Life, "Global Survey of Evangelical Protestant Leaders," June 22, 2011. Available at: www.pewforum.org/Christian/ Evangelical-Protestant-Churches/Global-Survey-of-Evangelical-Protestant-Leaders.aspx#global

21. Stafford, "Teeming Diversity."

22. The Cape Town Commitment. The full report is available at: http://www.lausanne. org/ctcommitment

23. Richard J. Mouw, *Abraham Kuyper: A Short and Personal Introduction* (Grand Rapids, MI: Eerdmans, 2011), 87.

24. Mouw, *Abraham Kuyper*, 87.

25. Quoted in Ronald J. Sider, *The Scandal of Evangelical Politics: Why Are Christians Missing the Chance to Really Change the World?* (Grand Rapids, MI: Baker Books, 2008), 19.

26. Mark Noll, *The Scandal of the Evangelical Mind* (Grand Rapids, MI: Eerdmans, 1994), 166.

27. Budziszewski, *Evangelicals in the Public Square*, 20.

28. Budziszewski, *Evangelicals in the Public Square*, 23.

29. Budziszewski, *Evangelicals in the Public Square*, 27–30.

30. Budzieszewski identifies four seminal thinkers who have influenced Evangelical political thought (Carl F. H. Henry, Abraham Kuyper, Francis Schaeffer, and John Howard Yoder), but claims that none of these provides an adequate framework for integrating reason and revelation to address public affairs.

31. Sider, *The Scandal of Evangelical Politics*, 11.

32. C. Henry, *The Uneasy Conscience*, 88.

33. Timothy Samuel Shah, "Some Evangelical Views of the State," in *Church, State, and Citizen: Christian Approaches to Political Engagement*, ed. Sandra Joireman (New York: Oxford University Press, 2009), 136–137.

34. Amy L. Sherman, *The Soul of Development: Biblical Christianity and Economic Transformation in Guatemala* (New York: Oxford University Press, 1997), 4–18.

35. Douglas Petersen, *Not by Might Nor by Power: A Pentecostal Theology of Social Concern in Latin America* (Oxford: Regnum Books International, 1996).

36. Glenn Tinder, "Can We Be Good Without God?," *The Atlantic Monthly*, December 1989, 71–72.

37. Lay Commission on Catholic Social Teaching and the U.S. Economy, *Toward the Future: Catholic Social Thought and the U.S. Economy* (New York: American Catholic Committee, 1984), 5.

38. Dietrich Bonhoeffer, *The Cost of Discipleship* (New York: Macmillan, 1961), 84.

39. For a description of Charles Colson's life and conversion, see Charles Colson, *Born Again* (Grand Rapids, MI: Chosen Books, 1976).

40. Examples of major crimes against humanity include Turkey's genocide against Armenians in the early twentieth century, the Khmer Rouge's genocide against the

educated urban peoples in Cambodia in the mid-1970s, and the Serbian ethnic cleansing against Muslim Bosnians in the early 1990s. Examples of widespread regime atrocities include Stalin's imposed famine in Ukraine in the 1930s that resulted from centralized control of agriculture and Mao Tse-tung's repression and famine of the 1950s caused by his "Great Leap Forward" program ostensibly designed to modernize Chinese society.

41. R. J. Rummel, "The Politics of Cold Blood," *Society,* November/December 1989, 33.
42. Alexander Hamilton, James Madison, and John Jay, *The Federalist in Great Books of the Western World,* ed. Robert Maynard Hutchins (Chicago: Encyclopaedia Britannica, 1952), 163.
43. Abraham Kuyper, *Lectures on Calvinism* (Grand Rapids, MI: Eerdmans, 1961).
44. Richard John Neuhaus, *"Christianity and Democracy: A Statement of the Institute on Religion and Democracy,"* Washington, DC: Institute on Religion and Democracy, 1981, 1.
45. Alexis de Tocqueville, *Democracy in America,* trans. Henry Reeve (New York: Appleton, 1904), 1: 334.
46. For example, two possible additional elements of Evangelical ethics are the tendency to view the state negatively and the propensity toward pietism, resulting in the spiritualizing of political issues. See Paul Henry, *Politics for Evangelicals* (Valley Forge, PA: Judson Press, 1974), 37–51.
47. "An Evangelical Manifesto: A Declaration of Evangelical Identity and Public Commitment," May 7, 2008, 15. Available at: http://www.anevangelicalmanifesto.com/
48. Michael Gerson and Peter Wehner, *City of Man: Religion and Politics in a New Era* (Chicago: Moody Publishers, 2010), 59.
49. Charles Marsh, *Wayward Christian Soldiers: Freeing the Gospel from Political Captivity* (New York: Oxford University Press, 2007), 27.
50. Cal Thomas and Ed Dodson, *Blinded by Might: Can the Religious Right Save America?* (Grand Rapids, MI: Zondervan, 1999).
51. James Davison Hunter, *To Change the World: The Irony, Tragedy, and Possibility of Christianity in the Late Modern World* (New York: Oxford University Press, 2010), 12.
52. Hunter, *To Change the World,* 274.
53. Hunter, *To Change the World,* 281.
54. Charles Colson, "More than Faithful Presence," *Christianity Today* (web only). Available at: www.christianitytoday.com/ct/2010/mayweb-only/29-52.0.html
55. Mouw, *Political Evangelism,* 48.
56. Mouw, *Political Evangelism,* 110.
57. P. Henry, *Politics for Evangelicals,* 50–51.

CHAPTER 5

1. "Government, Global Poverty and God's Mission in the World: An Evangelical Declaration," May 18–19, 2010, Wheaton, IL, 9.

2. Robert McNamara, *One Hundred Countries, Two Billion People* (New York: Praeger Publishers, 1973), 6–8.

3. These are listed in Jay W. Richards, *Money, Greed, and God: Why Capitalism Is the Solution and Not the Problem* (New York: HarperOne, 2009), 88–89.

4. UNDP, *Human Development Report, 1990*, chap. 2. See: http://hdr.undp.org/en/reports/global/hdr1990/

5. The index is a numerical coefficient between 0 and 1, with low numbers suggesting poverty and high numbers suggesting prosperity.

6. United Nations, *Human Development Report 2011*. The data are from "Human Development Index Trends, 1980–2011." Available at: http://hdr.undp.org/en/

7. Martin Wolf, *Why Globalization Works* (New Haven: Yale University Press, 2004), 44.

8. Paul Collier, *The Bottom Billion: Why the Poorest Countries Are Failing and What Can Be Done About It* (New York: Oxford University Press, 2007), 3

9. Wolf, *Why Globalization Works,* 172.

10. According to *The Economist*, the number of people who have been lifted out of poverty from 1981 to 2010 is 660 million. This unprecedented reduction in Chinese poverty has helped to meet the UN Millennium Development Goal of halving world poverty in 2010—five years ahead of schedule. See "A Fall to Cheer," *The Economist*, March 3, 2012, 81.

11. Andre Gunder Frank, *Latin America Underdevelopment or Revolution* (New York: Monthly Review Press, 1969), chap. 1.

12. Robert Heilbroner, "The Triumph of Capitalism," *The New Yorker,* January 23, 1989, 98.

13. UNDP, *Human Development Report 2007/2008* (New York: Palgrave Macmillan, 2007), 280.

14. Philip Jenkins, "Forward," in Peter Wehner and Arthur C. Brooks, *Wealth & Justice: The Morality of Democratic Capitalism,* (Washington, DC: AEI Press, 2011), xviii.

15. Amartya Sen, *Development as Freedom* (New York: Knopf, 1999). See especially, Introduction and chaps. 1 and 2.

16. Don Eberle, *The Rise of Global Civil Society: Building Communities and Nations from the Bottom Up* (New York: Encounter Books, 2008), 58–61.

17. Pope John Paul II, *On Human Work* (Washington, DC: U.S. Catholic Conference, 1981), 9–10.

18. The Lay Commission on Catholic Social Teaching and the U.S. Economy, *Toward the Future: Catholic Social Thought and the U.S. Economy* (New York: American Catholic Committee, 1984), 50.

19. Ronald J. Sider, *Rich Christians in an Age of Hunger* (Downers Grove, IL: InterVarsity Press, 1978), 84.

20. In the 1970s, the Roman Catholic Church responded to increased economic polarization in Latin America by popularizing the notion that God was partial to the poor. It called this partiality "the preferential option for the poor."

21. Sider, *Rich Christians,* 84.

22. Sider, *Rich Christians,* 162.

23. Ronald J. Sider, *Rich Christians in an Age of Hunger: Moving from Affluence to Generosity,* 5th ed. (Nashville, TN: Thomas Nelson, 2005).

24. Sider, *Rich Christians,* 5th ed., 230.

25. Sider, *Rich Christians,* 5th ed., 62.

26. Sider, *Rich Christians,* 5th ed., 135–136.

27. Sider, *Rich Christians,* 5th ed., 223.

28. Nicholas Wolterstorff, *Until Justice and Peace Embrace* (Grand Rapids, MI: Eerdmans, 1983).

29. Wolterstorff, *Until Justice and Peace Embrace,* 66 and 86.

30. See, for example, Brian Griffiths, *The Creation of Wealth* (London: Hodder and Soughton, 1984) and Herbert Schlossberg, *Idols for Destruction: Christian Faith and Its Confrontation with American Society* (Nashville, TN: Thomas Nelson Publishers, 1983), chaps. 2 and 3.

31. Four of the most important of these documents on Third World poverty are the following: the United Church of Christ's (UCC) 1987 study "Christian Faith and Economic Life;" the United Methodist Church's 1988 "Resolution on Economic Justice;" the Episcopal Urban Bishops Coalition's 1987 study guide, "Economic Justice and Christian Conscience;" and the Presbyterian Church's 1984 statement, "Christian Faith and Economic Justice." For an assessment of these statements, see Amy L. Sherman, "Christians and Economic Development," *First Things,* March 1990, 43–50. Additionally, the U.S. Conference of Catholic Bishops issued a pastoral letter titled "Economic Justice for All" that assessed poverty from a largely structuralist perspective. For a critique of the bishops' letter, see Mark R. Amstutz, "The Bishops and Third World Poverty," in *Prophetic Visions and Economic Realities: Protestants, Jews, and Catholics Confront the Bishops' Letter on the Economy,* ed. Charles R. Strain (Grand Rapids, MI: Eerdmans, 1989), 61–74.

32. During the Cold War, when the ideological conflict pitted Soviet state socialism against American democratic capitalism, many American church leaders sought to avoid either alternative economic system by calling for a "third way"—one that encouraged a mixture of governmental redistribution with some free enterprise to facilitate economic innovation and job creation. In practice, however, these initiatives tended to identify more with socialism than with capitalism.

33. Clark H. Pinnock, "The Pursuit of Utopia," in *Freedom, Justice and Hope: Toward a Strategy for the Poor and the Oppressed,* eds. Marvin Olasky, Herberg Schlossberg, Pierre Berthoud, and Clark H. Pinnock (Westchester, IL: Crossway Books, 1988), 66–76.

34. Pinnock, "The Pursuit of Utopia," 66.

35. Lawrence M. Mead, *From Prophecy to Charity: How to Help the Poor* (Washington, DC: AEI Press, 2011), 60.

36. Mead, *From Prophecy to Charity,* 62.

37. Mead, *From Prophecy to Charity,* 106.

38. "The Villars Statement on Relief and Development," in *On Moral Business: Classical and Contemporary Resources for Ethics in Economic Life*, eds. Max L. Stackhouse, Dennis P. McCann, and Shirley J. Roels, with Preston N. Williams (Grand Rapids, MI: Eerdmans, 1995), 471.

39. "The Oxford Declaration on Christian Faith and Economics," in *On Moral Business: Classical and Contemporary Resources for Ethics in Economic Life*, eds. Max L. Stackhouse, Dennis P. McCann, and Shirley J. Roels, with Preston N. Williams (Grand Rapids, MI: Eerdmans, 1995), 470–482.

40. "The Oxford Declaration on Christian Faith and Economics," 478.

41. "The Oxford Declaration on Christian Faith and Economics," 474.

42. James W. Skillen, "A Good Beginning, but Much More Needs to Be Done," in *Christianity and Economics in the Post–Cold War Era: The Oxford Declaration and Beyond,* eds. Herbert Schlossberg, Vinay Samuel, and Ronald J. Sider (Grand Rapids, MI: Eerdmans, 1994), 186.

43. For an overview of the effects of policies and practices that are conducive to economic growth, see Paul Kennedy, *Preparing for the Twenty-First Century* (New York: Random House, 1993), chap. 10, "Winners and Losers in the Developing World." For a more comprehensive overview of the sources of wealth creation, see Daron Acemoglu and James A. Robinson, *Why Nations Fail: The Origins of Power, Prosperity, and Poverty* (New York: Crown Publishers, 2012).

44. See, for example, William Easterly, *The White Man's Burden: Why the West's Efforts to Aid the Rest Have Done So Much Ill and So Little Good* (New York: Penguin Books, 2006). One of the early important critics of foreign aid was P. T. Bauer, who challenged the prevailing belief that foreign assistance was beneficial to poor societies. See P. T. Bauer, *Dissent on Development: Studies and Debaters in Development Economics* (Cambridge, MA: Harvard University Press, 1972) and P. T. Bauer, *Equality, the Third World, and Economic Delusion* (Cambridge, MA: Harvard University Press, 1981).

45. NAE, "US Foreign Aid and Humanitarian Assistance 1995." Available at: http://www.nae.net/fullresolutionlist

46. For further data on Accord, see their website: http://www.accordnetwork.org/

47. Rachel M. McCleary, *Global Compassion: Private Voluntary Organizations and U.S. Foreign Policy Since 1939* (New York: Oxford University Press, 2009), 16.

48. For information about World Vision, see its website: www.worldvision.org/

49. More than 1 million American donors were involved in supporting World Vision in 2010.

50. For information about Opportunity International, see its website: www.opportunity.org/

51. Eberle, *The Rise of Global Civil Society*, 151.

52. Until the mid-1990s, federal support of religious NGOs was difficult. Because of constitutional provisions that emphasized the separation of church and state, the federal government had been prohibited from allocating funds to faith-based

organizations that provided educational, social, medical, and other services. But with the Charitable Choice provision of the Welfare Reform Act of 1996 (formally called the Personal Responsibility and Work Opportunity Reconciliation Act), federal funding of faith-based initiatives became far more prevalent domestically.

53. J. Bruce Nichols, *The Uneasy Alliance: Religion, Refugee Work, and U.S. Foreign Policy* (New York: Oxford University Press, 1988), 3.
54. Eberle, *The Rise of Global Civil Society.*
55. McCleary, *Global Compassion,* 29.
56. Andrew F. Walls and Jim Punton, "Evangelical Views on Mission and Development, Viewpoint" (London: Christian Aid, 1975), 1.

CHAPTER 6

1. Timothy P. Weber, "How Evangelicals Became Israel's Best Friend," *Christianity Today,* October 5, 1998, 39.
2. Gary M. Burge, *Whose Land? Whose Promise?: What Christians Are Not Being Told About Israel and the Palestinians* (Cleveland: Pilgrim Press, 2003), 236.
3. Whereas the Roman Catholic Church had emphasized the role of clergy and church tradition in interpreting and applying Scripture, the Reformers—led by Martin Luther, John Calvin, John Knox, and others—claimed that the church priesthood was unnecessary in reading and interpreting Scripture. Indeed, since literate persons could apprehend the fundamental truths of Scripture, the gospel was directly accessible to them.
4. Gerald R. McDermott, "Evangelicals and Israel," in *Uneasy Allies? Evangelicals and Jewish Relations,* eds. Alan Mittleman, Byron Johnson, and Nancy Isserman (Lanham, MD: Lexington Books, 2007), 139.
5. Gary A. Anderson, "Israel and the Land: Does the Promise Still Hold?" *Christian Century,* January 13, 2009, 22.
6. Richard J. Mouw, "The Chosen People Puzzle," *Christianity Today,* March 5, 2001, 73.
7. The dispensational creed has several key elements. First, God's redemptive history is divided into distinct epochs or dispensations, with the millennium (Christ's one-thousand-year reign) culminating in the end of history. Second, God's redemptive plan involves two distinct covenants—one with Israel and the other with the Gentile church that has accepted Jesus as the Messiah. Although Jews have rejected Jesus, the Abrahamic covenant remains binding; unlike supersessionists, dispensationalists do not believe that the church has become the new Israel. Third, God's redemptive plan involves two distinct purposes—one earthly (Israel) and the other spiritual (the church). This belief explains why dispensationalists are strong supporters of the Jewish people and of Israel in particular. Fourth, prior to Christ's triumphant millennial reign, the world will experience a time of great suffering (known as the "tribulation") as the forces of good and evil confront each other, with

the war culminating in the Holy Land in the battle of Armageddon. This prophetic claim is important because it places Israel and the Jewish people at the center of the close of history.

8. The movement gained growing legitimacy when Oxford University Press published in 1909 the Scofield Reference Bible, which included notations from a dispensationalist perspective.

9. Timothy P. Weber, *On the Road to Armageddon: How Evangelicals Became Israel's Best Friend* (Grand Rapids, MI: Baker Academic, 2004).

10. Weber, "How Evangelicals Became Israel's Best Friend," 49.

11. "What It Means to Love Israel," *Christianity Today*, September 2007, 24.

12. Stephen Spector, *Evangelicals and Israel: The Story of American Christian Zionism* (New York: Oxford University Press, 2008), 165.

13. Spector, *Evangelicals and Israel*, 180.

14. Spector, *Evangelicals and Israel*, viii–ix.

15. According to Peter Berkowitz, the catalyst for the rise of political Zionism was not modernity itself but, rather, the growing persecution of Jews throughout Europe and Russia. Because of the rise in anti-Semitism, Jews were reminded that they were aliens and in need of a political home. The person most responsible for developing and legitimating this claim was Theodore Herzl, the father of political Zionism. His intellectual and organizational skills helped to create an international movement in support of a Jewish homeland. See "Israel and the Future of Zionism," Biannual Conference on Religion, Politics and Public Life, Sponsored by the Pew Forum on Religion and Public Life, Key West, Florida, December 4, 2006.

16. The declaration read in part: "His Majesty's Government view with favour the establishment in Palestine of a national home for the Jewish people...it being clearly understood that nothing shall be done which may prejudice the civil and religious rights of existing non-Jewish communities in Palestine...." It is significant that the British commitment to a Jewish homeland could not come at the expense of Palestinian rights.

17. Some observers, like Donald Wagner, believe that Christian Zionism arose from premillennial dispensationalism in the nineteenth century. This claim is unsustainable, however, since Protestants, in renewing an interest in the Old Testament law, began calling for the restoration of the Jews to their ancestral land long before dispensationalism emerged. See Donald E. Wagner, "Marching to Zion: The Evangelical-Jewish Alliance," *Christian Century*, June 28, 2003, 20. John J. Mearsheimer and Stephen M. Walt assert this claim as well in their provocative and widely read book on the Israel lobby. See John J. Mearsheimer and Stephen M. Walt, *The Israel Lobby and U.S. Foreign Policy* (New York: Farrar, Straus and Giroux, 2007), 132.

18. Stephen Sizer, *Christian Zionism: Road-map to Armageddon?* (Downers Grove, IL: IVP Academic, 2004), 135.

19. For a discussion of restorationist initiatives in the nineteenth century, see Michael B. Oren, *Power, Faith, and Fantasy: America in the Middle East, 1776 to the Present* (New York: W.W. Norton, 2007), 141–147.

20. Walter Russell Mead, "The New Israel and the Old: Why Gentile Americans Back the Jewish State," *Foreign Affairs* 87 (July/August 2008), 32.

21. Anderson, "Israel and the Land," 24.

22. One measure of the influence of the prophetic strand is the popularity of prophetic literature. In the 1970s, one of the most widely read Christians books was Hal Lindsey's *The Late, Great Planet Earth*, which used biblical prophesies to explain contemporary global developments. Published in 1970, by 1990 the book had sold more than 28 million copies. Timothy LaHaye's and Jerry Jenkins's novels on hypothetical "end-times" scenarios have been even more successful. Their collection of bestsellers—known as the Left Behind series because they focus on prophetic developments consistent with dispensationalism—have sold more than 60 million copies.

23. Mead, "The New Israel and the Old," 31.

24. Paul Charles Merkley, *Christian Attitudes towards the State of Israel* (Montreal: McGill-Queen's University Press, 2001), 4.

25. See: http://www.gallup.com/poll/1639/middle-east.aspx

26. Michael Novak, *On Two Wings: Humble Faith and Common Sense at the Founding* (San Francisco: Encounter Books, 2001).

27. Madeleine Albright, *The Mighty & The Almighty: Reflections on America, God, and World Affairs* (New York: HarperCollins, 2006), 134.

28. For some major critiques of the Mearsheimer-Walt thesis, see the following: Walter Russell Mead, "Jerusalem Syndrome: Decoding the Israel Lobby," *Foreign Affairs* 86 (November/December 2007), 160–168; Michael Massing, "The Storm over the Israel Lobby," *The New York Review of Books,* June 8, 2006, 64–73; and Jeffrey Goldberg, "The Usual Suspect," *The New Republic,* October 8, 2007, 40–50.

29. Dennis Ross, "The Mind-Set Matters: Foreign Policy Is Shaped by Leaders and Events, Not Lobbies," *Foreign Policy* (No. 155, July/August 2006), 61.

30. Goldberg, "The Usual Suspect." Available at: http://www.tnr.com/doc.mhtml?i= 20071008&s=goldberg100807

31. Quoted in Spector, *Evangelicals and Israel*, 166.

32. Some of its major objectives include: to show concern for the Jewish people and the state of Israel, to promote a biblical understanding of Israel, to encourage Christian leaders to become effective influences in their countries on behalf of Israel and the Jewish people, and to help bring the Jews back to their homeland. In the aftermath of the end of the Cold War, the ICEJ assisted Russian Jews to migrate to Israel, and by 1998 it had helped more than 40,000 persons make the journey. In seeking to promote appreciation for Jews and understanding of Israeli concerns, the ICEJ sponsors a fall festival at the Feast of Tabernacles that has become the largest annual tourist event in Israel, drawing an average of seven thousand visitors.

33. CFI's mission statement, for example, specifies three major goals: to comfort and support the people of Israel, to inform Christians of God's plan for Israel, and to make the Jewish people aware of Christians' solidarity with them.

34. The IFCJ, a Chicago-based organization headed by Rabbi Yechiel Eckstein, provides financial support for Jews migrating to Israel, as well as to recent immigrants in need of financial aid. Since its founding in 1983, IFCJ has provided nearly $100 million in humanitarian aid to Jewish immigrants.

35. Ya Hovel, a small Tennessee-based organization, for example, encourages American believers to assist Jewish settlement farmers in the West Bank with agricultural tasks, such as picking grapes.

36. John Mearsheimer and Stephen Walt argue that the Christian Zionist influence in supporting Israel has been overstated. For a discussion of why they believe that Christian Zionism has limited political impact on U.S. foreign policymaking, see Mearsheimer and Walt, *The Israel Lobby and U.S. Foreign Policy*, 138–139.

37. Joan Didion, "Mr. Bush & the Divine," *The New York Review of Books*, November 1, 2003.

38. Karen Armstrong, "Bush's Fondness for Fundamentalism Is Courting Disaster at Home and Abroad, *The Guardian*, July 31, 2006.

39. Spector, *Evangelicals and Israel*, ix.

40. Pew Forum on Religion & Public Life, "American Evangelicals and Israel," June–July 2003; available at: http://pewforum.org/Christian/American-Evangelicals-and-Israel.aspx

41. Pew Forum on Religion & Public Life, "Many Americans Uneasy with Mix of Religion and Politics," August 24, 2006, p. 20. Available at: http://pewforum.org/Politics-and-Elections/Many-Americans-Uneasy-with-Mix-of-Religion-and-Politics.aspx

42. Mark Harlan, "A Middle Way in the Middle East," *Christianity Today*, April 2003, 85.

43. Burge, *Whose Land? Whose Promise?*, 78.

44. Tom Strode, "Letter by 60 Christian Leaders Criticizes Pro-Israel Evangelicals," *Baptist Press*, August 9, 2002. Available at: http://www.bpnews.net/printerfriendly.asp?ID=13995

45. Pat Robertson, "Why Evangelical Christians Support Israel," available at: http://www.patrobertson.com/Speeches/IsraelLauder.asp

46. Spector, *Evangelicals and Israel*, 165.

47. Quoted in Spector, *Evangelicals and Israel*, 165.

48. Tarrence Group, "American Christians and Support for Israel," October 9, 2002. Available at: http://www.imra.org.il/story.php3?id=14013

CHAPTER 7

1. James W. Skillen, "Evangelicals and American Exceptionalism," *The Review of Faith & International Affairs* 4 (Winter 2006), 45.

2. Pew Forum on Religion & Public Life, Transcript on "God's Country," September 26, 2006. Available at: http://pewforum.org/Politics-and-Elections/Gods-Country-Evangelicals-and-US-Foreign-Policy.aspx

3. Allen D. Hertzke, *Freeing God's Children: The Unlikely Alliance for Global Human Rights* (Boulder, CO: Rowman & Littlefield, 2004).

4. Telephone interview with Paul Marshall, June 20, 2008.

5. Hertzke, *Freeing God's Children*, 35.

6. For an excellent overview of the role of Evangelicals in addressing the plight of Soviet Pentecostals and the role of the U.S. government in facilitating their emigration to the United States, see Kent R. Hill, *The Puzzle of the Soviet Church: An Inside Look at Christianity and Glasnost* (Portland, OR: Multnomah Press, 1989).

7. Hertzke, *Freeing God's Children*, 59.

8. National Association of Evangelicals, "1996 Statement of Conscience Concerning Worldwide Religious Persecution." Available at: www.nae.net

9. Paul Marshall, *Their Blood Cries Out* (Dallas: Word Publishing, 1997).

10. IRFA led to a number of institutional changes in the U.S. foreign policy establishment. First, the Department of State created the Office of International Religious Freedom, headed by an ambassador-at-large for religious freedom, to spearhead the cause of international religious freedom and to increase awareness of the religious component of American diplomacy; second, the new office was tasked with preparing an annual report on the status of religious freedom in foreign countries; and third, an independent, nongovernmental U.S. Commission on International Religious Freedom was established to monitor international religious persecution, call attention to the most egregious abuses, and make policy recommendations.

11. While the original law required mandatory sanctions on countries that were classified as CPC, the law was modified a year later in order to provide the president with greater discretion in applying sanctions. One of the key provisions of the 1999 law was that the president could waive punitive action if it would further religious freedom or promote the national security interests of the United States.

12. For an excellent 10-year assessment of the impact of IRFA, see *Faith & International Affairs*, vol. 6, no. 2 (Summer 2008), which is devoted to numerous articles on the development, evolution, and impact of IRFA by leading scholars and practitioners of religious freedom.

13. Thomas F. Farr, *World of Faith and Freedom: Why International Religious Liberty Is Vital to American National Security* (New York: Oxford University Press, 2008).

14. At times the IRF Office has considered the Commission's recommendations ill-advised. Indeed, Robert Seiple, after serving two years as the first ambassador-at-large of the IRF Office, concluded that the commission was far too punitive in its approach. See Robert A. Seiple, "Speaking Out: The USCIRF Is Only Cursing the Darkness," *Christianity Today*, October 2002 (web only). Available at: Christianitytoday.com/ct/2002/octoberweb-only/10-14-31.0.html

15. Laura Bryant Hanford, "The International Religious Freedom Act: Sources, Policy, Influence," *Faith & International Affairs* 6, no. 2 (Summer 2008), 38.

16. Open Door, "World Watch List 2012." Available at: www.opendoorsuk.org/resources/persecution/

17. Allen D. Hertzke, "International Religious Freedom Policy: Taking Stock," *Faith & International Affairs* 6, no. 2 (Summer 2008), 22.

18. Hanford, "The International Religious Freedom Act," 38.

19. See, for example, Farr, *World of Faith and Freedom,* especially chaps. 1 and 2.

20. Hanford, "The International Religious Freedom Act," 38.

21. Hertzke, "International Religious Freedom Policy," 22.

22. For a comprehensive introduction to contemporary human trafficking, see Ethan B. Kapstein, "The New Global Slave Trade," *Foreign Affairs* 85 (November/December 2006), 103–115.

23. Matthew O. Berger, "Human Trafficking Still Widespread, US Included," *Inter Press Service,* June 14, 2010. Available at: http://www.ipsnews.net/news.asp?idnews=51817

24. Human trafficking involves the use of deception and coercion to induce victims to cross national borders in search of a better life. But it also occurs when any person holds another person captive to compel some type of service. Human trafficking can therefore take a variety of forms, including sex trafficking, forced labor, involuntary servitude, and bonded labor.

25. UNICEF, "Child Protection Information Sheets," May 2006, p. 27. Available at: www.unicef.org/protection/files/Trafficking.pdf

26. The NAE resolution, adopted in 1999, states that sex trafficking "is a violation of the sanctity of life and of the God-given dignity and integrity of human persons."

27. Hertzke, *Freeing God's Children,* 330.

28. Hertzke, *Freeing God's Children,* 322.

29. U.S. Department of State, "Trafficking in Persons Report, June 2011." Available at: http://www.state.gov/j/tip/rls/tiprpt/2011/

30. Department of State's Human Trafficking Office classifies countries into three groups. Tier I includes countries whose governments comply with the minimum standards for ending human trafficking; Tier II includes countries that do not fully comply with those standards but which are making significant efforts to ensure compliance; and Tier III includes countries that do not meet minimum standards and are not attempting to comply with them. Countries that are classified as Tier III are subject to sanctions—principally termination of nonhumanitarian, non-trade-related assistance. The 2011 "Trafficking in Persons Report" classifies 21 states as Tier III countries, including Algeria, Iran, Libya, Saudi Arabia, Sudan, Venezuela, and Zimbabwe. See "Trafficking in Persons Report, June 2011," 53–58. Available at: http://www.state.gov/j/tip/rls/tiprpt/2011/

31. While South Korea welcomes refugees from North Korea, escaping to South Korea is nearly impossible because of the military surveillance maintained by North Korea. It has been estimated that fewer than 6,000 North Koreans have been successful in migrating to South Korea in the fifty years since the Korean War.

32. The growing concern with Chinese refugee policies eventually resulted in the U.S. House of Representatives adopting a resolution that called on China to halt forcible repatriation.
33. Nicole Hallett, "Politicizing U.S. Refugee Policy Toward North Korea, *Yale Journal of International Affairs* 1 (Winter/Spring 2006), 78–79.
34. NAE, "2002 Second Statement of Conscience Concerning Worldwide Religious Persecution with Special Examination of Sudan and North Korea." Available at: www.nae.net/government-relations/policy-resolutions/430-worldwide-religious-persecution-2002
35. Center for Religious Freedom, "Statement of Principles on North Korea," January 2003. Available at: www.hudson.org/index.cfm?fuseaction=publication_details&id=4696
36. This was a significant political achievement, especially since a number of groups opposed the proposed legislation. The South Korean government, for example, was against the measure because it believed that it would impair its own strategy of building increasing economic ties with its northern neighbor. Fundamentally, South Korea had been pursuing a "sunshine policy" of helping to sustain the North Korean regime lest its sudden collapse result in millions of citizens arriving in South Korea in need of work and social support. Department of State officials also opposed the law because they believed that the measure would impair diplomatic negotiations with North Korea on political and security concerns.
37. Interview of Michael Horowitz by Stan Guthrie, "North Korea Human Rights Act a 'Miracle,'" *Christianity Today,* October 1, 2004. Available at: www.christianitytoday.com/ct/2004/octoberweb-only/10-4-12.0.html
38. "Statement of Principles Regarding the Suffering People of North Korea and the Threats Posed by Its Regime to World Security," July 2005. Available at: www.uri.edu/artsci/wms/hughes/state_principles_nk.doc
39. The AEI speech is available at: http://www.aei.org/events/2008/01/17/the-north-korean-problem-toward-a-diplomatic-solution-in-2008-event/
40. Thomas Omestad, "Condoleezza Rice Hits Back at Critics of Her North Korea Nuclear Strategy," *U.S. News & World Report,* January 24, 2008. Available at: http://www.usnews.com/news/world/articles/2008/01/24/north-korea-strains-the-bush-administrations-strategy
41. "Dr. Barrett Duke on the Seoul Summit for North Korean Human Rights," *Christianity Today,* December 15, 2005. Available at: www.christiantoday.com/article/dr.barrett.duke.on.the.seoul.summit.for.north.korean.human.rights/4794.htm
42. While some human rights activists opposed the freeing of slaves with money in the belief that such a practice would only exacerbate the slave trade, in practice the campaign was beneficial in publicizing the horrific human rights abuses of the Khartoum government.
43. For an informative account of the politics involved in the passage of the Sudan Peace Act, see Hertzke, *Freeing God's Children.*
44. For an excellent overview of the challenge of implementing the CPA, see International Crisis Group, "Sudan's Comprehensive Peace Agreement: Beyond the Crisis," March 13, 2008.

45. Fundamentally, the war pits fur farmers against nomadic Arab herdsmen. Since the Darfur militia had periodically challenged government authority in the region, the Khartoum regime responded by arming and supporting Arab tribesmen, known as the *janjaweed*. The conflict exploded in 2003 and intensified in subsequent years, leaving some 300,000 civilians dead and displacing another 2.5 million. See Neil MacFarquhar, "Why Darfur Still Bleeds," *New York Times*, July 13, 2008, WK5.

46. The Darfur dispute took center stage again in early 2010 when the International Criminal Court issued an arrest warrant for Sudan's president, Omar al-Bashir, for crimes that he is alleged to have committed in Darfur. Specifically, the court's prosecutor, Luis Moreno-Ocampo, charged that al-Bashir had committed crimes of genocide, crimes against humanity, and war crimes in Darfur.

47. For an analysis of the conflict over Abyei, see Roger Winter, "Abyei Aflame: An Update from the Field," Center for American Progress. Available at: www.american progress.org/issues

48. First diagnosed in 1981 in the United States, AIDS (acquired immune deficiency syndrome) is a disease of the immune system caused by a virus known as HIV (human immunodeficiency virus). The disease impairs people's immune systems, making them far more likely to get infections and tumors.

49. HIV can also be spread through other means—such as direct contact with the blood or fluids of an HIV-positive person, tainted needles, or breastfeeding.

50. In the late 1980s, I recall hearing a sermon by an Evangelical preacher who claimed that the high death rates among homosexuals with AIDS was God's way of dealing with people who disregarded divine precepts.

51. National Association of Evangelicals, "AIDS 1988." Policy resolution adopted by NAE's Board of Directors in 1988.

52. "The Age of AIDS: Interview with Franklin Graham," *Frontline*, May 30, 2006. Available at: http://www.pbs.org/wgbh/pages/frontline/aids/interviews/graham.html

53. "Statement of Conscience of the Evangelical Church on Global AIDS," June 2003. Quoted in Chan Woong Shin, "Are Culture Wars Over? U.S. Evangelicals and the Global AIDS Crisis," Religion, Media and International Affairs, Syracuse University. Available at: http://sites.maxwell.syr.edu/luce/ChanWoong.html#_edn3

54. Shin, "Are Culture Wars Over? U.S. Evangelicals and the Global AIDS Crisis."

55. Mark Stricherz, "ABC vs. HIV," *Christianity Today*, April 1, 2003, 30.

56. George W. Bush, *Decision Points* (New York: Crown Publishers, 2010), 335.

57. Bush, *Decision Points*, 338.

58. Bush, *Decision Points*, 340.

59. "President Discusses the Fight Against Global and Domestic HIV/AIDS," January 31, 2003. Available at: http://georgewbush-whitehouse.archives.gov/news/releases/2003/01/20030131-4.html

60. The Focus Countries included Botswana, Cote d'Ivoire, Ethiopia, Guyana, Haiti, Kenya, Mozambique, Namibia, Niger, Rwanda, South Africa, Tanzania, Uganda, and Zambia. Vietnam was added in mid-2004, bringing the total to fifteen countries.

61. John W. Dietrich, "The Politics of PEPFAR: The President's Emergency Plan for AIDS Relief," *Ethics & International Affairs* 5 (Fall 2007), 280.
62. Holly Burkhalter, "The Politics of AIDS: Engaging Conservative Activists," *Foreign Affairs* 83 (Jan/Feb 2004), 9.
63. "The AIDS Team," *Christianity Today*, August 2006, 15.
64. Condoleezza Rice, *No Higher Honor: A Memoir of My Years in Washington* (New York: Crown Publishers, 2011), 229.
65. After becoming an Evangelical Christian, Wilberforce concluded that slavery was inconsistent with God's created order. As a result he decided to make the abolition of slavery his calling as a member of the British Parliament, and for more than two decades he led the campaign to end this practice. But rather than seeking to eliminate slavery, he adopted a more modest strategy for tactical reasons: he would first seek to eliminate the slave trade. Since most British institutions had an economic stake in the slave trade, he faced significant opposition to his efforts. Eventually he succeeded in this heroic effort with the passage of the Slave Trade Act of 1807. Some 26 years later, after Wilberforce had retired from Parliament, slavery was made illegal with the passage of the Slavery Abolition Act of 1933.
66. Ironically, in one of his earliest acts as president, he had reinstated this policy after President Clinton had voided it. In exempting AIDS programs from the Mexico City policy, Bush decided that while he remained committed to the policy itself, it was more important to ensure widespread and effective anti-AIDS monies to halt the pandemic.

CHAPTER 8

1. Peter Berger, "Moral Judgment and Political Action," Vital Speeches of the Day 56 (December 1, 1987): 120.
2. Mark. R. Amstutz, *International Ethics: Theories, Concepts, and Cases in Global Politics*, 4th ed. (Boulder, CO: Rowman & Littlefield, 2013).
3. *New York Times*, February 3, 2007, A1.
4. U.S. opposition to Kyoto was fueled in part by the fear that the failure to involve the emerging economies was not only "unfair" but would also cancel whatever gains were realized by the North's emissions reductions. Not surprisingly, the U.S. Senate overwhelmingly passed a resolution (95–0) that required developing nations to accept binding emission targets before it would consider ratification.
5. One of the most important outcomes of the UN conference was the promise by rich countries to transfer $30 billion over a three-year period to poor countries threatened by rising sea levels and other environmental changes resulting from global warming. As of mid-2011, only $12 billion had been budgeted by donor governments and only $4 billion had been delivered to poor countries.
6. In his study of the ethics of globalization, philosopher Peter Singer argues that there is no moral reason why developed countries should be entitled to a greater

share of global pollution. As a result, he claims that developed nations have a moral responsibility to greatly reduce their carbon emissions to achieve a fairer distribution of the costs of using fossil fuels. See Peter Singer, *One World: The Ethics of Globalization* (New Haven: Yale University Press, 2002), chap. 2.

7. Stephen M. Gardiner, "The Global Warming Tragedy and the Dangerous Illusion of the Kyoto Protocol," *Ethics and International Affairs* 18, no. 1 (2004), 36.

8. "A Deeper Partisan Divide Over Global Warming," *Pew Research Center*, May 8, 2008. Available at: http://people-press.org/2008/05/08/a-deeper-partisan-divide-over-global-warming/

9. "Evangelicals Go 'Green' with Caution," The Barna Group, September 22, 2008. Available at: http://www.barna.org/barna-update/article/13-culture/23-evangelicals-go-qgreenq-with-caution

10. The Evangelical Climate Initiative, "Climate Change: An Evangelical Call to Action." Available at: http://christiansandclimate.org/learn/call-to-action/

11. The major opposition to this initiative came from a group of Evangelical leaders that included Charles Colson of Prison Fellowship, James Dobson of Focus on the Family, and Richard Land of the SBC. In a letter submitted to Ted Haggard, NAE president, they argued that climate change was "not a consensus issue, and our love for the Creator and respect for His creation does not require us to take a position."

12. The Evangelical Climate Initiative, "Climate Change: An Evangelical Call to Action," February 2006. Available at: www.npr.org/documents/2006/feb/evangelical/calltoaction.pdf

13. The Evangelical Climate Initiative, "Principles for Federal Policy on Climate Change." Available at: http://christiansandclimate.org/policy-makers/

14. The Cornwall Alliance, "A Renewed Call to Truth, Prudence, and Protection of the Poor: An Evangelical Examination of the Theology, Science, and Economics of Global Warming." Available at: http://www.cornwallalliance.org/articles/read/a-renewed-call-to-truth-prudence-and-protection-of-the-poor/

15. In 1970, the NAE leadership adopted "Ecology 1970," a resolution pledging support for environmental protection; a year later, the NAE adopted a similar resolution titled "Environment and Ecology 1971." Like the earlier statement, this later resolution calls for prudent use of the earth's resources, thereby limiting long-term degradation. Available at: http://www.nae.net/fullresolutionlist

16. See Adelle M. Banks, "Dobson, Others Seek Ouster of NAE Vice President," *Christianity Today*, March 2, 2007. Available at: www.christianitytoday.com/ct/2007/marchweb-only/109-53.0.html

17. SBC, "On Environmentalism and Evangelicals," June 2006. Available at: http://www.sbc.net/resolutions/amResolution.asp?ID=1159

18. SBC, "On Global Warming," June 2007. Available at: http://www.sbc.net/resolutions/amResolution.asp?ID=1171

19. Banks, "Dobson, Others Seek Ouster of NAE Vice President."

20. For an overview of the Evangelical debate over climate change, see the following: John Copeland Nagle, "The Evangelical Debate Over Climate Change,"

University of St. Thomas Law Journal 5, no. 1 (2008), 53–86; Benjamin B. Phillips, "Getting into Hot Water: Evangelicals and Global Warming," *Journal of Markets & Morality* 12, no. 2 (Fall 2009), 315–335; and Brian McCammack, "Hot Damned America: Evangelicalism and the Climate Change Policy Debate," *American Quarterly* 59, no. 3 (2007), 645–668.

21. Phillips, "Getting into Hot Water," 321.

22. This condition is similar to admission in other types of human communities, from corporations and universities to professional associations. For example, at the liberal arts college where I teach, students are selected from a pool of applicants. Typically, the pool of applicants is much larger than the number admitted. Students can join the college community only after their applications have been accepted. Those that are not accepted must find an alternative institution.

23. See Hedley Bull, *The Anarchical Society: A Study of Order in World Politics* (New York: Columbia University Press, 1977); and Michael Walzer, *Just and Unjust Wars: A Moral Argument with Historical Illustrations,* 4th ed. (New York: Basic Books, 2006), and *Spheres of Justice: A Defense of Pluralism and Equality* (New York: Basic Books, 1984), chap. 2.

24. John Rawls, *The Law of Peoples* (Cambridge, MA: Harvard University Press, 1999).

25. See Singer, *One World: The Ethics of Globalization*, especially chaps. 4 and 5; Charles Beitz, *Political Theory and International Relations* (Princeton, NJ: Princeton University Press, 1979); and Allen Buchanan, *Justice, Legitimacy, and Self-Determination: Moral Foundations for International Law* (New York: Oxford University Press, 2004).

26. George W. Bush, *Decision Points* (New York: Crown Publishers, 2010), 303.

27. NAE, "Immigration 2006." Available at: http://www.nae.net/fullresolutionlist

28. NAE, "Immigration 2009." Available at: http://www.nae.net/fullresolutionlist

29. Mark Amstutz and Peter Meilaender, "Public Policy & the Church: Spiritual Priorities," *The City,* Spring 2011, 4–17. Available at: http://www.civitate.org/2011/03/the-city-spring-2011-full-edition/

30. For example, Evangelicals who support amnesty for illegal aliens appeal to Bible verses like "When a stranger resides with you in your land, you shall not oppress the stranger. The stranger who resides with you shall be to you as the citizen among you. You shall love the stranger as yourself, for you were strangers in the land of Egypt. I am the Lord your God" (Lev. 19:33–34). But those who oppose amnesty cite St. Paul's appeal in Romans 13:1, which declares: "Let every person be subject to the governing authorities. For there is no authority except from God, and those that exist have been instituted by God."

31. M. Daniel Carroll R., *Christians at the Border: Immigration, the Church, and the Bible* (Grand Rapids, MI: Baker Academic, 2008).

32. Matthew Soerens and Jenny Hwang, *Welcoming the Stranger: Justice, Compassion and Truth in the Immigration Debate* (Downers Grove, IL: IVP Books, 2009).

33. James K. Hoffmeier, *The Immigration Crisis: Immigrants, Aliens, and the Bible* (Wheaton, IL: Crossway Books, 2009), 158.

34. For an excellent critique of the misuse of Scripture, see Manfred T. Brauch, *Abusing Scripture: The Consequences of Misreading the Bible* (Downers Grove, IL: IVP Academic, 2009).

35. The NRCAT's mission statement reads: "Torture violates the basic dignity of the human person that all religions, in their highest ideals, hold dear. It degrades everyone involved—policy-makers, perpetrators and victims. It contradicts our nation's most cherished ideals. Any policies that permit torture and inhumane treatment are shocking and morally intolerable."

36. The declaration, along with a series of essays on religion and torture, is in *The Review of Faith & International Affairs* 5 (Summer 2007). See especially John C. Green, "Religion and Torture: A View from the Polls," and James Turner Johnson, "Torture: A Just War Perspective." The declaration is also available at: http://newevangelicalpartnership.org/?q=node/14

37. Pew Research Center, "The Religious Dimensions of the Torture Debate," May 7, 2009. Available at: http://pewresearch.org/pubs/1210/torture-opinion-religious-differences

38. Richard A. Posner, "Torture, Terrorism, and Interrogation," in *Torture: A Collection*, ed. Sanford Levinson (New York: Oxford University Press, 2004), 291.

39. Jean Bethke Elshtain, "Reflection on the Problem of 'Dirty Hands,'" in *Torture: A Collection*, ed. Sanford Levinson (New York: Oxford University Press, 2004), 79.

40. Quoted in Erin Roach, "Ethicist: NAE Torture Declaration 'Irrational,'" *Baptist Press*, March 15, 2007. Available at: http://www.bpnews.net/bpnews.asp?id=25190

41. Keith Pavlischek, "Human Rights and Justice in an Age of Terror: An Evangelical Critique of an Evangelical Declaration Against Torture." Available at: http://www.booksandculture.com/articles/webexclusives/2007/september/ept24a.html

42. Pavlischek, "Human Rights and Justice in an Age of Terror."

43. Stephen L. Carter, *The Violence of Peace: America's Wars in the Age of Obama* (New York: Beast Books, 2011), 41.

44. Paul W. Kahn, *Sacred Violence: Torture, Terror, and Sovereignty* (Ann Arbor: University of Michigan Press, 2008), 13 and 21–41.

45. Zachary R. Calo, "Torture, Necessity, and Supreme Emergency: Law and Morality at the End of Law," *Valparaiso University Law Review* 43 (2009), 1612.

46. Johnson, "Torture: A Just War Perspective," 31.

47. For a superb, compelling biography of this extraordinary Christian leader, see Eric Metaxas, *Bonhoeffer: Pastor, Martyr, Prophet, Spy* (Nashville, TN: Thomas Nelson, 2010), 323.

48. Quoted in Calo, "Torture, Necessity, and Supreme Emergency," 1598–1599.

49. Bernard Brodie, "Implications for Military Policy," in *The Absolute Weapon: Atomic Power and World Order*, ed. Bernard Brodie (New York: Harcourt Brace, 1946), 76.

50. Major Cold War arms-control accords include SALT I, the ABM Treaty, SALT II, and the INF Treaty.

51. According to the new agreement, the United States and Russia are each entitled to deploy a maximum of 1,550 nuclear warheads, with a maximum of 700 of them deployed on strategic delivery vehicles (ICBMs, SLBMs, and bombers). Additionally, each country can possess a maximum of 800 deployed and nondeployed strategic delivery vehicles.

52. Although some 190 countries are party to the NPT, four nuclear countries—India, Pakistan, North Korea, and Israel—are not part of the accord. And Iran, a party to the treaty, is currently believed to be close to acquiring a small nuclear arsenal. Iran has been cited by the International Atomic Energy Agency (IAEA) for noncompliance with the accord's provisions.

53. U.S. Department of Defense, "Nuclear Posture Review Report, April 2010." Available at: www.defense.gov/npr

54. U.S. Department of Defense, "Nuclear Posture Review Report," 48–49.

55. George P. Shultz, William J. Perry, Henry A. Kissinger, and Sam Nunn, "A World Free of Nuclear Weapons," *Wall Street Journal*, January 4, 2007, A15. For earlier antinuclear sentiments, see George F. Kennan, *The Nuclear Delusion: Soviet-American Relations in the Atomic Age* (New York: Pantheon) and Jonathan Schell, *The Abolition* (New York: Knopf, 1984).

56. The three additional articles, all published by the *Wall Street Journal*, were: "Toward a Nuclear Free World," January 15, 2008; "How to Protect Our Nuclear Deterrent," January 20, 2010: and "Deterrence in the Age of Nuclear Proliferation," March 7, 2011. They are available at: www.nuclearsecurityproject.org/publications. Given the unusual and surprising collaboration by former Cold War officials responsible for the development and nuclear strategy, a leading journalist has written an account about this important joint initiative. See Philip Taubman, *The Partnership: Five Cold Warriors and the Quest to Ban the Bomb* (New York: HarperCollins, 2012).

57. One of the most important NGOs is Global Zero, which issued an important report on further cuts in the U.S. strategic arsenal. The report was prepared by a commission of noted former public officials and headed by retired Gen. James Cartwright, the former vice chair of the Joint Chiefs of Staff. The commission's principal recommendations include reductions in the total U.S. strategic arsenal to 900 nuclear weapons, only half of which would be deployed, and the elimination of all nuclear ICBMs and tactical weapons. See Global Zero U.S. Nuclear Policy Commission Report, "Modernizing U.S. Nuclear Strategy, Force Structure and Posture," May 2012.

58. For data on strategic nuclear arms, see Department of State, "New START Treaty Aggregate Number of Strategic Offensive Arms," December 1, 2011. Available at: www.state.gov/t/avc/rls 178058.htm; for data on tactical nuclear arms, see Arms Control Association, "Nuclear Weapons: Who Has What at a Glance." Available at: http://www.armscontrol.org/factsheets/Nuclearweaponswhohaswhat

59. NAE, "Nuclear Weapons 2011." Available at: http://www.nae.net/government-relations/policy-resolutions/703-nuclear-weapons-2011

60. The NAE resolution boldly declares that "hundreds of thousands of Americans, both military and civilian, are directly or indirectly involved in the design, manufacture and deployment of nuclear weapons." Since the United States is not making new warheads and continues to reduce its arsenal, this assertion is clearly false. To be sure, significant numbers of military and scientific personnel will be required to maintain a small, credible deterrent. In particular, significant scientific resources will be needed, as the 2009 Strategic Posture Commission noted, to extend the life of existing warheads.

61. The NAE expresses its concern about dehumanization as follows: "When a state relies on nuclear weapons for its security, it may dehumanize citizens of other countries by targeting noncombatants for threatened nuclear destruction." This declaration fails to reflect contemporary strategic doctrine, which emphasizes accurate, limited destruction of military targets and the protection of civilian populations.

62. National Conference of Catholic Bishops, *The Challenge of Peace: God's Peace and Our Response* (Washington, DC: US Catholic Conference, 1983).

63. For data on drone strikes, see the *Long War Journal* website on the War on Terror. Available at: http://www.longwarjournal.org/pakistan-strikes.php For an insightful critique of the Obama administration's reliance on drones, see Tom Junod, "The Lethal Presidency of Barack Obama," *Esquire* magazine, August 2012, 98-105+.

CHAPTER 9

1. Alexis de Tocqueville, *Democracy in America*, trans. Henry Reeve (New York: Appleton, 1904), 1:334.

2. Quoted in Kenneth Thompson, *Morality and Foreign Policy* (Baton Rouge: Louisiana State University, 1980), 147.

3. Richard J. Mouw, "Carl Henry Was Right," *Christianity Today,* January 2010, 31.

4. Richard John Neuhaus, "Christianity and Democracy: A Statement of the Institute on Religion and Democracy" (Washington, DC: The Institute on Religion and Democracy, 1981), 1.

5. The Editors, "Editorial: Putting First Things First," *First Things*, March 1990, 12.

6. Paul Ramsey, *Who Speaks for the Church?* (Nashville: Abingdon Press, 1967), 152.

7. Reinhold Niebuhr, one of the most influential twentieth-century American theologians, had a profound impact on mainline Protestant denominations by challenging their progressive assumptions about human nature and political and social change. Niebuhr did not chart a new approach to politics but, rather, challenged the false faith of rational, optimistic religion of his time. Indeed, Niebuhr became the most influential political ethicist during the early Cold War years because he undermined the pervasive liberal faith that assumed that reason, love, and cooperation were the foundation of a human social and political order,

both domestically and internationally. Because of his influence among American cultural elites, *Time* dedicated a cover story to him in March 1948.

8. For an overview of Niebuhr's views of sin and human nature, see Reinhold Niebuhr, *The Nature and Destiny of Man—Vol. I: Human Nature* and *Vol. II: Human Destiny* (New York: Charles Scribner's Sons, 1964). According to Roger Epp, Niebuhr renewed four key ideas: the duality of human nature, the purposive nature of history, the need for order in political life, and the priority of love in human life. For a discussion of these principles, see Eric Patterson, "Christianity and Power Politics: Themes and Issues," in *Christianity and Power Politics Today: Christian Realism and Contemporary Political Dilemmas*, ed. Eric Patterson (New York: Palgrave Macmillan, 2008), 4.

9. Reinhold Niebuhr, "Why the Christian Church Is Not Pacifist," in *The Essential Reinhold Niebuhr: Selected Essays and Addresses,* ed. Robert McAfee Brown (New Haven: Yale University Press, 1986), 111.

10. Emil Brunner once noted that love is always just, while justice is not necessarily love. See Emil Brunner, *Justice and the Social Order* (New York: Harper and Brothers, 1945), 261.

11. Reinhold Niebuhr, *Moral Man and Immoral Society: A Study in Ethics and Politics* (New York: Charles Scribner's Sons), 1960, xx.

12. It should be noted that Niebuhr was a vocal pacifist during his early years, but the evil realities of Nazism made him change his position in the late 1930s. For this reference, see Niebuhr, "Why the Christian Church Is Not Pacifist," 111.

13. Reinhold Niebuhr, *The Irony of American History* (New York: Charles Scribner's Sons, 1952), 72.

14. Reinhold Niebuhr, *The Children of Light and the Children of Darkness* (New York: Charles Scribner's Sons, 1944), xiii.

15. Reinhold Niebuhr, *The Structure of Nations and Empires* (New York: Charles Scribner's Sons, 1959), 298.

16. In his short study of American history, Niebuhr develops this perspective, arguing that American history is ironic precisely because the hopes and ideals are unconsciously betrayed by the collective behavior of its people and government. See Niebuhr, *The Irony of American History*.

17. Niebuhr, *Nature and Destiny*, Vol. I, 220.

18. Kenneth Thompson, "The Political Philosophy of Reinhold Niebuhr," in *Reinhold Niebuhr: His Religion, Social and Political Thought*, ed. Charles W. Kegley (New York: Pilgrim Press, 1984), 249.

19. Niebuhr, "Why the Christian Church Is Not Pacifist," 114.

20. Reinhold Niebuhr, "Repeal the Neutrality Act!" in *Love and Justice: Selections from the Shorter Writings of Reinhold Niebuhr*, ed. D. B. Robertson (Philadelphia: Westminster Press, 1957), 177–178.

21. Peter Berger, "Moral Judgment and Political Action," *Vital Speeches of the Day*, December 1, 1987, 120.

22. NAE, "Nuclear Weapons 2011." Available at: http://www.nae.net/government-relations/policy-resolutions/703-nuclear-weapons-2011

23. The Evangelical Climate Initiative, "Climate Change: An Evangelical Call to Action." Available at: http://christiansandclimate.org/learn/call-to-action/

24. On the abuse and misuse of the Bible, see Manfred T. Brauch, *Abusing Scripture: The Consequences of Misreading the Bible* (Downers Grove, IL: IVP Academic, 2009).

25. D. James Kennedy, "Surviving the Nuclear Age," a sermon preached in the mid-1980s at Coral Ridge Presbyterian Church, Fort Lauderdale, Florida.

26. Evangelical Covenant Church, "Immigration 2006." Available at: http://www.covchurch.org/who-we-are/beliefs/resolutions/resolutions-from-2000-2009/2006-immigration/

27. John Buchanan, "Borderline Solutions?," *The Christian Century*, June 15, 2010, 7.

28. Richard J. Mouw, *Abraham Kuyper: A Short and Personal Introduction* (Grand Rapids, MI: Eerdmans, 2011), 110.

29. D. G. Hart, *From Billy Graham to Sarah Palin: Evangelicals and the Betrayal of American Conservatism* (Grand Rapids, MI: Eerdmans, 2011), 193–194.

30. H. Richard Niebuhr, *Christ and Culture* (New York: Harper Torchbooks, 1951), 2.

31. U.S. Catholic Bishops, "The Challenge of Peace: God's Promise and Our Response," The Pastoral Letter on War and Peace, *Origins*, May 19, 1983. Available at: www.osjspm.org/the_challenge_of_peace_1.aspx. The pastoral letter has four parts: (1) theological, biblical, and moral perspectives on peacekeeping, including an assessment of the just war tradition; (2) the problem of peacekeeping through nuclear deterrence; (3) proposals and policies for promoting peace in the nuclear age; and (4) the role of the church and selected constituencies in fostering moral analysis of national security concerns.

32. U.S. Bishops, "The Challenge of Peace," 3.

33. U.S. Bishops, "The Challenge of Peace."

34. Paul Henry, *Politics for Evangelicals* (Valley Forge, PA: Judson Press, 1974), 74.

35. For an overview of some major moral issues in the SDI debate, see Mark Amstutz, "The Morality of SDI," *Christian Scholar's Review* 28, no. 1 (September 1988), 7–24.

36. NAE, "Immigration 2009." Available at: http://www.nae.net/resolutions/347-immigration-2009

37. "Joint Statement regarding Immigration Concerns, 2006." Available at: http://www.gracelutheran-hsv.org/immigration

38. Paul Raabe, "Theological Thoughts on Illegal Immigrants," May 2006. Available at: http://www.ifire.org/phpbb3b/viewtopic.php?f=2&t=2250

39. Hart, *From Billy Graham to Sarah Palin*, 223.

40. Ross Douthat, *Bad Religion: How We Became a Nation of Heretics* (New York: Free Press, 2012), 6.

41. "An Evangelical Manifesto: A Declaration of Evangelical Identity and Public Commitment," May 7, 2008, 15. Available at: http://www.anevangelicalmanifesto.com/

42. Douthat, *Bad Religion*, 284.

INDEX